ACPL ITEM

DISCARDED

Y0-BVQ-072

FEB

MYSTERIES OF THE MIND

The Drama of Human Behavior

Other Books by Dr. Robert M. Goldenson

HELPING YOUR CHILD TO READ BETTER
UNDERSTANDING CHILDREN'S PLAY (coauthor)
ALL ABOUT THE HUMAN MIND
THE COMPLETE BOOK OF CHILDREN'S PLAY (coauthor)
THE ENCYCLOPEDIA OF HUMAN BEHAVIOR

Mysteries of the Mind

THE DRAMA OF HUMAN BEHAVIOR

ROBERT M. GOLDENSON, PH.D.

GARDEN CITY, NEW YORK

DOUBLEDAY & COMPANY, INC.

1973

ISBN: 0-385-05789-X
Library of Congress Catalog Card Number 72–76162
Copyright © 1973 by Robert M. Goldenson
All Rights Reserved
Printed in the United States of America
First Edition

ACKNOWLEDGMENTS

American Anthropological Association for "Voodoo Death" by W. B. Cannon, 44 (1942), pp. 169–81, issue of the *American Anthropologist*. Reproduced by permission of the American Anthropological Association.

Psychiatric Quarterly for excerpts from "Folie à Trois-Psychosis of Association" by S. R. Kesselman, 18 (1944), pp. 138–52. (New York State Department of Mental Hygiene, Albany, N.Y.)

American Psychological Association for "Automatic Writing as an Indicator of the Fundamental Factors Underlying the Personality" by A. M. Mühl, 17 (1922), pp. 166–83, issue of *Journal of Abnormal Psychology*. Copyright 1922 by the American Psychological Association, and reproduced by permission.

American Psychological Association for "An Unusual Case of Auto-Scopic Hallucination" by Cornelis B. Bakker, 69, ＃6 (1964), pp. 646–49, issue of *Journal of Abnormal and Social Psychology*. Copyright © 1964 by the American Psychological Association, and reproduced by permission.

American Psychological Association for "Four Cases of 'Regression' in Soldiers" by W. McDougall, 15 (1920), pp. 136–56, issue of *Journal of Abnormal Psychology*. Copyright 1920 by the American Psychological Association, and reproduced by permission.

Appleton-Century-Crofts for excerpts from *The Psychology of Suggestion* by Boris Sidis. Copyright 1909. By courtesy of Appleton-Century-Crofts, Educational Division, Meredith Corporation.

Appleton-Century-Crofts for excerpts from *Wish and Wisdom* by Joseph Jastrow. By courtesy of Appleton-Century-Crofts, Educational Division, Meredith Corporation.

Herman Behr for excerpts by Patience Worth from *Light from Beyond*.

Chapman and Grimes, Inc., for excerpts from *Philistine and Genius* by Boris Sidis.

Cornell University Press for excerpts from Henry E. Sigerist: *Civilization and Disease*. Copyright 1943 by Cornell University. Used by permission of Cornell University Press.

E. P. Dutton & Co., Inc., for excerpts from the book *Clowning Through Life* by Eddie Foy and Alvin F. Harlow. Copyright 1928 by E. P. Dutton & Co., Inc. Renewal, © 1956 by Alvin F. Harlow. Published by E. P. Dutton & Co., Inc., and used with their permission.

Faber & Faber, Ltd., for excerpts from *Tibetan Adventure* by H. Tichy.

International Universities Press, Inc., for excerpts from *Psychoanalysis and Culture* by G. B. Wilbur and W. Muensterberger. Excerpts from the article "Totemic Aspects of Contemporary Attitudes Towards Animals" by K. A. Menninger which appeared in *Psychoanalysis and Culture,* edited by G. B. Wilbur and W. Muensterberger, 1951.

The M.I.T. Press for excerpts from *Ex-Prodigy: My Childhood and Youth* by Norbert Wiener. Reprinted by permission of The M.I.T. Press, Cambridge, Massachusetts.

Maclean's for excerpts from "Is There a Miracle at Uptergrove?" by F. Hamilton, September 15, 1950, issue of *Maclean's* Magazine.

Holt, Rinehart and Winston, Inc., for excerpts from *Clever Hans* (The Horse of Mr. Von Osten) by Oskar Pfungst and edited by Robert Rosenthal. Copyright © 1965 by Holt, Rinehart and Winston, Inc. Reprinted by permission of Holt, Rinehart and Winston, Inc.

Psychiatry for adaptation of Account 23, of "An Experimental Investigation of the Possible Anti-Social Use of Hypnosis" by Milton H. Erickson, (1939) 2:391–414; p. 407. Reprinted by permission of *Psychiatry* and the author.

The Psychoanalytic Quarterly for "Unconscious Mental Activity in Hypnosis: Psychoanalytic Implications" by Milton H. Erickson and Lewis B. Hill, Vol. XIII, 1944, pp. 60–78. Reprinted by permission.

D. H. Rawcliffe for excerpts from *The Psychology of the Occult* by D. H. Rawcliffe. Reprinted by permission of Dover Publications, Inc. and the author.

Sandford & Greenburger Associates, Inc., for excerpts from *Encyclopedia of Aberrations,* edited by E. Podolsky. © Copyright 1953 by Philosophical Library, Inc. Used by permission of Philosophical Library, Inc.

Williams & Wilkins for excerpts from "Piblokto or Hysteria Among Peary's Eskimos" by A. A. Brill, 40 (1913), pp. 514–20, issue of *Journal of Nervous and Mental Disease.* Copyright 1913 by The Williams & Wilkins Co., Baltimore. Reprinted by permission.

To my friends
Flossie and Max Green

Foreword

Long before man ventured into the boundless regions of outer space, psychologists and psychiatrists were actively probing the equally vast expanse of inner space. For over a hundred years these scientists have used the techniques of laboratory and clinic to explore the intricate workings of the human mind. In the course of their efforts, they have accumulated an array of observations, experiments, and case studies that makes one thing clear: Nothing in this world is more varied, more astonishing, or more baffling than the human personality.

During the past few years the psychological sciences have become statistically oriented, and have emphasized the universal more than the unique. In so doing, they have tended to turn attention away from the more dramatic aspects of man's experience. One of the prime objects of MYSTERIES OF THE MIND, with its subtitle *The Drama of Human Behavior,* is to counterbalance this tendency by bringing together a wide variety of unusual human-interest cases, and by presenting them in story, rather than textbook, form.

In spite of its title, the book does not deal with the occult or supernatural. In fact, one of its themes is that many mysterious phenomena such as water divining and automatic writing can be explained on perfectly natural grounds. But even though we will not be drawing upon the occult, we will in some instances be dealing with behavior that is distinctly abnormal—which raises the question of the distinction between the normal and the abnormal. Granting that there is no hard and fast line between the two, let us say a normal person is one who can meet the everyday demands of life without extreme emotional distress or clear-cut symptoms such as obsessions, compulsions, delusions, or sexual deviations.

Certainly some of the cases described in this book, such as the man who preferred his horse to his bride, would come within the sphere of the abnormal. Similarly, the individual who splits into two or more distinct selves, each with its own name, handwriting, and personality, is bound to be considered abnormal. Moreover, we do not have to go into the supernatural to search for behavior that is extreme in character. We could hardly classify as normal the person who insists that everyone, including himself, is exactly one inch high.

No matter how strange and inconceivable they might appear, all the cases reported in these pages have been thoroughly authenticated. And in the interest of clarity, they have been grouped under such headings as "A Quartet of Prodigies" and "Animals and Men." Some of these cases are recognized classics in the psychological literature; others, dredged up from obscure sources, have never received the attention they deserve; a few have had their day in the news media. But all have been chosen for the light they shed on the complexities of the mind and the infinite variations on the human theme.

Another object of this book, then, is to explore as many dimensions of the human personality as possible within the limits of a single volume. Each of the case stories will illustrate a different facet of behavior. Three of them describe disorders occurring in exotic cultures such as pibloktoq and voodoo death. Three others deal with man's relations with animals: a unique case of bestiality, a so-called "talking horse," the tiger-men of Hindustan. Several others are concerned with the extraordinary power of suggestion—its negative aspects in cases of mass hysteria, and its positive aspects in hypnotic treatment. Two of the stories show the remarkable feats performed by *idiots savants,* and the equally remarkable productions of automatic writers and child prodigies. Three deal with identical twins, their likenesses and differences, and a fourth presents a rare type of psychosis in which the patient encounters his double everywhere he goes. Among the other stories is one that describes, and attempts to explain, the amazing exploits of the most versatile impostor on record.

These case reports are offered with several other objectives in mind: to enlarge the reader's appreciation of the richness and variety of human behavior . . . to evoke the inherent drama of cases hitherto reported only in technical language . . . to answer the reader's natural questions by giving scientific explanations wherever possible.

Finally, the author has chosen cases which are not only intriguing in themselves, but which tend to satisfy the reader's curiosity about important problems of human behavior. Here are a few samples:

Are the same mental disorders found in all societies?

Can a hypnotist make a subject perform a criminal act?

How can mass panic be prevented?

Do child prodigies usually "burn out" in adulthood?

Is there such a thing as photographic memory?

What is the truth about stigmata, or the wounds of the cross?

What is the largest number of selves found in cases of multiple personality?

The reader will find that some of the cases raise questions that cannot yet be answered—hence the title MYSTERIES OF THE MIND. But it is the author's hope that in reading them there will be ample proof that truth can be stranger than fiction, and far more enlightening.

Contents

Masquerade

According to many young people of today, the greatest problem in life is the "search for identity," the discovery of who and what they are. This is not a new question—in fact, it is characteristic of the lengthy adolescent period in Western society. But today it is raised more insistently than ever before.

Some people deny that they have a single self, since they deal with different situations and different people in such different ways. To them life is a masquerade in which they take many parts, not just one. They remind one of the young child who pretends to be a bus driver on Monday, an airplane pilot on Tuesday, and his Uncle Dudley on Wednesday. Most of us, however, settle down as we grow; one self gradually becomes dominant and holds the rest of us in check. But what about those other people who *don't* settle down to a first person singular?

The theme of the stories in this section is that some people have to be described in terms of first person *plural*. These are the people—few and far between—who split into two or more selves or who, chameleon-like, take on the selves of others. In some instances this may happen on a conscious, deliberate level; in others, the split is due to unconscious, subterranean forces deep within the mind. But whatever the source of these multiple selves, they are bound to open our eyes to the infinite diversity of the human personality and the drama of human behavior.

WALTER MITTY IN THE FLESH

On a blistering afternoon in August 1926, Pola Negri, "the last great siren of the silent screen" was languishing between silken sheets in her lavish suite at the Hotel Ambassador. She had come to New York to attend the funeral of the man to whom she was "formally though secretly" engaged, Hollywood's—and the world's—greatest idol, Rudolph Valentino.

As she lay in bed, resting for the ordeal that was to begin the following day, the grief-stricken star heard a knock at the door of her suite and sent her personal maid to answer. Standing in the hallway was a short but distinguished-looking gentleman dressed in dark clothes and carrying a small black bag. "I am Dr. Sterling Wyman," he said, "a close friend of the late Mr. Valentino. Would you kindly tell Miss Negri I am here?"

The maid ushered Dr. Wyman into the parlor, excused herself, and in a few moments returned to escort him to Miss Negri's bedroom. Sitting up in bed, she stretched out both hands to greet him. "Ah, Dr. Wyman, you were his close friend. It was so thoughtful of you to come."

"Not only his friend, Miss Negri, but his doctor when

he came to New York. Rudy would have wanted me to take care of you, my dear, and that is why I am here."

"How kind of you!" exclaimed the star. "I am almost out of my mind with grief, and my head is positively splitting."

"Yes, yes, I know. It is too much for you to bear alone," said the doctor, as he put his fingers lightly on her wrist and took her pulse. "Mmmm. Here, you must take one of these tablets. It will make you feel better. Miss, would you please bring Miss Negri a glass of water?"

Sitting on the edge of her bed, the doctor continued to soothe the disconsolate star. She was immensely grateful for his attention, and when he offered to devote all his time to her during the trying days to come, she readily accepted. She was even more appreciative when he offered to relieve her of some of the stress by interviewing the press and issuing bulletins on her health and other matters related to the funeral. "I shall be at your service at all times, day and night," he assured her.

"Day and night? In that case, I must make it as easy as possible for you. There is an extra bedroom in my suite, and I would be honored if you would make use of it."

"Yes," said the doctor, thoughtfully, "that would be more practical." And before the day was over he had sent for his baggage and moved into the elegant suite.

The next day, when the body of the famous star was placed on view, Dr. Wyman became the busiest man at Campbell's funeral parlor. He attended to Miss Negri's needs in a private room, permitting only selected visitors to see her in her hour of grief. He prepared bulletins on the state of her health and included statements quoting her public relations man. Between these responsibilities he kept an eye on the thousands of mourners who filed past the bier, and set up an informal first-aid clinic in an anteroom. There he dispensed aspirin and words of comfort to the more hysterical women and adolescent girls, without charging a fee. And, as if that were not enough, he always found time to answer the questions of the press, and to give his expert analysis of Valentino's fatal illness. His comments were reported verbatim in the city's newspapers, including the New York *Times*, which identified him not only as Miss Negri's New York physician, but as the author of *Wyman on Medico-Legal Jurisprudence.*

Shortly after the funeral a curious fact was brought to the attention of the newspaper editors. The learned doctor, whom they had been so liberally quoting, was not a doctor at all, but an impostor whose exploits they themselves had reported several times before. At first they were reluctant to admit publicly that they had been duped once again, but within a few days they decided that Wyman's latest caper was too good a story to ignore. They therefore exposed him as a fraud, and made certain that Pola Negri saw their articles. Her reaction was classic. She maintained that, fake or no fake, Dr. Wyman was the best doctor she ever had, and she would continue to use his services whenever she was in the city!

This incident occurred about midway in the multifaceted career of the most dedicated and the most successful impostor in history. The man who called himself Sterling Wyman, and a dozen or so variations on that name, was actually Stanley Jacob Weinberg, born in Brooklyn in 1890. His childhood was not particularly eventful, but during his years in high school he developed an engaging manner and a persuasive use of language—in fact so persuasive that he won a debate on women's suffrage and as a reward was sent to Washington. When he returned, his head was full of plans for the future: he would attend Princeton, get his B.A., see the world by taking positions in the Foreign Service and diplomatic corps, then return to study medicine at Johns Hopkins, and after obtaining his M.D., he would complete his preparation for life by taking a degree at the Harvard Law School.

Stanley's father, a moderately successful real estate broker, admired his son's ambition, but felt that he should concentrate on a single career; and until he made his choice, it might be best for him to get some practical experience. He therefore got Stanley a clerical job with a friend who was also in the real estate business. The young man did well for a few months—but when he devised a scheme which he insisted would expand the business by leaps and bounds, his employer refused to carry it out, and he quit his job in a huff. Discouraged and despondent, he took to bed for a month, then suddenly regained his customary vivacity and announced that he was ready to prepare himself for his triple career as diplomat, doctor, and lawyer. When his father still insisted that he narrow his choice to one field, he decided to earn his own way through college. He ran away from home and took a series of odd jobs, as a messenger boy, office boy, photographer's assistant. However, he left each of them within a few weeks since they were not only boring but failed to advance him rapidly enough toward his goal.

Frustrated but not defeated, it suddenly dawned on Stanley that he could realize his dreams without going to all the trouble of attending a series of colleges and universities. Starting with the Foreign Service, the first step in his master plan, he visited a leading stationer, and ordered a hundred engraved invitations to a bon voyage banquet at the Hotel St. George in honor of S. Clifford Weinberg, the newly designated United States Consul General to Algiers.

When the appointed day came, more than seventy-five doctors, lawyers, politicians, and other notables arrived in full dress, with their wives in elegant evening gowns. The guests enjoyed the elaborate dinner immensely, and at an appropriate moment, the young consul made a charming speech in which he thanked his friends, whom he did not mention by name, for arranging the banquet. A number of guests, including a justice of the New York Supreme Court, responded with cordial speeches in which they wished him well on his mission. The justice, in fact, was so impressed with the young consul that, as the party was breaking up, he invited him to sit on the bench with him the next day. The invitation was readily accepted.

The young consul arrived at the court in morning coat and striped trousers, and was ushered to the bench. He spent an interesting hour watching the judge dispose of case after case. During a recess, the justice told his guest that he had a surprise for him. In a moment, his clerk brought in a photographer to take their picture for the newspapers. The man arrived, set up his tripod, and disappeared under his hood to focus the camera. A moment later he emerged, flung back his hood, and shouted, "Your Honor, that fellow sitting beside you stole one of my best cameras!" Taken aback, the judge retired to his chambers with his guest trailing after him.

When they were alone, the "consul" calmly and unabashedly explained that he had worked for the photographer for a month, but that the man had refused to pay him a cent, and he had indeed taken the camera to teach him a lesson. He then went on to explain in a disarming manner that he was not really a consul general, but Stanley Weinberg of Brooklyn, and that he had arranged the banquet in his own honor in order to convince his father that he really *could* become a consul general if only he would agree to send him to Princeton to prepare for a diplomatic career. From there he went on to describe his plans to become a doctor and lawyer, but the justice grew strangely impatient, and finally called in a policeman, instructing him to take the young man home to get the stolen camera.

While Stanley was having his day in court, a messenger had arrived at his father's office with a sheaf of bills from the St. George Hotel, totaling about four hundred dollars. He telephoned the hotel and learned that a banquet had been given in honor of the consul general to Algiers—Weinberg by name. Since he had not seen Stanley for several months, he at once concluded that his son had been taking courses on his own, had passed the State Department examinations, and had been appointed to the post. His admiration for his son's initiative was so great that he paid the bills without further question.

But when Mr. Weinberg returned home, things took on a slightly different hue. Stanley was standing there with a camera under one arm and a policeman grasping the other. He listened to his son's "explanation," accompanied the two of them to Magistrate's Court, and put up the required bail. A few weeks later the trial was held and Stanley pleaded guilty to grand larceny. Since it was his first offense, the judge gave him a suspended sentence and placed him on probation.

The incident precipitated another period of despondency, and Stanley was sent to a sanitarium. The doctors diagnosed his condition as manic-depressive psychosis, and gave him what psychotherapy they could. He enjoyed the attention, the easy life, and the conversations with the staff so much that his spirits began to rise almost immediately. However, he remained six months, and by that time he seemed to have shed his grandiose ideas.

When he was released, he took a job as a cub reporter and quickly advanced to writing feature stories. But he soon forgot that he was still on probation, was arrested for failure to report, and sent to Elmira Reformatory for violating parole. There he had plenty of time to develop his Walter Mitty fantasies, and when he came out embarked on one impersonation after another. He began by buying a uniform and posing as a naval officer. While strolling in Prospect Park in this attire he met a girl who appealed to him, and aroused her interest by telling her exciting tales of his voyages. Suddenly, however, he stopped and confessed that he wasn't an officer at all, but a Brooklyn boy looking for work. He then proceeded to say that he wanted to marry her—if only she would have faith in him. Just at this point a couple of officers from the Brooklyn Navy Yard picked him up for impersonating an officer. He was immediately taken to court, and in spite of the fact that he had committed a federal offense, he talked the judge down to a ten-dollar fine. Shortly after paying the money, he married the girl—and remained married to her for the rest of his life, with substantial time out for prison sentences and affairs with other women.

Stanley's next escapade was prompted by an article in the papers stating that the USS *Wyoming* was lying at anchor in the Hudson River. Recalling his brief diplomatic triumph at the Hotel St. George, he suddenly decided that he would become both a lieutenant commander in the Rumanian Army and consul general from Rumania. He then telephoned the United States Navy Department in Washington, introduced himself in a convincing accent, and announced that the Queen of Rumania had instructed him to pay his respects to the United States Navy.

In a few hours appropriate arrangements were made for him to visit the *Wyoming*, whereupon he acquired an impressive uniform adorned with plenty of gold braid, rented a launch, and arrived at the flagship. Though still only twenty-four years of age, he had grown a mustache and conducted himself with such dignity that he appeared much older. He spent a half hour inspecting the sailors as they stood stiffly at attention, then chatted pleasantly with the officers. The captain was so taken by the young commander that he ordered a twenty-one-gun salute to be fired for him. Weinberg (now calling himself Stanley Clifford Weyman) then took his launch back to Manhattan and from there rode the subway home to Brooklyn.

Still intrigued with uniforms, Weyman, as we shall call him from now on, commissioned himself a lieutenant in the Army Air Corps when the United States entered the First World War. For a few days he walked about town accepting salutes from enlisted men and sighs from young ladies. Then, having wasted enough time, he decided to make a formal inspection of the 47th Regiment in its armory in Brooklyn. With the commanding officer at his side, he was in the midst of his inspection, when he was rudely interrupted by two detectives who had been trailing him about town. He spent the next two years in jail.

Free again, and looking for a job, Weyman noticed an advertisement for a doctor who would take charge of sanitation work to be carried out by a large company for the Peruvian Government. Here, at last, was an opportunity to achieve another of his aspirations. Overnight he became a medical officer in the United States Navy, with full credentials showing that he had served eighteen months overseas. As luck would have it, the final interview for the position was conducted by a Columbia University Medical School professor whom Weyman immediately recognized. Without hesitation, he stepped out of

the group of applicants, cordially shook hands with the
professor and told him how much he had enjoyed attending his clinics at the medical school. This may have had a
grain of truth in it, for a few years before, Weyman had
hung around the school posing as a medical student.
Under the mistaken impression that the young man had
been one of his students, the professor chose him for the
job.

No one knows how "Dr." Weyman got a passport, but
he managed to do so, and was soon off to Lima with an
attractive young woman as his companion. There he immediately rented a lavish marble residence, bought a
limousine on credit, and hired a chauffeur to drive it.
During the following few weeks he apparently performed
his technical duties creditably and also gave a number of
parties which made him and his companion favorites with
Peruvian society. As a medical officer in the Navy, he also
hobnobbed with American naval officers in the area, and
gave a tea in their honor. Interestingly, he took the trouble
to write a letter to one of the officers from the Brooklyn
Navy Yard who had arrested him for his previous impersonation, telling him about the tea and about his
success as a sanitation expert. The intelligence officer informed the company that he was an impostor, and he
was immediately recalled. In the interest of public relations, his employers decided not to prosecute him.

During the next few months Weyman worked at honest
jobs, then departed from his list of aspirations by taking a
position as head accountant for a manufacturer, a job
he obtained by stating that he was a good friend of a
leading senator and that he had been employed by the
chairman of the Republican National Committee. The
job, however, did not offer enough excitement and he
vanished after six weeks, leaving behind bills for several
hundred dollars' worth of flowers charged to his em-

ployer's account at Goldfarb's by Captain Sterling C. Wyman of the United States Navy. Apparently the job had been so dull that he had to look for stimulation on the side.

At this point Weyman noticed a vivid account of the arrival of Princess Fatima of Afghanistan. The accompanying picture showed her clad in a long, variegated robe and wearing a large sapphire in her left nostril. In the interview with the reporters she stated that she had come to America for a double purpose—to meet "that handsome man," President Warren G. Harding and to dispose of a huge diamond she had acquired in India in order to have sufficient funds to send her three sons to college. The following day, a dispatch from Washington indicated that she might have a problem seeing the President, since Prince Mohammed Wali Khan of her country had tried in vain to arrange a meeting with the Secretary of State as a prelude to signing a treaty with his country. The reason for the Secretary's coolness was that Great Britain had asked him to hold off since that country felt Afghanistan was still in its sphere of political influence and wanted to establish the treaty before any was signed by the United States. Here, then, was a challenge worthy of Weyman. Could he arrange a meeting for the princess in spite of the fact that the prince had failed?

Weyman had long wanted to shake the hand of the President of the United States, and decided at once to accept the challenge. Filled with anticipation, he selected an appropriate uniform from a costume wardrobe that by now had grown to theatrical proportions. The fact that the uniform was actually that of an officer of the United States Junior Naval Reserve (a non-governmental organization on the level of the Boy Scouts) did not matter any more than the fact that he bestowed on himself the non-existent title of State Department Naval Liaison Officer.

In an hour or so, he was in the princess's suite at the old Waldorf Astoria. As soon as he had introduced himself and kissed her hand, he asked if she and her three sons would be ready to go to Washington within a week. Delighted at this recognition from a State Department official, the princess immediately agreed, and within a few days the Third Assistant Secretary of State received a call from Rodney S. Wyman, the State Department Naval Liaison Officer, informing him that Princess Fatima would be happy to see President and Mrs. Harding on or about July 25, and that he himself would make the necessary arrangements with the White House.

The official assumed that the Secretary of State had authorized Weyman to arrange the interview, and in due time the princess was formally received in the Red Room of the White House. On the following day, the Washington *Post* published a long article, complete with photographs, that began "Royalty touched hands with democracy at the White House yesterday when Princess Fatima, Sultana of Afghanistan, and her three sons were received by President Harding in special audience." The article went on to describe the "brilliant hues of the princess's gown and jewels," the cashmere shawls and gossamer veils she brought to the First Lady, and included the interesting detail that "she takes out her nose jewel when she goes to bed at night, as other women remove their earrings." The article also mentioned that the introductions were performed by her adviser and interpreter, Commander Rodney Sterling Wyman who, of course, was standing beside her in the group picture.

A few months after the Fatima coup, Weyman returned to his doctor role when he learned that Dr. Adolf Lorenz, the famous Viennese "bloodless surgeon," was about to arrive in the United States. When the ship docked he went aboard, introduced himself as Dr. Clifford Weyman, and informed him in excellent German that the New York City Health Commissioner had asked him to welcome the doctor to the United States and offer his services as private secretary. The offer was immediately accepted and the newspaper photographers took pictures of the two together.

The new secretary proved to be an excellent guide during Dr. Lorenz's first bewildering days in America, and would no doubt have continued to be helpful had not one of Princess Fatima's sons noticed his picture in the paper. He was promptly exposed and, though Dr. Lorenz maintained that he was satisfied in every way with his services, the Health Commissioner had to let him go because he had misrepresented himself not only as a doctor but as his representative. The exposé hit the front pages, and Weyman was soon picked up by a federal agent—not for impersonating a doctor, but for impersonating a naval officer in the Fatima affair. In court, he insisted that he could not be guilty of this offense, since he was not wearing a uniform of the United States Navy, but one of the United States Junior Naval Reserve—and besides, he was really a manic-depressive and not completely accountable for his actions. Despite this double plea, he was sentenced to two years in the Atlanta Federal Penitentiary.

Safely ensconced in the pen, Weyman at last had enough time on his hands to turn to another of his aspirations. With the assistance of the warden he studied law, and did so well that despite his convict status, he was permitted to take the bar examination and became an accredited attorney under the laws of the state of Georgia. His sentence was shortened for good behavior, and when he returned to New York, he took a job as

legal clerk in a title and mortgage company. Since his
work involved real estate transactions, he managed to
give his father a few inside tips on foreclosures. Both of
them made a good deal of money on these deals, and
Weyman bought himself a bright red Daimler roadster
and a Pierce Arrow limousine, which he decorated with
a special plate he had made, containing the legend "Special Deputy Attorney General—New York."

In 1925, Weyman added yet another title to his lengthy
pedigree. He read that a major medical meeting was to
be held at Middlesex College of Medicine in Cambridge,
Massachusetts, and decided to attend. Within an hour or
two he put on his most conservative suit, got his little
black bag out of a closet, and was on his way to the
station. During the five-hour train ride he jotted down
some notes on a favorite subject of his, the need for improved psychiatric care in penitentiaries and prison
hospitals, a subject on which, by now, he had considerable firsthand experience. When he arrived at the meeting
he introduced himself to his "colleagues" as Dr. Allen
Stanley Wyman, a member of the New York State Lunacy
Commission, and casually mentioned some of his ideas
on the psychiatric care of prisoners. They were so impressed that he was invited to speak at the evening meeting. He made use of the notes he had prepared on the
train, and his talk was enthusiastically received by his
unsuspecting audience.

The following year Weyman achieved his greatest triumph as a physician during the funeral of Rudolph Valentino, and from then on he played many variations on
his former roles. These were intermingled with brief periods during which he held legitimate jobs, and longer
periods spent in Sing Sing and other penal institutions.

One of these variations will indicate the full extent of

his resourcefulness. In April 1928, the papers were head-
lining the flight of the Bremen fliers, who were attempting to duplicate Lindbergh's world-shaking flight, but in
the reverse direction. Taking off from Ireland, they successfully flew the Atlantic; but their gas ran low, and in
landing on a barren island off the coast of Canada, their
plane was damaged. Two great aviators, Bernt Balchen
and Floyd Bennett, flew to the rescue of the stranded
fliers, but unfortunately Bennett contracted pneumonia
and died en route. He was later buried at Arlington
National Cemetery in Washington, and shortly afterward
the Bremen fliers announced that they would fly to Washington and lay a wreath on his grave. They agreed to
stop over in New York on the way, and arrangements
were made for the city's official greeter Grover Whalen
to welcome them. He was in the midst of his speech when
a natty officer dressed in cavalry boots marched onto the
platform and announced that Mayor James J. Walker
had personally assigned him the honor of welcoming the
fliers to the city. Introducing himself as Captain Stanley
Wyman of the United States Volunteer Air Service, the
officer brushed the sputtering Whalen aside and proceeded to make an eloquent and moving speech of his
own.

After the fliers had taken their leave, a reporter with
a memory for faces approached Weyman and accused
him of being the impostor who had taken over Valentino's funeral. Weyman drew himself up to his full five
feet two, scornfully remarked that this accusation was
totally irrelevant, and indignantly stalked off. The next
day, when the photographs of the ceremony appeared
in the paper, his imposture came to the attention of the
police. However, they chose to ignore the whole em-
barrassing episode, probably because any action on their

part would have focused attention on the laxity of their supervision, and would have harmed their own reputation more than Weyman's.

The entire series of exploits—and we have reviewed only the highlights—leaves no doubt that Weyman was past master of the art of imposture. And "art" seems to be the proper word, for he unquestionably possessed in very high degree the qualities we associate with the art of acting—particularly a sense for the dramatic moment, and an ability to throw himself convincingly into different roles. It is interesting that A. A. Brill, a leading psychiatrist of the time, made these comments: "No man living has gotten away with the grand gesture more often than he has. In his way he is an artist. It is impossible to study his career and not take off one's hat to his persistent cleverness, audacity, and aplomb." It is interesting, too, that another psychoanalyst, Dr. Phyllis Greenacre, has drawn a parallel between the impostor and the artist: "In both the creative artist on the brink of a new surge of creativity and in the impostor between periods of imposture, there is a sense of ego hunger and a need for completion—in the one, of the artistic self; in the other, of a satisfying identity in the world."

These comments raise some questions that beg for an answer. Did Weyman's desire for recognition—his "ego hunger"—go beyond normal bounds into the realm of the truly pathological? Were his impersonations motivated by a search for identity—that is, was he a confused, lost soul trying vainly to find himself and his place in the sun? Did his "grand gestures" stem from grandiose ideas, the kind of delusions that are typically found in the mental illness known as manic-depressive psychosis?

There is a great deal of evidence that Weyman was subject to periods of exhilaration and periods of discouragement bordering on despondency—and he *was* diagnosed as a manic-depressive more than once. Yet that diagnosis appears highly questionable for several reasons. In the typical manic phase of this psychosis the patient talks a blue streak, concocts harebrained schemes which he never carries out, acts in an uncontrolled and frequently violent manner. And in the depressive state he wears a look of despair, speaks in a monotone, and constantly bemoans his lot. Yet, while Weyman was subject to "mood swings," they were never as extreme as in the psychosis. He did not talk wildly or lose control of himself, and though he was unrealistic in many of his aspirations and subject to Walter Mitty fantasies, he dwelled in the actual world and was not out of touch with reality. Moreover, as pointed out above, he recovered from his depression almost overnight in the first sanitarium he visited, and in others later on; and his rapid recoveries were apparently due to the fact that his ego hunger was satisfied by the extra attention he received. This is far from the usual pattern in the mental illness in question.

This does not mean that Weyman was a perfectly normal human being. It merely indicates that he was probably a borderline case. During the twenties, when the manic-depressive diagnosis was made, the categories of emotional disorders were far more fixed and limited than they are today, and there was far less recognition of disorders lying in the gray area between normality and pathology. More specifically, Weyman was probably afflicted with a form of disturbance known today as psychopathic or antisocial personality: "This type of personality occupies a twilight zone between the ordinary individual and the hardened criminal. The category includes a varied assortment of unscrupulous businessmen, confidence men, shyster lawyers, quack doctors, crooked politicians, prostitutes, and impostors." (*The Encyclopedia of Human Behavior,* article on "Antisocial Reaction.")

Antisocial personalities have been exhaustively studied in recent years, and their major features have been identified by such investigators as H. M. Cleckley, W. A. Heaton-Ward, and R. D. Wirt. Let us look at some of these characteristics with Weyman in mind. The first two, *defective conscience* and *absence of guilt feelings,* are so important that the disorder was once known as "moral insanity" and "moral imbecility." Certainly Weyman did not accept or even fully appreciate the ordinary ethical standards. During an interview with a reporter, he glibly maintained: "I am not doing anything wrong. Get this straight, and you may be able to understand me and my position better. I am an American boy, one hundred per cent, born in Brooklyn. From my early days as a kid, I have been imbued with the go-gettem spirit. Now one of the first things that an ambitious lad learns is that every opportunity for increasing his fame must be taken advantage of . . . and if the opportunities don't materialize spontaneously there is just one thing to be done and that is to create them. That's been my motto all along, and people who have made up their minds that I am cracked or have some sinister motive are simply deluding themselves."

That quotation is a good illustration of a third characteristic which the American Psychiatric Association includes in its description of the disorder: "*An ability to rationalize their behavior* so that it appears warranted, reasonable, and justified." It also illustrates a fourth feature, *good intelligence,* which in this case Weyman used primarily to get around the law and to talk his way into and out of situations he "created." The next characteristic, a *good front,* with an engaging manner is so obvious in his case that it does not require elaboration. The same goes for *irresponsibility* (though he remained married to the same woman, he frequently left her for weeks, was an erratic provider, and became such a notorious character that his only child, a daughter, left home and changed her name as soon as possible). Equally clear is *lack of foresight,* which in his case was accompanied by a desire to "be somebody" and "have everything" without planning or working for these goals. Weyman's intense ego hunger fits into the picture at this point.

The next three characteristics also fit like a glove: *disregard for truth,* which includes lying or glossing over the truth even when detection is certain; *self-defeating behavior,* illustrated by the fact that he frequently courted disaster even at the height of success, as in having his picture taken at every opportunity, never disguising his face, and wearing elaborate but inappropriate uniforms; and *failure to learn from experience.* The latter quality is exemplified by the fact that Weyman spent about one third of his adult life behind bars, and continued his impersonations for over thirty years even though he frequently promised to change. Some feel that a pattern of this kind is indicative of a deep-lying sense of guilt and an unconscious need for punishment; his self-defeating behavior, as in blithely violating parole and writing the letter from Peru, could be used as evidence for this need. Others would insist that he persisted in his impostures primarily to satisfy an urge for drama and change.

Placing Weyman in a broad psychiatric category is one thing; *explaining* his behavior is another. But this is not too surprising, since there is virtually no agreement on the origin of the antisocial personality. Some specialists have maintained that the disorder is inborn, since the tendencies come to the fore early in life—and for this reason such labels as "constitutional psychopath" and "constitutional psychopathic inferior" have been used in the past. A few claim that the condition may be due to abnormal brain functions, though brain-wave tests with the electroencephalograph are not regarded as conclusive.

Others attempt to find the causes in early life, and particularly in faulty relationships with the parents. One theory holds that many psychopaths find themselves caught between a strict, hard-driving father and a lenient, overindulgent mother, and as a consequence rebel against ordinary ethical standards and take the easier, more comfortable way of the mother. At the same time, they develop a charming façade not only to get what they want but to conceal their inner conflicts from the world. What we know about Weyman's parents seems to support this theory, but it is not sufficient to explain his total behavior. We therefore have to end with a question mark and the hope that the next great imposter will submit to a closer and more productive scrutiny.

PERSONALITY PARADE

The Ouija board has long been out of fashion, though there are signs that it is coming back into use. About fifty years ago it was one of the most popular and intriguing parlor games. The apparatus consisted of a large wooden board on which the letters of the alphabet and the words "yes" and "no" were printed, plus a triangular wooden pointer mounted on wheels. In playing the game, the pointer was placed on the board and the player put his fingers lightly on it, then closed his eyes or looked in another direction. An onlooker or the player himself then asked a question, and the pointer was supposed to move to yes or no or to the letters of the alphabet that spelled out an answer.

Some people had little if any success with the Ouija board, but others became so adept at it that they answered questions not only rapidly but, it appeared, automatically, for they insisted that the pointer moved entirely by itself as if controlled by an invisible force. This peculiar phenomenon soon came to the attention of psychologists and psychiatrists, who immediately suspected that the invisible force was actually the subconscious mind, or "unconscious," of the player. A few of them performed experiments with patients and found that the Ouija board helped them to identify individuals who could readily "dissociate"—that is, separate conscious from unconscious levels of thinking. Some even used it as a technique for bringing buried memories and repressed impulses to the surface where they could be examined and analyzed.

One of these students of the unconscious was Dr. Winifred Richmond, a psychiatrist in the Boston area. One day, while exploring the use of the Ouija board, she discovered that the technique was working unusually well for one of her subjects, a young English teacher named Violet X. When she was asked a question, the pointer moved so quickly from letter to letter that it was hard to transcribe what she was spelling out. This gave Dr. Richmond an idea: Why not dispense with the board altogether, and see if Violet would record her thoughts directly on paper? She therefore placed a pencil in the girl's hand and proceeded to ask her a few questions. Sure enough, the hand began to write automatically, without any conscious intent on Violet's part. The writing was hesitant at first, but after several practice sessions, she developed an extraordinary facility, and page after page was rapidly filled with notes. Violet was astonished at this strange outpouring, and felt as if there were two parallel streams of mental activity going on concurrently—one of which she could call her own, the other expressing itself through her hand.

Even more astonishing was the material that Violet's hand produced. Over a period of three months, no less than seven distinct personalities, plus several minor ones, made their appearance. They did not emerge once and disappear, but recurred periodically and unpredictably— each with its own name, its own unique style of expression and its own individual handwriting. According to an account written by Dr. Anita Mühl, an associate of Dr. Richmond's, "Each spoke of herself or himself in the first person, giving detailed answers to questions, coherent accounts of themselves, and admonitions and advice to the experimenters. Half a dozen different personalities might come at one sitting, interrupting one another unceremoniously, and sometimes even rudely. The personalities, once established, would often appear when called, coming with the remark: 'So and so is here, what do you want?' Miss Violet X maintained the same attitude as the other experimenters, questioning or replying to what the hand was writing. Any levity on the part of the subject or the others was apt to call forth scathing remarks from the secondary personalities. Miss X with one exception retained her own personality and was fully aware of what was going on, although she by no means always knew what the hand was writing."

We will describe the seven major personalities in the order of their first appearance, and then consider their significance for the primary personality Violet. Number One burst upon the scene in letters three inches high: "Hello! I am ANNIE MCGINNIS." Violet was taken completely by surprise and made some remark such as "Who?

I never heard of you." Her hand then proceeded to produce a well-drawn portrait of a rather tough-looking girl, labeling it "ANNIE." When she looked down at the drawing, Violet was completely mystified, for she had never shown any artistic talent whatever.

Annie then began to tell her story, which was continued in various installments throughout the week's experimentation. In brief, she had been raised in poverty and had taken the downward path through no fault of her own. She had simply been befriended and led astray by a man who had made glowing promises not only of food and shelter but a life of comfort and ease. Once she had become a "fallen woman," she continued downward until she became a prostitute. Finally, according to Annie, she had died while giving birth to a child, and after that her spirit had wandered aimlessly in limbo, suffering pangs of remorse for the sins she had committed. Then, fortunately, she had discovered Violet X, with whom she took up her abode "because," as she wrote, "you are so good, I love to be with you."

Annie was the most dominant and persistent of all the personalities that appeared in the automatic writing, and she had by far the most to say. Each time she took over Violet's pencil, she "took charge in a whirlwind fashion," and wrote diatribes against men in a crude, flowing hand. Her hatred was expressed in large capital letters, and when one of the male personalities appeared, she would try to interrupt or obliterate all traces of his writing by scribbling over the entire page. True to type, she was "coarse, rude, quick-tempered, resentful, reckless, and passionate". Although anger was her predominant mood, she would occasionally be in a good humor, and at those times told crude jokes and was "a great blarney."

Violet's reaction to Annie was one of tension and revulsion. Whenever she made her appearance, the girl raised her eyebrows, gritted her teeth and pressed her lips together in a mixture of anger and fright. As her hand wrote, she would be seized with a near convulsion; her arms would stiffen and the fingers would grasp the pencil tightly. At other times, her feet would pound on the floor while her arm, totally out of control, would repeatedly bang itself on the table with enough force to cause her considerable pain. When Violet asked Annie why this happened, her hand wrote that she had to hit something whenever she thought of what men had done to her.

The next personality to appear was quite the reverse of Annie McGinnis. Announcing herself as "Mary Patterson," her handwriting was quite similar to Violet's normal script. This resemblance went even further, for she used excellent English and in general was more like the primary personality than any of the others. Mary insisted that she was Violet's "most familiar spirit," and though she came to the surface infrequently, it was generally after one of the more aggressive personalities had been in control of her hand. However, Mary was too quiet and reserved to hold the stage for any length of time, for one of the more dominant characters was sure to oust her and take over the pencil.

The third personality, Mary Minott, contrasted sharply with this "familiar spirit." Self-assured to the extreme, she described herself as "a woman of the world." She was bitterly antagonistic to Mary Patterson, who was anything but cosmopolitan in her tastes, and would also upbraid Violet X for preferring that "puritanical prig" to herself. Her grand passion was dress design, and she insisted that if Violet would only listen to her, she would make her famous in the field. To prove her point, Mary Minott produced drawing after drawing of beautiful and original dresses, with a talent that bordered on genius. Violet was completely taken aback when she looked at the drawings which her own hand had created, for in her normal state she had never shown any skill or even any particular interest in the field of fashion.

The fourth personality, Alton, differed from all the rest in one important respect. He was an actual person, and a friend of Violet's fiancé whom she had met the previous summer. Apparently he was also a would-be suitor, for he would address her in the most endearing terms, and attempt to win her away from the man she loved. These attentions were met with a cold shoulder, and Violet tried to banish him from the scene. But he persisted in the face of these rebuffs, and soon developed a new approach by maintaining that if she would let him be her guide, she could become a first-class medium. He insisted that she had a special talent for this work, and that the spirits of both the living and the dead could speak through her. It was a dangerous business, he recognized, but if she would only put herself in his hands, he would protect her from all possible harm.

Annie McGinnis was not the only personality who purported to be dead. In the course of the experimental sessions, Violet's father, who had actually passed away some time before, appeared on the scene a number of times. Like the other personalities, he wrote in the first person, and when the handwriting was compared with that of Violet's father, it was found to be remarkably similar. His appearances, however, were brief, and consisted only of hurried comments on family affairs.

The sixth personality was more abstract than any of the others, labeling itself simply "The Spirit of War and Desolation." It arrived on the scene at a particularly timely period, for America was on the verge of entering the First World War. The Spirit's writing alternated between two themes. First, it sounded dreadful warnings about the decimation of the world and urged Violet to relieve the inhuman suffering by working for the Red Cross. Second, it tried to prevail upon her to give up automatic writing and take up the study of mediumship. As in the case of Alton, The Spirit of War and Desolation insisted that she had a rare gift for this activity.

The last of the subconscious selves was in many ways the most significant. Unlike the others it did not arrive on the scene full blown, but made many tentative and shadowy appearances before it developed a characteristic handwriting and point of view. It merely referred to itself as "Man," and first came to attention by interrupting other conversations with completely irrelevant remarks. When questioned by Violet or the observers, it would give only ambiguous answers or none at all. Within a few weeks, however, this new male personality developed a marked antagonism toward the lovesick Alton and vied with him for the center of the stage. At first, the two would appear alternately, but later on Man succeeded in crowding out Alton altogether.

This cleared the stage for a final battle of personalities. Man developed an even greater dislike for Annie McGinnis than for Alton, and attempted to banish her as well. But that was not an easy task, for Annie "hated him in return in letters two inches high," and considered him the "reincarnation of all her enemies." Whenever Man tried to take over, she would intrude irrepressibly and write a tirade against the men who had "done her wrong"—and when Man would try to eliminate her from the scene, she would take particular delight in scribbling all over whatever he wrote.

Man, however, became more and more persistent and dominating, and a change seemed to come over Violet whenever he was in control. In her own words, "I feel different when Man is present than I do with any of the others; there is a feeling of power and vigor and I don't want to sit still, I want to run or express myself in some vigorous way." The urge for action began to express itself in an interest in dancing, which Violet had never displayed before, and Man would fill sheet after sheet with a choreography of rhythmic lines. As time went on, the lines became increasingly energetic and were interspersed with "Let's dance, Violet!" Though she tried to resist at first, she began to believe that she could actually dance spontaneously if she could only let herself go—but she had always been emotionally inhibited and was afraid to try.

Then came the final, climactic scene. One evening, as Violet was quietly writing, Man appeared and as usual began to dance—on paper. "In a moment Miss X spoke loudly and said 'Oh—I want to dance—I believe I can dance,' and getting to her feet she began to sway rhythmically back and forth. The swaying became more and more violent, her arms began to wave and her feet to execute a curious shuffling movement. Suddenly her body gave a violent wrench and she cried out in a sharp high voice. Her face depicted the emotions of a tremendous struggle, ecstasy and terror contending for expression. She was taken to a couch by the experimenters where for about ten minutes she remained stiff and moaned in an unnatural voice."

Violet gradually returned to normal, but for some time remained terrified by her experience. As she later related, she felt that she was losing control over herself, and that another personality was threatening to take over completely. In her own words, "I wanted to give myself up to it and yet I didn't want it. I can't describe it, but I felt as though I were two people."

The psychiatrist, who had had considerable experience with dissociation, felt that there was a genuine danger that this conflict might actually split Violet's personality, and therefore decided that it was high time to terminate the experiment. Violet took it upon herself to make a few further attempts, but found that Man always came to the surface and always tried to persuade her to express her love of action by dancing. But his power seemed to diminish, especially when she married and was distracted from the automatic writing. However, one day when she was alone, she decided to try it again, and this time Mary Patterson, her "most familiar spirit," made an appearance and explained that all the other personalities had become so completely submerged that they lacked the power to express themselves. After this no further attempts were made.

What explanation can be given for this unexpected parade of personalities? From a psychological viewpoint, it is important to recognize that practically everyone has some capacity to dissociate—that is, to separate one part of the mind and have it express itself *by* itself. We all do exactly that when we dream at night or fantasize during the day. Normally we put aside these dreams and daydreams in the interest of ongoing activities that direct our attention to outward reality; and in some cases we unconsciously repress them because they express urges or revive experiences that are distasteful or threatening to our ego. But we must also recognize that this capacity to dissociate, and to express the unconscious, can be cultivated—and there is little doubt that Violet's experiments with the Ouija board were actually a training process in which she gained practice in tapping her unconscious. As Dr. Mühl put it, "The first attempts were not so brilliantly successful, but with repeated attempts a marvelous facility for writing developed, and with this an increased tendency to dissociate."

It is very probable that Violet's increase in skill was due not only to practice, but to encouragement and suggestion on the part of the experimenters. Dr. Mühl also points out that Violet was run down because of overwork at the time of her automatic behavior, which suggests that fatigue may have played a part in loosening the controls over her unconscious or over that part of the unconscious (sometimes called the paraconscious or fore-conscious) which can most readily be called to the surface.

Frequently individuals who are extraordinarily capable of automatic writing have a history of other forms of dissociation such as somnambulism, amnesic episodes, or hysterical symptoms. The investigators compiled a care-ful life history of Violet but were unable to find evidence for any of these tendencies. She had lived a normal, healthy life as a child, had received excellent schooling, and had graduated from a college for women. Although she had taken a course or two in psychology, she knew practically nothing about abnormal behavior. Her major had been English, the subject which she was teaching at the time of the experiments, but she also had a deep interest in sociology and had done some social service work in Boston. All the evidence indicated that she was a stable person with a "fine intellect and charming personality."

We can only conjecture that Violet's ability to write automatically was a latent capacity which had never had an opportunity to exhibit itself. Perhaps, too, her tendency to dissociate had been obscured by her busy intellectual life, or had been expressed unconsciously through identification with the personalities she encountered in her literary and social work.

Violet was intrigued and mystified by the seven personalities, and made every effort to help the experimenters discover their origin. Annie McGinnis, she felt, was easily explained by her experience in social work and the fact that she had been strongly impressed by the idea that she herself had been saved from treading the downward path only by the accident of birth and training. Annie's hatred of men, according to Dr. Mühl, was probably "the outcome of the ambivalent opposite emotional tendency"—i.e., it was a denial of her own desires. The Spirit of War and Desolation, which urged her to join the Red Cross, was a further expression of her social work interests. Mary Patterson was her own dominant self, who appeared on the scene as a "familiar spirit" to remind and reassure her that the other personalities were only secondary expressions of her primary self. Mary Minott represented a secret desire for elegance and a latent capacity for design, both of which had been suppressed or ignored in the interest of a strait-laced intellectual existence as a teacher of English. Miss X's father probably represented a double tendency: First, it revealed a hidden desire to become a medium—which Alton insisted on—and communicate with the dead. (Mediums are frequently dissociated personalities who speak or write automatically.) And second, it indicated a strong identification with her father, which may have been the source of what the psychiatrist diagnosed as a "bisexual trend." Her masculine tendencies were even more fully expressed by Man's vigor, aggressiveness, and freedom of expression. The last episode, in which Man induced her to let go and engage in a wild dance, produced such a violent anxiety reaction that there can be little doubt that these masculine urges were real.

Finally, it seems clear that all seven selves represented different facets of a personality that was far more complex than appeared on the surface. The fact that each of them was given a name and had a characteristic handwriting can only be explained as an attempt to give expression to latent tendencies in personified form. This histrionic urge was probably acquired through wide reading of novels and plays in preparation for her career as an English teacher. Probably, too, the "case approach" utilized in her social service work reinforced her tendency to express impulses and feelings in dramatic form.

Violet's experiments with automatic writing demonstrate the fact that the human personality is often, or perhaps always, made up of a more or less rich diversity of urges, talents, and capacities. Most of these remain hidden and unexplored, though in some cases we gain an outlet in the form of fantasies, daydreams, and visions of a better self. In rare cases, these divergent impulses crystallize into two or more organized selves which exist side by side. Violet's experience stands midway between the normal world of fantasy and the abnormal world of the dual or multiple personality.

FORGOTTEN LIFE

Few if any psychological disorders have received greater attention from specialists and public alike than amnesia. Practically everyone has heard or read about the disheveled man who staggers up to the police desk in a dazed condition, pleading, "Sergeant, please help me. I don't know who I am or what my name is!" Equally familiar is the case of the fighter who takes a hard blow on the head and goes down for the count of nine. Later, in the locker room, he bemoans the loss of the fight, whereupon his trainer gleefully informs him that he struggled to his feet, and not only finished the round but went on to win the fight. Even more widely publicized is the *Random Harvest* type of case in which a man forgets his identity, wanders off to another town, assumes a new name, marries and has children, is eventually discovered by his first wife, and perhaps regains his original identity to boot.

It would be hard to equal such situations for sheer human drama. Yet they can not only be equalled but surpassed by the case of the Reverend Thomas Carson Hanna of Plantsville, Connecticut, a case which has become a landmark not only in the study of amnesia, but in the exploration of the subconscious levels of the human mind.

The Reverend Hanna was a vigorous, healthy man of twenty-five years of age, just starting his career in the ministry. His family background was excellent; he had received the finest university education; and he was considered a person of extraordinary ability and high promise. Yet within the space of less than half an hour this young clergyman underwent a change so profound that it was impossible to recognize him as the same person except by outward appearance. Here is how this change occurred, as described by an outstanding psychologist of the time, Dr. Boris Sidis:

On April 15, 1897, Mr. Hanna met with an accident; he fell from a carriage and was picked up in a state of unconsciousness. When the patient came to himself he was like one just born. He lost all knowledge acquired by him from the date of his birth up to the time of the accident. He lost all power of voluntary activity, knew nothing of his own personality, and could not recognize persons or objects. He had, in fact, no idea whatever of the external world. Objects, distance, time did not

exist for him. Movements alone attracted his involuntary attention, and these he liked to have repeated.
Nothing remained of his past life, not even a meaningless word, syllable, or articulate sound. He was totally
deprived of speech, he had lost all comprehension of
language. The conversation of the people around him
was to him nothing but sounds without any meaning.
He had lost all sense of orderliness in his responses to
calls of nature. The patient was smitten with full mental blindness, with the malady of complete oblivion.
Impressions coming to him from the external world had
lost their meaning; the patient did not know how to
interpret them. He was like a newborn babe.

The case of the Reverend Hanna was brought to the
attention of Dr. S. P. Goodhart of New York shortly after
the accident occurred. Suspecting a brain injury, he immediately conducted a thorough clinical examination. His
tests failed to reveal any signs of organic lesion, and he
therefore referred the case to Dr. Sidis, who was engaged in research at the Pathological Institute of the
New York State Hospitals.

When Dr. Sidis first examined the patient, a few weeks
after the accident, he found him in "a state of complete
amnesia": "H. has absolutely no recollection of any experience previous to the accident. His former life is completely gone from his memory. He has recollections only
for such events of his life as have occurred since the
injury. . . . Patient says 'I know' of events that have
occurred since the accident; of experiences previous to
that time he knows from reports of what 'others tell him.'
He regards the history of his life before the accident
as an experience that had occurred in the life of quite
a different person. . . . The accident may be considered
the boundary line separating two distinct lives of the

same individual. What had occurred in his former life before the accident is unknown to the personality formed after the accident. *Two selves seem to dwell within H.* One seems to be deadened, crushed in the accident, and the other is a living self whose knowledge and experience are but of yesterday. It seems to be a case of double consciousness, and the patient is now in a secondary state."

This initial diagnosis was fully verified by the exhaustive examinations that followed. Dr. Goodhart's observations were also confirmed: No evidence of tissue damage of any kind could be found—"There was not the least disturbance in his sense organs, no sign of peripheral or central injury. His sensibility and reactions to sense stimuli were fully normal." This finding was impressive enough, but far more striking was Sidis' verdict that even though Mr. Hanna behaved like a baby who had just entered upon life, his intellectual *capacities* had not suffered the slightest damage. Like a baby, he would reach out for his own image in the mirror, stretch out his hand to grasp far-off shining lights, and attempt to devour a cake of soap. Moreover, all the knowledge he had acquired in years of schooling seemed to have been wiped out by the accident. Words, numbers, and scientific theories meant nothing to him, and "no object, no person, however intimate and near, awakened in him even the vaguest sense of familiarity." He could not even recognize his own parents nor the young lady to whom he was devoted. And, like a baby, he had no special interest in the opposite sex, and no idea about sexual functions or the difference between men and women.

In view of these observations, one might ask, how did Dr. Sidis know that his patient's basic intelligence was still intact? By the simple fact that he found the young clergyman capable of learning and learning rapidly.

The learning process, however, had to start from scratch. The first evidence of progress was the same as it is for any infant: the control of movement. Within a few days, Mr. Hanna began to regain the use of his voluntary muscles as a result of experiencing his own involuntary movements as well as simple instruction from his doctors and nurses. Next, he learned to perceive depth and distance by stretching out his hand toward objects. Then he went through the usual stages of creeping, crawling, and toddling, and within a few weeks had learned to stand, walk, and run as well as a two-year-old child. Soon, too, he was able to eat by himself, and began to recognize different articles of food. By this time he no longer attempted to eat soap or devour an entire apple, core, stem and all. **1725496**

Progress was equally swift in communication. To make known his wants, he would imitate words and phrases used by other people. But this method proved too slow and cumbersome, and the psychologist found that he could teach his patient to speak more effectively by showing him objects and carefully pronouncing their names. The academic skills of reading and writing, however, presented special problems: "In reading, he asked for the meaning of nearly every third word, and his writing was like that of a child who had just begun to learn the formation of letters. His reading was extremely slow, hesitating, and his handwriting awkward. Curiously, he proved to be ambidextrous and could write equally well with either hand—something he could not achieve before the accident." The reason may be that he had regressed to the earliest infancy, long before children establish hand preference, which ordinarily begins to manifest itself at about eighteen months.

All through the learning period, which lasted for several weeks, Mr. Hanna demonstrated the superiority of his mentality in a variety of ways. He was as inquisitive as the brightest child, constantly asking questions, constantly showing his eagerness to learn new things. His memory was remarkably tenacious, and he retained everything he learned or observed in the minutest detail. His acuteness in distinguishing fine points, as well as his powers of reasoning, were unexcelled. His sense of proportion and appreciation for beauty were equally remarkable. Numbers came easily to him and, after a few weeks of teaching, Sidis found that "although he had not yet learned (in this state) his fractions, nor did he know anything of geometry, he still could solve very complicated problems in a simple way, making the best use of the knowledge he acquired."

Mr. Hanna's progress was, on the whole, so rapid that it soon became evident to the psychologist that his past had not been completely obliterated by the accident, and that he was actually not starting from scratch, as originally supposed. This led him to a theory that can best be expressed in his own words: "His keen sense of the proportionate, the harmonious, and the musical, his delicate appreciation of the good and the beautiful, his remarkable logical acumen, his great power of carrying on a long train of reasoning, the facility with which he acquired new knowledge, the immediate use to which he put it, the significant fact that in the course of a few weeks he learned to speak English correctly, pronouncing well and making no mistakes—all that, taken as a whole, confirmed me in the conclusion that the old personality was not crushed to death, that it was only dissociated from the rest of conscious life, and that from the subconscious depth in which it sunk it still exerted a great influence on the newly formed personality of the patient."

To test this theory, Sidis proceeded to explore Mr. Hanna's "subconscious self," using techniques that anticipated Sigmund Freud's emphasis on the dream as "the royal road to the unconscious," as well as Morton Prince's use of hypnosis in treating cases of multiple personality. The date of Freud's great work *The Interpretation of Dreams* was 1900, and it was not translated into English until several years later; the date of Prince's classic study of Christine Beauchamp, *The Dissociation of a Personality,* was 1906. The date of Sidis' investigation of the Reverend Hanna was 1897.

When the patient was asked to relate his dreams, he answered that they seemed to be of two kinds. One type was relatively indistinct, and turned out to be commonplace dreams of everyday life. A study of these dreams revealed that they were all based on experiences which had occurred *after* the accident, and therefore reflected only his current life. The other type was characterized as "clear picture dreams" or "visions," and depicted events which had occurred in his *former* life. Mr. Hanna, however, did not recognize these visions as past experiences, nor did he have any idea of their meaning. To the psychologist, on the other hand, they were of the highest importance, since they enabled him to "catch a glimpse into the darkness of the subconscious life," and gave him hope that he would eventually be able to draw back the veil that separated the patient from his past.

To verify the idea that these "visions" were reflections of his patient's past rather than fantasies or fabrications, Dr. Sidis invited Mr. Hanna's father to be present when the young man described them. Mr. Hanna, Sr., was able to identify practically all the events, persons, and places that occurred in these so-called dreams, even though his son insisted that he had never encountered them before. As an example, his father was able to identify a house on which his son claimed to see a sign reading "N-e-w B-o-s-t-o-n J-u-n-c." The younger Mr. Hanna spelled out the letters as he saw them, and knew the meaning of the word N-e-w since he had learned this word by then, but the rest of the sign was entirely unfamiliar and unintelligible to him. At another point, "When the father accidentally happened to mention the name 'Martinoe,' the patient's amazement knew no bounds. 'That is the name of a place I passed in my dream (vision),' he exclaimed, 'but how do you know it? It is only a dream!'"

In addition to the study of his patient's visions and dreams, Dr. Sidis used a variant of hypnosis to revive his preaccident memories. He had found this method, which he termed "hypnoidization," particularly effective in cases of amnesia. The patient was asked to close his eyes, remain as quiet as possible, and then attend to some stimulus such as either reading or singing. In the case of reading, he was asked to repeat what he had heard with his eyes still shut and tell what came to mind during or after the reading and repetition. In response to the song stimulus, he was simply to describe the ideas or images that passed through his mind.

This technique elicited a great deal of valuable material. In Sidis' own words, "Events, names of persons, places, sentences, phrases, whole paragraphs of books totally lapsed from memory, and in languages the very words of which sounded bizarre to his ears and the meaning of which was to him inscrutable—all that flashed lightning-like on the patient's mind. So successful was this method that on one occasion the patient was frightened by the flood of memories that rose suddenly from the obscure subconscious regions, deluged his mind, and were expressed aloud, only to be forgotten the next moment. To the patient himself it appeared as if another being took possession of his tongue."

The success of the hypnoidization method prompted

Dr. Sidis to go a step further. By asking leading questions, he encouraged his patient not only to envisage experiences from his former life, but to act them out. This technique appears to be an anticipation of the method of "abreaction" which Freud later developed. There is a difference, however, in their use of this method. Freud's emphasis was on reliving traumatic events and the harmful repressed feelings associated with them. By this means he sought to clear these feelings and the symptoms they produced out of the patient's system—a form of "emotional catharsis." Sidis, on the other hand, used the acting-out process primarily as a means of bringing forgotten events closer to the surface in order to break through a state of amnesia.

The breakthrough, however, was slow in coming. For several weeks Mr. Hanna relived earlier experiences, such as a storm that occurred on Mount Jewett, Pennsylvania, "sitting up in bed, with his eyes firmly shut, blind and deaf to all impressions that had no relation to the 'vision' . . . His environment is that of the past, and in it he lives and moves." A little later, he "fell into a state of double consciousness or double personality . . . The 'primary state' included the patient's whole life up to the time of the accident; the 'secondary state' dated from the accident, and included all the knowledge and experience acquired in that state. In the primary state the patient was discussing metaphysics, philosophy, theology, and even once wrote for me a concise statement on the science of pathology; in the secondary state he did not even know the meaning of these terms. In the primary state his handwriting was fine and delicate; in the secondary state it was awkward and childish, and he could only *print* capitals, as he had not yet learned to write them."

The two personalities were completely separated by

a wall of amnesia. Neither was aware of the other. There was, however, one bridge between the two: In his ordinary waking state (the secondary state), the patient vividly recalled the "visions" which occurred in his primary state. Moreover, the psychologist found that by the skillful use of suggestion and indirect questioning, he could begin to control the alternation of the two personalities. Then, as the patient lived through more and more of his past experiences, and as the secondary personality "matured," the two came closer and closer together. Slowly the visions acquired a sense of familiarity when Mr. Hanna recalled them in his waking state, and soon he began to recognize them as his own experiences. This breakthrough was the beginning of the end of the amnesia, and in time "the two personalities were finally run together into one. The patient is now perfectly well and healthy, and has resumed his former vocation."

In presenting the case of the Reverend Hanna in his book, *The Psychology of Suggestion,* Boris Sidis described it as "unique in the annals of psychiatry." On the whole this characterization still applies after seventy-odd years. Nevertheless a few other cases of sudden reversion to infancy have been reported, and one in particular deserves mention not only because it parallels the Hanna case in some respects, but because it offers a possible key to the cause of the disorder.

During World War I, Dr. William McDougall, one of America's leading psychologists, was in charge of psychiatric treatment at a hospital in England. In January 1918, one of the patients transferred to his care was an Australian private, M.B., who had been in a hospital a few months previously for complete loss of speech, or "mutism," which had apparently been precipitated by a heavy bombardment of the area in which he was stationed at the front. Under treatment he had recovered his voice, but in view of his previous reaction, was evacuated to Dr. McDougall's hospital when the air raids began over London.

When he was admitted to the hospital, M.B. spoke with a severe stutter and showed some tremor of the limbs—otherwise he behaved quite normally. On the second night, however, he was startled by the noise of a falling object, became extremely excited and frightened, and insisted that someone was "after" him. The next morning, Dr. McDougall found him "in a completely childish condition. He sat in bed alert and lively like a young child taking a keen interest in new surroundings. He childishly displayed his few bits of property and pointed inquiringly towards various objects. He showed no trace of comprehension of spoken or written language and uttered no sound other than 'oh sis-sis-sis'; this was frequently repeated and used partly as an emotional expression, partly to call our attention to the object of his curiosity. Given a pencil he made no attempt to write; and he seemed to have little or no understanding of the use of ordinary objects and utensils, most of which he examined with mingled expressions of curiosity and timidity. All his motor functions seemed to be intact, save that when he was put on his feet he walked jerkily, with short hurried steps, the feet planted widely apart. As soon as allowed to do so, he slipped down upon the floor and crawled about on his buttocks with the aid of his hand, as some young children prefer to crawl."

This behavior was startling in itself, but appeared even more astonishing when it was learned that the strapping M.B., who had suddenly been reduced from the age of twenty-two to the age of fourteen or fifteen months, had enjoyed a reputation as a roughrider and breaker of horses before entering the service.

Further investigation revealed that the patient could

not feed himself and would not take any food unless the nurse tasted it first. He failed to grasp the simplest commands such as to put out his tongue, even when conveyed by gesture; and he showed no interest in letters or photographs of his relatives and friends which were found in his pockets. Most of his time was spent in playing with various objects as toys, and with a small doll which a neighbor on the ward kept as a mascot. At one point he wept like an infant when a nurse accidentally stepped on a picture of a horse which he treasured. He was very easily frightened, and shrank from dogs, the stuffed head of a stag, and any sudden noise that occurred without obvious cause.

As in the case of the Reverend Hanna, M.B. gave some indications that he retained hidden memories of his normal life. When offered a lighted cigarette, he immediately smoked it—although he proceeded to stick it, still glowing, behind his ear. When shown a picture of a steeplechase, "he became very excited and animated, straddled across a chair and made as though riding a horse race, and then by gesture and the help of various small objects gave a vivid description of a steeplechase upon a miniature course indicated on the floor." After he had been in the hospital for a few weeks, he toddled out to the swimming pool, stripped off his clothes, dived in and swam like an expert. He also tried to kiss some of the nurses on the sly.

During the three months that followed his admission, in January, M.B. passed through many of the stages of early childhood. By March he had achieved great facility in describing daily events through gestures, and a little later he made a few sounds to accompany the gestures. He had become a universal pet on the ward, and one man patiently taught him to spell out a few words on the typewriter, while others taught him to copy pictures with a pencil in the crude style of a five- or six-year-old. Toward the end of the month, he ceased to crawl and learned to walk about the ward, humming as he went. In April, however, he was frightened by the rumbling of beds being moved about on the ward above him, and "promptly relapsed to complete mutism and crawling, with loss of all his gains."

M.B. recovered spontaneously from the relapse and continued to make progress. By May he began to use names of his own making for people and objects around him. He also took an interest in basket weaving and other forms of occupational therapy. At about this time, McDougall made several attempts to hasten his improvement by means of hypnosis and narcotherapy (ether rather than sodium amytal was used at the time). These efforts were unsuccessful because the patient was still unable to use or understand the spoken word to any great extent.

Progress, however, continued on a spontaneous basis, and by July M.B. had learned to copy printed words and numbers, but without attaching any meaning to them. Although he could not use words in making calculations, he was able to count a small number of articles by placing them in pairs. He also seemed to understand "in a very vague way" a good deal that was said to him or in his presence.

Shortly afterward he was shipped back to Australia, where he failed to recognize his relatives. A year or so later, however, he was reported to have "gradually returned to an approximately normal condition."

The two cases described in this chapter have much in common since both involve a complete regression to infantile behavior. Moreover, they both seem to have been brought on by traumatic experiences—an accident in one case and heavy bombardment in the other. Would they therefore be classified as the same type of disorder?

The answer seems to be no. M.B. is probably an example of "hysterical puerilism," and is so categorized in Henderson, Gillespie and Batchelor's *Textbook of Psychiatry*. This is a disorder in which the patient reverts to behavior characteristic of early childhood, apparently in response to pressures and anxieties. In M.B.'s case the regression may have been due to an unconscious desire to escape the risks of war by regressing to the safety of childhood. Mr. Hanna's case, on the other hand, would probably be classified today as an "acute traumatic disorder," a reaction that sometimes immediately follows a severe blow to the head. In this type of disorder the patient suffers a temporary impairment of brain function, and two of the common symptoms are loss of consciousness and amnesia, both of which occurred in Mr. Hanna's case. The unusual character of the case, however—and the reason for including it in this book—is that the amnesia did not simply involve recent events, as it ordinarily does, but extended all the way back to infancy.

NOM DE PLUME

Fifty years ago the name of Patience Worth was a household word, and her novels evoked the highest praise from the country's leading critics. *The Sorry Tale* was hailed by the New York *Mirror* as a "world literary marvel" and described by the New York *Times* as "a wonderful, a beautiful and a noble book, constructed with the precision of a master hand." Another of her longer novels, *Hope Trueblood*, was compared to the works of George Eliot, and her plays and poems—fifteen hundred in all —were acclaimed as literary gems.

Today the name of Patience Worth is all but forgotten, and her books survive, if they survive at all, only as dusty relics. Yet she cannot be dismissed as just another author who failed to stand the test of time. Patience Worth deserves to be remembered perennially—not for the merit of her works, but for the manner in which they were written and the light they throw on the human mind.

Our story of these works begins with a scene in 1916. One evening Mrs. John Curran, a St. Louis housewife, was sitting at her desk gathering her thoughts together before starting a letter. Suddenly she felt distracted and "far away," and her hand began to write by itself, as if guided by an unseen being. As she wrote, her pen gathered speed until it fairly flew over the paper—without hesitation and apparently without thought. When she finally put it down and gathered up the sheets of paper, she found that they contained the first chapter of a new book "by Patience Worth," written in language entirely foreign to her own way of speaking or writing.

Mrs. Curran's writing, under the name of Patience Worth, covered twenty-four years. Over three and a half million words were produced, always following the same general pattern. She would suddenly feel a compelling urge to write and would begin without preparation or intimation of what was coming. She would work on several manuscripts at a time, in each case starting precisely where she had left off a week or so before. As she herself described it, the entire panorama of a story would move before her "like pictures on a screen," and she would simply record the action in words. What is more, she did not work over the material, as practically every author does; once it was written, not a word was changed. In one instance, when a chapter of one of her books was mislaid by the publisher, she sat down and wrote it out, word for word, even though she had written the original months before.

The strange case came to the attention of a leading psychologist of the time, Dr. Charles E. Cory, and he conducted a thorough investigation over a period of many months. Mrs. Curran gave him her full co-operation, for she was completely mystified by her totally unexpected role as an author of renown. She had never had any experience or practice in writing, nor any aspiration to authorship. In fact, as Dr. Cory stated, "The one ambition of her life has been to sing. She has a good voice, and until Patience Worth 'arrived,' her entire energy was given to its cultivation." As to her intellect, he found her to be intelligent and intuitive, but much inferior to Patience Worth: "A conversation with her, though based upon an extended acquaintance, does not give the impression that one is in the presence of the mind that wrote *The Sorry Tale*."

This impression was fully supported by an examination of the many works she produced. Most of them reflected the life and times of bygone eras—ancient Rome, early England, the Middle Ages—and contained a richness of detail that could normally be acquired only through prolonged study and research. In each case the language appeared to be thoroughly in keeping with the times depicted and sometimes so archaic that it was difficult for the average reader, including Mrs. Curran herself, to understand. Moreover, these historical tales were not constructed simply, but were "intricately woven" and amazingly varied not only in style but in content. Some were powerful and dramatic in impact, others full of subtle humor or seasoned wisdom, but all reflected the skill of an author who seemed to have completely mastered her craft. To illustrate these points, let us look at some brief excerpts from her works:

From *The Sorry Tale*

The morn spread forth the golden tresses of the sun, and lo, a star still rested on a cloud bar. And Jerusalem slept. The temples' stood whited, and the market's place shewed emptied. Upon the temple's pool the morn-sky shewed, and doves bathed within the waters at its edge.

Beside the market's way camels lay, sunk upon their folded legs, and chewed, their mouths slipping o'er straw, and tongues thrust forth to pluck up more for chewing. The hides shewed like unto a beggar's skull, hair fallen off o'er sores.

The day had waked the tribes, and narrowed streets shewed bearded men, and asses, packed. The temple priests stood forth upon the stoned steps and blew upon the shell that tribesmen come. From out the pillared place the smoke of incense curled, and within the stone made echo of the chants and sandal's fall of foot.

From *Telka*

A-swish the pot-broth. A-whang the bowl. A-kick the hearth-log. A-flush the cheek and a-snap the eye. A-jerk the reed-wove basket from off the cupboard top. A-thud the bare soles. A-whack up on the flags with scows, a-slammed from 'neath the bench. A-clatter scow-shod feet, and kirtle jerked o'er middle o' the smock. A-toss

the curls, and maid, a-hot by anger, off adown the path
unto the river's bend.

Formal Poem
Into the Purple Sea Would I Cast My Nets

Oh, into the purple sea would I cast my nets.
I would drag its depths for the vagrant songs
That sink to rest therein.
I would trap the whisper o' the shells
And the moaning of the reefs.
I would catch the silver sprays
As they trickle back upon the sea's breast,
Losing them in one great mightiness.
I would listen to the waters
Of the young morning, when they wake
Fresh sounding of the wind's caress.
Into the purple sea would I cast my net
To bring it forth so laden.

How did Mrs. Curran—or "Patience Worth"—acquire
the astonishing skill and wealth of information that made
these stories and poems possible? To answer these questions Dr. Cory made a careful survey of Mrs. Curran's
reading from childhood on, and found little or nothing
that would account for her intimate acquaintance with
the life and customs of the people she so vividly described.
The answer was the same when he examined the interests
that dominated her life, and the contacts she had made
throughout the years. Moreover, he found that Mrs. Curran herself could throw no real light on the problem. She
could not recall books, conversations, or schoolwork that
would explain her fund of information and her ability to
tell a tale. She did, however, offer an "explanation" of
a different order. She suggested, with some reservations,

that Patience Worth was actually the reincarnation of
a gifted Englishwoman who had lived several centuries
before. During that life, she theorized, Patience must
have read about or in some cases actually experienced the
events which later inspired the stories that so mysteriously
flowed from her pen.

In discussing this theory, Mrs. Curran revealed an interesting fact. In 1913 she spent many evenings with a
spiritualist friend, Mrs. Hutchings, in an effort to contact
the dead. A short time after these sessions, Patience made
her first appearance. She was born—or if you like, reborn
—on a Ouija board operated by Mrs. Hutchings and
herself, announcing her arrival with the sentence "Many
months ago I lived. Again I come—Patience Worth my
name." Mrs. Curran drew the one conclusion that seemed
plausible to her: The séances had put her in touch not
only with a person who was no longer living but one
who now resided in her own body!

Dr. Cory also saw a connection, but used it to reinforce
a theory of his own. He had long suspected that Patience
Worth came into being as the result of a dissociation in
Mrs. Curran's personality, a condition in which a subconscious segment of the mind splits off and assumes
a life of its own. Unlike other cases of split or multiple
personality, the secondary self in this case (Patience
Worth) was of a distinctly higher order of mentality
than the primary self (Mrs. Curran). Apparently this
self had been developing for some time beneath the level
of consciousness, and was brought to the surface by the
sessions with the medium and the Ouija board. Later
on, however, Mrs. Curran found the Ouija board too
slow, but discovered that she could take down Patience
Worth's dictation directly or use her husband as recorder.

It is a well-known fact that many mediums are themselves dissociated, but in this highly unusual case the

medium was instrumental in arousing the dissociative tendency in her *subject*, Mrs. Curran, during the séances. The case of Patience Worth is also a striking illustration of the fact that creative thinking can occur below the level of consciousness. There is other evidence that this can happen: The idea of analytic geometry came to Descartes during a dream; Coleridge claimed that he created his great poem *Kubla Khan* in a drug-induced sleep; and Mozart maintained that some of his works burst upon his consciousness in finished form, and he simply wrote them down without changing a note. The writings of Patience Worth, however, differ from these examples in one important respect: They were apparently the product of a split consciousness and the formation of an incipient second self. Dr. Cory regarded this split as the key to the case. As he put it, "The division of the self has resulted in a division of labor. To Mrs. Curran falls the care of the needs of the body, and the interests of social life. . . . This sets free and unfettered the mind of Patience Worth. . . . She is beyond the reach of perturbation and confusion, and therein lies her strength. Her mind seems to possess the effortless activity and facility of a dream, a dream without chaos." In a word, Patience Worth could dwell in a realm of creative imagination because Mrs. Curran took care of the day-to-day problems of life.

This suggests that many people may have the germ of creativity in them, and that it might grow and flourish if, somehow, their minds could be freed from everyday demands and distractions. But the theory still leaves one important aspect of the case unexplained—how Mrs. Curran acquired the huge fund of information which her second self drew upon.

To answer this question another psychologist, Joseph Jastrow, made an exhaustive study of Mrs. Curran's background and early experience. He found some "clues" in the following facts. Her lineage on both sides was English. Her father was a newspaper editor, and not only her friend Mrs. Hutchings, but an uncle, were spiritualist mediums. Part of her youth was spent playing the piano in her uncle's church, and part was spent in the Ozarks. Jastrow states:

> Inevitably she absorbed some knowledge of English ways from her parents. Her father's editorial office may well have been a center for miscellaneous information. The constant association with Mr. Yost, editor, a voracious reader with a large fund of general knowledge, encouraged the development of Patience Worth. Mrs. Hutchings, a writer, introduced the Ouija board as a medium of expression. Mrs. Curran found that she could make it go. The possibility of mediumship or control was familiar to her; also, that at séances mediums speak in affected language. Her own religious occupations appear throughout. The Ozark dialect fell upon a sensitive ear and retentive memory; it is a quaint speech with many archaic usages . . . It is then my hypothesis—and admittedly such—that Mrs. Curran welcomed the Ouija board as a mode of release of a literary facility and an imaginative trend. To launch upon an uncertain sea of writing on her own account would hardly be a venture that would come within her consideration.
>
> Patience Worth was a mask; and even the diffident become bold when their personality is safeguarded . . . Mrs. Curran did not devise this outlet or plan the career which came to be hers; she drifted into it, and from drifting came to steer the craft with all the zest of a successful navigator. That form of motivated drifting is favorable to freedom of improvisation, which is con-

genial to ready rather than elaborately skilled minds
. . . She is unaware of any preparation; the material
seems to come spontaneously and impromptu; but as
in all such cases of subconscious performance, there is
convincing evidence of long incubation; the hatching is
not as sudden as it appears.

Dr. Jastrow goes on to show that the dialects used by
Patience Worth in her stories and poems were not as
authentic as her admirers and even the critics thought
them to be. He submitted many of her writings—including
the samples given above—to an outstanding Elizabethan
scholar, Professor Schelling, whose verdict was that "The
language employed is not that of any historical age or
period; but where it is not the current English of the
part of the United States where Mrs. Curran lives, is a
distortion born of a superficial acquaintance with poetry
and a species of would-be Scottish dialect . . . The prose
shows no sense of style beyond a certain feeling for the
swing of our English Biblical phrase, and I find nothing
in the way of genius either in the plots or the stories or the
realization of the personalities of the characters involved.
Improvisation, now a lost art among lettered folk, is not
dead; and it is under such conditions as those surrounding Mrs. Curran that it is likely to be revived: not too
much education, an interest in music, an existence, shall
we say, upon the fringes of culture, a memory for the
phrase, and a tendency for reverie. I raise no point as to
the candor in this as in any such case; it is as easy to
deceive one's self as others; and deliberate deception does
not enter into it."

This analysis not only throws light on Mrs. Curran's
literary output but also explains why her novels and
poems, so impressive at first, did not stand the test of
time. Jastrow himself concludes on an amusing note: "The

performance is significant not as trick authorship but as
an interesting form of release which is not likely to be
duplicated—not with the same setting. To Mrs. Curran,
Patience Worth has been worth the patient devotion she
spent upon it. Many a writer, including the present one,
would gladly adopt a mythical ghost, if in compensation
he received the fluency of output along the direction of
his desires, and thus became his own ghost-writer."

There is little doubt that Jastrow has put his finger on
some of the sources of Mrs. Curran's inspiration. But an
additional possibility comes to *this* author's mind. If we
accept the idea that Mrs. Curran wrote her novels and
poems during episodes of abstraction or dissociation, we
suspect that previous episodes had occurred during which
she read books dealing with people and events in the
distant past. Since this reading was done in a split-off
state of mind, she would have remained unaware of it
in her normal waking state. Nevertheless, the material
might well have been stored in her memory and worked
over by her unconscious until it came to the surface in
the form of novels, plays, and poems written under the
nom de plume of Patience Worth.

While there is no actual proof of this theory in Mrs.
Curran's case, it is supported by the fact that many
people—especially dissociated personalities—experience
episodes of temporary amnesia during which they perform
unusual actions or undergo experiences which they cannot
remember in their normal state of mind. This theory is
also supported by an additional fact which Jastrow men-
tions but glosses over: The name Patience Worth was
traced to a contemporary novel *which Mrs. Curran did
not recall reading.* Our theory is that the same thing may
have occurred many times over. Certainly an explanation
of this kind is far more acceptable than the theory of
reincarnation.

There is a striking parallel between Mrs. Curran and two other cases, one from the turn of the century and the other from the present day. The older case revolves around a spiritualist medium in France named Hélène Smith and her alter ego, Leopold. Like Mrs. Curran, there was nothing extraordinary about Hélène when she was in her normal state, but when she spontaneously fell into a dissociated, somnambulistic state, a man who called himself Leopold appeared before her so vividly that she never doubted his reality. According to the psychologist Théodore Flournoy, who investigated her case, Leopold "speaks for her in a way she would have no idea of doing, he dictates her poems of which she would be incapable. He replies to her oral or mental questions, converses with her, and discusses various questions. Like a wise friend, a rational mentor, and as one seeing things from a higher plane, he gives her advice, counsel, orders, even sometimes directly opposite to her wishes and against which she rebels . . . In a word, it would be impossible to imagine a being more independent or more different from Mlle. Smith herself, having a more personal character, an individuality more marked, or a more certain actual existence."

But that is not all. Like Patience Worth, Leopold introduced his host personality, Hélène, to worlds that appeared to be completely foreign to her, all the way from medieval times to the planet Mars. During her séances she would envisage complex scenes and even act them out. In her Martian period, for example, she not only described in detail the landscape, inhabitants, fauna and flora of that distant planet, but even spoke and wrote in a strange language which she called "Ultra-Martian" and which, she insisted, she had learned directly from Leopold. Undoubtedly Leopold was not only an incipient second personality, but one that represented the young woman's hidden impulses and repressed desires.

The other case—the current one—is that of an English-woman named Rosemary Brown who claims that she is visited periodically by the spirits of long-dead composers. Among them are some of the greatest of all time: Chopin, Schubert, Beethoven, Brahms, Bach, Mozart, Debussy, and, above all, Liszt. Their visits are always in spirit form and imperceptible to others. During these visits they rarely engage in idle conversation, but instead dictate what she calls their new compositions, either communicating them directly from mind to mind or guiding her hands over the piano keys. During the past six years she has accumulated over four hundred compositions ranging from songs and sonatas to symphonies and opera—including the missing last movement of Schubert's *Unfinished Symphony*. She has had a limited musical education, and plays these compositions without a great deal of artistry, but nevertheless a number of musical authorities have asserted that they conform closely to the individual style of each of the composers.

Many people dismiss Mrs. Brown and her coterie of composers as sheer hoax. Many others, including the lady herself, accept her experiences as clear and cogent proof that the dead can communicate with the living. But there is a third alternative: Mrs. Brown may be receiving messages not from the spirits of the composers, but from the depths of her own mind. As in the cases of Mrs. Curran and Hélène Smith, she may have an extremely active unconscious, in which the music "incubates" for some time, and then, when she is in a dissociated state, it is delivered to consciousness in finished form. And again like Mrs. Curran and Hélène Smith, her hidden fantasies take dramatic, personalized form like figures in a dream.

The Power of Suggestion

Of all the influences on men's minds, suggestion is probably the most universal. We see it in the wide-eyed responses of native Africans to the incantations of the medicine man, and in the confessions of witches brought before medieval tribunals. At the dawn of the modern era it took a different form in the carefully staged "treatment" of Anton Mesmer. Dressed in purple robes, he attempted to cure his patients by having them dip iron rods in a tub of magnetized water and apply them to the ailing parts of their bodies.

Today, in spite of the fact that we live in a century that prides itself on rationality, suggestion appears to be as prevalent as ever. Most of us are still affected by emotion more than by reason. Suggestion has merely changed its form, but its power is virtually undiminished. The whole of our economy is built on advertising, and advertising is built on suggestion. Our political scene would be far different if campaigners no longer used the band-wagon appeal, and no longer kissed little babies and sprinkled their speeches with "glittering generalities" about clean government and a better world ahead. Many people would be overdosed with sleeping medicines if doctors did not prescribe placebos, those dummy pills that contain nothing but sugar or bread, yet work nevertheless.

Each of the following topics involves suggestion in one form or another. One will describe dramatic experiments designed to determine the limits of suggestion—that is, where does it work and where does it prove ineffective? Another will deal with its power to produce changes in the body such as scars and blisters. A third will illustrate, and attempt to explain, the ancient practice of water divining. The fourth will describe a unique and unexpected use of hypnotic suggestion in solving a personal problem. These case studies—all true—will, we hope, take the reader into territory he may not have explored before, and introduce him to some of the mysteries that lie in the outer reaches of the mind.

THE LETTER

It is a well-known fact that under hypnotic suggestion an apt subject can be induced to do all kinds of curious and outlandish things such as eating a lemon without wincing when told it is an orange. But is it possible to induce him to commit a crime or violate his ethical code?

To put this important question to the test, Dr. Milton H. Erickson, then a psychiatrist at the Eloise Hospital in Michigan, selected as one of his subjects a young man whom he knew well and who was "no more conventional than the average college student." While carrying out a series of hypnotic demonstrations, he developed this subject—we'll call him Andrew—to a point where he could be readily put into a deep trance. After that he instructed Andrew, over a period of months, "in accord with a carefully planned technique of suggestion, to read his roommate's love letters, without the subject's knowledge that the experimenter had secretly made contact with the roommate [we'll call him Jim] and had arranged for the leaving of personal letters readily accessible." Further, Dr. Erickson took pains to give Andrew a good reason to read the letters: "Every effort was made to convince him of the legitimacy of the act as a worthy scientific procedure, related to the investigation of the ability to remember unpleasant things, and connected, in turn, with an investigation of memory processes as affected by hypnosis."

After this preparation, Dr. Erickson hypnotized Andrew and instructed him to read Jim's mail when he was alone in their room. The first trial failed. The mail was not moved and Andrew insisted that he had not read it. On subsequent trials he also failed to obey instructions and even suggested an alternative. He "offered to do any number of disagreeable tasks which could be used as a memory test and which involved himself only." However, Dr. Erickson persisted in his original intent of inducing him to read the letters, and "Finally a promise was secured from the subject that he would do as asked on a particular evening if the experimenter would be present."

When the appointed evening arrived, Dr. Erickson arranged to visit him when Jim was out of the room. He immediately placed Andrew in a deep trance state and asked him to get one of the letters and read it. At this point a new form of resistance developed: "Extreme difficulty was experienced by the subject in finding that letter. He overlooked it repeatedly and searched in all the wrong places, since no overt move was made by the experimenter to direct his search. Eventually, he had to be forced to find the letter and open it. He immediately discovered that he could not read it because he had mislaid his glasses. In searching for his glasses, he succeeded in mislaying the letter, and when both the glasses and the letter were at hand, he opened the letter in such fashion that he was confronted by the blank sides of the pages. These he kept turning around and around in a helpless fashion, explaining that the pages were blank. After being told insistently to turn the pages over, he yielded, but did this in such fashion that the writing was then upside down. When this error was corrected, the subject developed spontaneously a blindness and became unable to read."

Andrew had indeed become psychologically blind, his final defense against betraying his roommate and his own ethical principles. But since he was still under the influence of hypnosis, Dr. Erickson was able to eliminate this reaction by suggestion, and he immediately regained his sight. However, when a further effort was made to get him to read the letter, "the blindness returned and it finally became necessary to discontinue the attempt."

There is an interesting sequel to this experiment, which Dr. Erickson has reported in the journal *Psychiatry,* under the title "An Experimental Investigation of the Possible Anti-Social Use of Hypnosis." Some weeks later he again enlisted Jim's co-operation and instructed him to remark to Andrew, "I just got a letter from my girl that I want you to read." Andrew at once replied, "I would like to. It's a funny thing, but for a long time I have wanted to read your mail. I don't know why. I've just had an awfully strong urge and it has disturbed me a lot, and I will be glad to do it and get that urge out of my system." Dr. Erickson goes on to say, "He then read the letter, of

which fact the experimenter was notified by the roommate. On the occasion of the next trance, the subject was
asked the general question about having read his roommate's mail. He stated that he had done so one day in
the waking state *at the roommate's but not at the experimenter's request.* He was then questioned extensively for
the content of the letter, but he was found unable to
remember any of it. When it was suggested that he re-
read the letter, he agreed, but demanded insistently the
privilege of asking his roommate's permission first, nor
would he consent to re-read the letter unless this conces-
sion were made."

In his comment on this experiment, one of several reported in his article, Dr. Erickson states: "Despite a
hypnotic technique of suggestion sufficient to hold an
offensive task before the subject for a period of months,
an exceedingly plausible and acceptable justification, and
obviously worthy motives, the entire attempt was so
complete a failure that he could not be induced hypnotically to repeat the waking performance authorized
in a socially acceptable manner except under the precise
conditions of that waking performance." This telling experiment therefore strongly suggests that under hypnosis
a person of good character cannot be induced to abandon
his moral code and commit an antisocial act.

The question of whether hypnosis can be used to induce
immoral or criminal acts has been hotly debated ever
since the end of the last century when two French doctors, Hippolyte-Marie Bernheim and A. A. Liébeault, began to use this technique in treating emotional disorders.
It is not a question that can be settled once and for all
by a single experiment, even if it appears to be as
compelling as the one just described. The only way we
can come near answering it is by performing a variety

of experiments on a variety of subjects. Fortunately many have already been performed; let's look at some outstanding examples.

One of the best-known series of experiments was performed by L. W. Rowland in 1939. In one experiment, subjects were deeply hypnotized and told to reach into a box and pick up a deadly rattlesnake; in another, several hypnotized subjects were ordered to throw sulphuric acid at the experimenter's face, after having been reminded that it could sear the skin and put out the eyes. In both cases some of the subjects obeyed the hypnotist and attempted to carry out the command. However, no harm was done, since both the snake and the experimenter were actually behind a sheet of invisible glass.

W. Lyon performed experiments along similar lines with somewhat similar results. Ten hypnotized subjects were ordered to pour sulphuric acid on the hands of an observer and on their own hands as well. They were also ordered to tear up a folder marked "Confidential Report." Out of a total of thirty trials (three for each), eleven of the suggested actions were carried out—but seven were ruled out because there was evidence that the subjects would not have carried them out if they had been more certain that the tasks were as dangerous or antisocial as the operator said they were.

Dr. Erickson, who performed the "letter" experiment, conducted a series of other trials that included stealing small sums of money, purloining important papers from a desk, and telling deliberate lies to a friend. His results were consistently negative: The subjects all refused to carry out the objectionable acts.

Milton V. Kline had four hypnotists put a twenty-eight-year-old male student into a deep trance, one after the other, and then order him to behave in a manner that was "not only antisocial but punishable by law." (The act consisted of self-exposure.) None of the experimenters could induce the student to comply. In a second experiment another subject was instructed to hallucinate a socially acceptable situation (having normal sexual intercourse with his wife) while being directed to perform the same act. This time he complied with the directions of three male hypnotists but refused to do so with a fourth, who was a woman. In a third experiment the act was again performed, but only for an experimenter who had worked with him for eight months, and who assured him that "It is all right to do this, you can do it, I would like you to do it." The other experimenters could not get him to do it.

W. R. Wells hypnotized a subject and ordered him to perform the following act as soon as he was awakened (posthypnotic suggestion): He would go to Wells's overcoat, which was hanging on a wall in the office, perceive it as his own, take a dollar bill from its pocket, and spend it just as if it belonged to him. His subject "stole" the money and spent it exactly as commanded.

Margaret Brenman repeated this experiment with six women selected as good subjects, and also had them perform other objectionable acts such as "stealing" a pen from a desk and examining the contents of a stranger's purse. The subjects were all deeply hypnotized and ordered to perceive these articles as their own. The acts were performed exactly as suggested.

J. G. Watkins, then an Army officer, performed three experiments on a corporal in his command. In the first, he told the corporal that another officer, Captain S, would give him information which he was not to divulge to him under any circumstances: "Remember, if you tell me, you are directly disobeying a military order." After receiving the secret information, the corporal was placed in a deep trance by Watkins, and told, "I am Captain S. I just gave you a piece of information you were not to divulge. I want to see if you remember it, Corporal. What is it?" The corporal revealed the information. So did his other subjects, seven in all.

In a second experiment, a member of the Women's Army Corps was chosen as the most suggestible he could find. Again an officer gave secret information, but this time Watkins placed his subject in a very light trance without inducing an hallucination, and instructed her as follows: "You have a message given to you by your commanding officer. You are working in a military intelligence office and know the seriousness of not being able to keep confidential information. Furthermore, you know the consequences of disobeying a military order from a superior. Yet, in spite of this, you are going to tell me that message. It is rising in your throat and you will not be able to keep it down. It is getting higher and higher . . . You will endure the most extreme suffering until you release it and speak the message. Speak it! Speak it!" The subject revealed the message.

The third experiment performed by Watkins was even more dramatic and nearly resulted in tragedy. He hypnotized an Army private and instructed him as follows: "In a minute you will slowly open your eyes. In front of you you will see a dirty Jap soldier. He has a bayonet and is going to kill you unless you kill him first. You will have to strangle him with your bare hands." A lieutenant colonel then took up a position directly in front of the subject, and "It took the instantaneous assistance of three others to break the soldier's grip, pull him off the officer, and hold him until the experimenter could quiet him back into a sleep condition." When the experiment was repeated with another subject, the man not only attempted to strangle the "Jap," but unexpectedly pulled out and opened a pocket knife and was prevented from stabbing him only by an upward wrist parry by the officer and quick action on the part of the witnesses.

At first sight it may appear that a number of these experiments achieved positive results—that is, they seem to have demonstrated that some subjects, at least, will perform objectionable or antisocial acts under the influence of hypnotic suggestion. However, there are at least three factors that cast doubt on this conclusion. First, many of them were carefully selected as "good" hypnotic subjects—individuals who could readily be put into a deep trance and comply with the hypnotist's instructions. In other words, they had already had special practice in obeying commands, and this might carry over to further experiments.

More telling than this objection is the fact that in prior situations the hypnotist had not asked his subjects to do anything against either their moral code or the legal code, and consequently the subjects had established a trusting relationship with him. Since that trust had never been violated before, it is likely that the subjects assumed that the experimenter would not ask them to perform acts that were really harmful to themselves or other people, however harmful or unlawful they might appear to be. Lyon found definite evidence for this point: "Hypnotized subjects . . . who performed the acts later testified that they did so because they trusted the experimenter and did not believe he could ask them to do something actually wrong." To be specific, there must have been an undercurrent of confidence that the experimenter would not jeopardize his subject's life by having him pick up a rattlesnake or jeopardize his own life by having a glass of acid thrown in his face. And the same would apply to the other experiments as well.

The third objection applies primarily to the experiments in which hallucination was employed. True, subjects did take money that did not belong to them; they also gave away confidences, exhibited themselves, and even attempted to kill another human being. However, in all these cases the subjects had been hypnotized before and knew they were being hypnotized again. And they further knew that they were engaged in an experiment, and that the suggested actions served an experimental purpose. Surely this would be enough to reassure them to some degree.

But even if it did not, and they actually believed in the suggested hallucinations, their acts were not unethical or punishable by law. They were acting under the control of another person rather than themselves, and they had no intent to violate the moral code or perform antisocial actions. Taking one's own money is not a crime. Neither is attacking a war enemy in self-defense, or exposing oneself in a situation where it is ethically done (and note that the man refused to do so with a lady hypnotist present). As another investigator, A. M. Weitzenhoffer, has pointed out: "In the past there has been general agreement that subjects could carry out antisocial acts if and when they a) felt protected, b) had latent criminal tendencies, c) had an implicit trust in the hypnotist . . . [There is] a fourth possible situation: The subject does not perceive the suggested act as being antisocial in nature."

We can conclude, then, in answer to whether or not antisocial acts can be induced under hypnosis, not only that practically all such attempts have been successfully resisted by the subjects, but that in the rare instances where the suggestion was carried out, some special cir-

cumstance prevailed: great confidence in the hypnotist, a
close relationship plus reassurance, or disguising the act
through hallucination. It appears that no one has demonstrated that a hypnotist can induce a person to perform
an antisocial act merely by ordering him to do it.

THE UNHEALING WOUNDS

The time was early Friday evening, and the place a
simple red-brick farmhouse in Uptergrove, a tiny town
in Ontario, Canada. Mrs. Donald McIsaac was hurriedly
finishing the supper dishes, for she knew what was coming. Putting the last plate away, she took off her apron
and climbed the stairs to her room and went to bed.
Downstairs the grandfather clock struck six—and the pain
began.

All that afternoon the scars on the back of Mrs.
McIsaac's hands, and others on her feet, head, back, and
side had begun to lose their hardness. But now, as she
lay in bed, they gradually took on the appearance of
fresh wounds. Soon blood began to form on the surface,
drop by drop; as it did, the pain mounted to excruciating
intensity and she moaned in agony. A half hour later the
woman slowly turned her eyes to heaven; she appeared to
lapse into a trance, and the agony in her face gave way
to an expression of ecstasy.

The appalling scene continued for three hours, and
Mrs. McIsaac's entire body became bathed in blood. But
as nine o'clock approached, the pain and bleeding grad-

ually subsided, and as the hour struck, they vanished completely and she fell into a deep, restful sleep.

Mrs. McIsaac's wounds were stigmata (Greek for "brand marks"), a term applied to scars which resemble the wounds inflicted on Jesus during the crucifixion. Those on the hands and feet represented the nails of the cross; those on the head, the crown of thorns; those on the back, the marks of the lash; and the one in the side, the thrust of the spear after he was crucified.

Mrs. McIsaac's wounds have been carefully examined by medical specialists of all three major faiths. The description given above is based directly on an eyewitness account of a Protestant doctor who participated in one of these examinations.

A few more details from this account will complete the picture: "During the early part of the week Mrs. McIsaac was in very good health despite the marks . . . perfectly normal, except that she is fairly deaf and has weak eyes . . . She talked easily and cheerfully. She talked a good deal about her religion, Roman Catholicism, in which she is obviously a devout believer, but she also talked of other things . . . She was bright, lively and full of energy right up until late Friday afternoon." Then, at six o'clock, the pain and bleeding started. "At times during the three-hour period," the account goes on, "she raised up to a sitting position, stretched her arms out in front of her . . . She did not respond to questions during the times when she was apparently in a coma . . . She was insensitive to the touch of a hand or to sudden motion. But there were pauses during which the pain apparently subsided, and during these lapses she answered questions and described what she said she had seen while in the comatose condition." Later, after the episode was over, and she had slept for a short while, "she remembered all that she had said during the pauses between the trance states and described in greater detail what she had seen and heard while in the comas . . . She seemed very tired. That night she slept well and on Saturday morning she appeared surprisingly fresh and youthful-looking and in very good health."

What *had* she seen and heard during the apparent comas? According to a priest who investigated this aspect of the case, she experienced ecstatic visions of the Sacred Passion and other scenes from church history: "Nearly all the contents conform to the liturgical season in which they occur. Visions of the Passion do not take place on Fridays on which the church does not specially commemorate the suffering of Christ such as the Fridays between Christmas and Ash Wednesday, and those between Easter and Corpus Christi. The wounds bleed less on these Fridays, too. But on Good Friday the pain is worse than at any other time and the wounds bleed more." According to the priest, her visions are accurate with regard to the architecture, dress, customs, and language of the particular period: "In the visions of the Passion, for instance, not only does she hear the vernacular of the time and place, Aramaic, but distinguishes between dialects of this tongue. She describes the pots of pitch, lamps, Roman eagles, fasces, and other objects in very simple language but in great detail."

Mrs. McIsaac's stigmata began to appear in 1937, and the investigations we have cited took place in 1950. Looking back, she recalls that she experienced a vision, and at the same time the first of the marks appeared as a small painful sore on the back of her right hand. At first she tried to hide it, but her family discovered it and insisted that she see a doctor. Many treatments and many doctors were tried, but the sore did not heal. During the following three years wounds began to form on the other hand, feet, and side, and she found it increasingly difficult and painful to hold objects and walk. But gradually the pain eased off six days a week, and by 1940 was confined to the hours between 6 and 9 P.M. on Fridays, and from 11 P.M. on Holy Thursday to midnight on Good Friday. During Holy Week an additional wound appeared on her right shoulder, the one on which the cross was carried. This wound bled profusely on Good Friday and was healed by Easter Sunday.

Stigmatization is not an unknown phenomenon. According to church history, the first stigmatic (or stigmatist) was St. Francis of Assisi, who is said to have received the wounds on Monte Alverno in 1224. By 1894, according to the leading lay authority on the subject, Dr. A. Imbert-Gourbeyre of Paris, 321 authentic cases had been discovered, forty-one of whom were men. Catholic Church authorities have challenged some of his examples, and have suggested that there were many others he overlooked. Since his investigation, there have been a few new cases which appear to be authentic, including the celebrated Therese Neumann of Konnersreuth, Germany, and the Capuchin monk Padre Pio of Fuggia, Italy. Mrs. McIsaac appears to be the first true stigmatic in North America, but there have been rumors of several others.

The Catholic Church conducts an exhaustive investigation of all claims, and has exposed many as fraudulent. Genuine stigmatization is considered supernatural in origin, but no final pronouncement is made until long after the person's death. Approximately sixty stigmatists have been canonized to date, but none in the twentieth century as yet.

The Church has been active in Mrs. McIsaac's case since 1940, when the last of the scars appeared. Her parish priest, convinced that her wounds were authentic stigmata, brought the phenomenon to the attention of

Cardinal McGuigan. He has adopted the same attitude that is invariably taken by the Church when new cases appear: "The Church takes no official notice of any happenings such as those attributed to the McIsaac home in Uptergrove. The Church always treats such matters with great reserve. It is well known that many such manifestations may be explained by natural causes. The authority of the diocese disapproves of the visits of priests and other religious people not connected with the family." Mrs. McIsaac herself regards her stigmata as a gift of God, though she makes no claims to sainthood. She has continued to live the same simple frugal life, has never sought publicity of any sort, and has never encouraged visitors. Thousands of people from all parts of the Western world, however, have come to Uptergrove, but she sees very few of them, and then only after careful screening.

While discouraging any premature conclusions, the Archdiocese of Toronto has actively investigated Mrs. McIsaac's case. During 1945 and 1946, the Church arranged to hold lengthy examinations at St. Michael's Hospital in Toronto, and at Bresica Hall, a Catholic women's college in the area. Catholic, Protestant, and Jewish physicians and psychiatrists were invited to conduct the examinations on condition that they submit signed statements for the files of the Church. The files are not open to the public, but interviews with some of the doctors have indicated that the investigation was indeed a thorough one. During the five weeks of tests, Mrs. McIsaac was not left alone for a moment either day or night. Her reactions were closely observed, and she was questioned before, during, and after her trance states. The wounds were carefully examined and described in detail. Blood smears were taken during the spontaneous bleeding that occurred every Friday night, and analysis revealed that it was the same as blood taken on other days. Even the timing of the episodes was put to test. In one experiment, the time was surreptitiously advanced and Mrs. McIsaac was given her meals four and a half hours later than usual —but though there was no clock or watch in her room, the bleeding began at six and ended at nine by the correct time.

The most famous European stigmatist of recent times was Therese Neumann. Born in 1898, she lived all her life in the small Bavarian town of Konnersreuth. There was nothing unusual about her childhood except the fact that after an illness she became nervous, irritable, and subject to attacks of vertigo. After completing her elementary schooling, she became a servant in the home of a neighbor.

In 1918, a fire broke out on the farm adjacent to her employer's home, and for two hours she helped to pass along pail after pail of water to dampen the buildings and prevent the flames from spreading. Then suddenly she grew weak and numb, and a pail slipped from her hands. After this she could only perform light tasks. However, her employer grew impatient with her and at one point ordered her to bring a heavy sack of potatoes from the cellar. On the way up the stairs her legs gave way and she fell backward, striking her head against a stone ledge. She then became so weak that she had to give up the job and return home.

Soon after, Therese had to be hospitalized for a period of seven weeks, but her condition grew worse instead of better. During the next few years she suffered from a series of disorders which included convulsions, temporary blindness, deafness in the left ear, anesthesia on one side of the body, abscesses, appendicitis, and pneumonia. She later claimed to have recovered completely from all these illnesses without medical help, and attributed her recovery to the miraculous intervention of God.

The Lent of 1926 signaled a new phase of Therese's life. She began to experience "Friday ecstasies" in which she saw visions of the Passion of Christ, with many details not mentioned in the Gospel. These visions were divided into fifty separate episodes (Stations of the Cross) lasting from two to fifteen minutes each, and were followed by a state of "exalted repose" during which she is said to have given the counsels of Jesus and predictions of future events—all in biblical language she was not accustomed to use. These Friday ecstasies were associated with a trancelike state of mind and the appearance of stigmata on her hands, feet, and left side. Here is her own description of her first vision: "All at once I saw the Redeemer before me on the Mount of Olives. Suddenly I felt such pain in my side that I thought I would die. At the same time I felt something hot running down my side. It was blood."

From that point on until she died in 1962, Therese Neumann's wounds were said to bleed every Friday except during Eastertide. When the newspapers learned about this "miracle," they printed story after story, and as a result people began to flock to Konnersreuth. On many Fridays as many as two thousand persons stood in line to gaze at the unpretentious peasant girl who was ecstatically beholding the Passion of Christ while at the same time suffering almost unbearable torture from her bleeding wounds. Many dignitaries of the Church, including bishops and cardinals, visited her and were uplifted by the sight. As E. Beyer states in an article in *Catholic World*, "Not one member of the hierarchy who visited her has ever publicly denounced her. Not one has ever hinted at the possibility of a 'pious fraud.' Not one has ever implied that she is not a true mystic who has already attained to a close union with God."

There were two aspects of Therese's life which appear even more phenomenal than her ecstatic visions and bleeding wounds. One was her reputed ability to speak a variety of languages, predict events, and describe the contents of unopened letters while she was in a brief somnambulistic state after the vision and bleeding were over. The other was the claim that she did not take any nourishment whatever—neither food nor water—since her first mystical experience in 1926. Many in the Church regarded her telepathic powers and her total fast, or "inedia," as conclusive proof that she could perform miracles.

The life of Therese Neumann has long been a controversial subject in both ecclesiastical and lay circles. A number of books and articles have been written on the theme that she should be recognized as holy and even sainted; an equally large number reject her claims on grounds of chicanery, self-deception, or hysterical disorder. Even the investigations conducted under the supervision of Archbishop Henle have been accepted by some and rejected by others. The story goes that the commission appointed by the Archbishop wanted to put Therese in a neutral clinic for observation, but her father refused permission on the grounds that his daughter might be used as a guinea pig. However, he did agree to placing her under twenty-four-hour surveillance by four Franciscan sisters for a two-week period under the supervision of the Neumann family physician, Dr. Seidl. The Archbishop of Regensburg published the doctor's findings and stated in his report that "During the whole period of the inquiry the reception of any form of nourishment was the object of strict observation . . . In spite of this meticulous invigilation she was never found taking food or drink, nor even trying to do so." After the two-week period, Dr. Seidl stated that she was in excellent condition, and that her weight was exactly the same as on the day the sisters arrived. A few weeks later the Archbishop delivered a sermon in the parish church in which he praised her "heroic patience, holiness, and obedience." He then sent an official report of his observations to the Pope himself, who later gave her his apostolic blessing.

Many writers such as Hilde Graef, author of a book entitled *The Case of Therese Neumann,* label her visions and stigmata as symptoms of a very advanced case of hysteria. On the other hand, D. H. Rawcliffe, in his book, *The Psychology of the Occult,* states categorically that she was "a deliberate fraud aided and abetted by her father." Others point out suspicious aspects of her story, and argue for either a complete rejection of her claims or, at most, a suspension of judgment. As one example, P. Siwek, author of *The Riddle of Konnersreuth,* is inclined to be skeptical without ruling out the possibility of her sanctity. In his article for the *Catholic Encyclopedia,* he states: "Therese's marvelous recoveries from her various illnesses could have been miraculous, but the certain judgment that they were seems unwarranted . . . There is insufficient evidence either that alleged organic illnesses existed or that their cure could not have been effected by natural forces. Regarding her Friday ecstasies, their supernatural character cannot be confidently affirmed according to the rules laid down by Benedict XIV and by mystical authorities such as Saint Therese of Avila and John of the Cross." And as for the wounds themselves, he goes on to say that "Again, stigmatization carries with it no guarantee of its miraculous origin. It could well have been, it seems, a natural effect of her 'ecstatic emotion' . . . Moreover, an impressive number of modern theologians believe that stigmatization as such can be explained without a direct miraculous intervention on the part of God. Her visions also are susceptible of a natural psychological explanation." And regarding the fasting, he states, "Unfortunately Therese's family never allowed the thorough examination of this point that the Catholic hierarchy insistently demanded. The refusal to co-operate with the church on this decisive point created serious suspicions. The observation of Therese's fasting by four Franciscan nuns for a two-week period during July, 1927 was accomplished in conditions that make it impossible to regard it as a guarantee that Therese's fast was absolute."

What kind of "natural psychological explanations" can be given for both of the stigmatists discussed in this chapter—and how convincing are they? The issue is not a simple one, but psychologists have advanced a number of relevant considerations.

First, Therese's history appears to include a number of illnesses that might have been psychogenic—especially her vertigo, temporary blindness, convulsive attacks, paralysis of the left arm, anesthesia of the entire left side of her body, and a throat pain which kept her from swallowing solid food. Every one of these symptoms is frequently found in hysterics; for instance, the last mentioned may well have been the common symptom of "lump in the throat" which is technically termed globus hystericus. As for Mrs. McIsaac, we do not have sufficient data on her health history to draw any conclusions on this point.

Second, one of the major characteristics of hysteria is heightened suggestibility and a tendency to dramatize feelings and events. Together, these tendencies might explain the ecstatic visions experienced by these women. They were both deeply devout, and focused rapt attention on the events surrounding the death of Jesus, probably to a point where their fantasies became so vivid and real that they identified with their Savior and lived through his sufferings as if they were their own. And as for the stigmata, there is a possibility that during their ecstatic visions the wounds were so greatly desired that they were unconsciously self-inflicted, and then reopened every Friday. This theory gains some support from the biography of the nun Lukardis of Aberweimar who, as Rawcliffe points out, developed the nervous habit of repeatedly stubbing her palms with the tips of her fingers, and chafing the upper part of her feet with her big toes. He also suggests that the first stigmata might have been intentionally inflicted either in a waking state or during an attack of hystero-epilepsy, and comments that "With hysterical individuals, a deliberate infliction of wounds on the hands and feet could easily develop into a delusion that the wounds were in fact conferred supernaturally. Delusion has played a very large part in the production of historical cases of stigmatization."

Third, it is also possible that some stigmata were preceded by minor irritations of the hands and feet, which gave rise to the nervous habit of scratching until the blood flowed. Highly suggestible individuals who become absorbed in the drama of the cross might overlook the actual origin of their wounds because of their strong desire to experience the agonies of their Lord, and perhaps at the same time to reap the benefits, or "secondary gains," of sympathy, attention, and reverence which their sufferings excited in others. Quite possibly, too, the skin irritations might have been symptoms of neurodermatitis, a condition that is frequently found in hysterical individuals. Again quoting Rawcliffe, "It is by no means improbable that certain hysterical mystics who contemplated the crucifixion felt the intense itching or irritation of neurodermatitis in the hands and feet—whether the underlying cause of the irritation was a subconscious desire for the miracle of the stigmata or a subconscious fear aroused by the contemplation of a realistically painted image of the crucified Christ."

It is an interesting and indicative fact that in some cases if the spear wound was shown on the left side of a painting or statue contemplated by the stigmatist, it appeared on his left side; and if it was on the right side, as it is in some cases, the bleeding occurred on that side.

A fourth possibility is that the wounds might have been due to either voluntary or involuntary scratching and excoriation of the skin to obtain relief from irritating conditions due entirely to psychosomatic factors. While the evidence for this explanation is more indirect than direct, it should certainly be considered. We know that warts, urticaria, and other localized rashes may be psychologically produced. We also know that red blotches (erythema) and blisters can be produced by hypnotic suggestion. F. A. Pattie, a psychologist, has reviewed all available reports and experiments designed to test this point. In a typical experiment, the hypnotist suggests that a pencil or his own finger is a red-hot iron which will produce a blister when it touches the subject's arm or back. In some of the most carefully controlled experiments, a metal letter or some other irregular object was applied to the skin, and the area was covered tightly with a bandage or plaster cast with a glass window through which it could be observed, to see whether the blister would be formed spontaneously. In many cases this result was achieved within a few hours. There have also been claims that not only blisters, but bleeding as well, could be produced by hypnotic suggestion, especially in cases where a lesion had already occurred. Such experiments were most successful with hysterical subjects, though they also seemed to produce results in highly suggestible normal subjects.

It may well be that in some cases stigmata were originally produced by a physical or psychogenic skin condition, and in others by self-mutilation, and that autosuggestion caused the scars to reopen and bleed every Friday. As Rawcliffe remarks, "In any event it seems possible that intermittent hemorrhage may be produced by psychogenic factors, in the case of certain hysterical individuals with chronic lesions on the hands or feet."

These, then, are the major arguments in favor of a natural rather than supernatural explanation of stigmata. At this point we can only say they strongly suggest that stigmatization is basically a hysterical phenomenon—but so far the evidence is not sufficiently conclusive to clear up the mystery completely.

THE FORKED STICK

For the greater part of India 1925 was a year of famine, and the suffering was unimaginable. The British did what they could to relieve the frightful conditions, but their efforts were totally inadequate, since the country had been afflicted with a drought, and where there is no water to irrigate the land, the food refuses to grow. In three districts—Ahmednagar, Sholapur, and Bijapur—the water scarcity was most acute, and well after well had been dug without yielding so much as a drop.

The Bombay Legislative Council was called into session to meet the crisis. The government reported that ships were already bringing in what water they could, but the amount was insignificant in the face of the great and growing need. Delegates who had advocated building a system of canals agreed that they could not be dug in time to save the populace—and, besides, they would be as empty as the river beds, since the available sources had all dried up. There seemed to be no solution whatever to the problem—"Except," as one delegate put it, "to make an even greater effort to find the water that lies beneath the surface of the land." This suggestion was met with an angry outburst: "What! We have already bored hundreds of wells without success. Why compound our failures? We have tried everything along that line!" "Everything except one thing, gentlemen. You have not tried Major Pogson."

The session became even stormier when the delegate explained that Major C. A. Pogson was a water diviner, a dowser. Member after member jeered at the idea. "Everyone knows those fellows are frauds preying on ignorant country folk!" Why don't we just perform a rain dance, like the American Indians? It would work just as well!" "His Majesty's Government has a corps of trained geologists with every modern instrument at their disposal. If they have failed to find water, how can you expect an untrained army man to locate hidden springs with nothing but the branch of a tree in his hands?"

The delegate held his ground, citing Pogson's long record of successes in other parts of India. He could not, of course, be expected to guarantee results, especially since he was unacquainted with the terrain of the Bombay area. "Yet," said his defender, "why not give the method a chance? There are too many lives at stake for us to sit by and ignore any possibility, no matter how farfetched it may appear!"

Some of the members objected that the Council would become a laughingstock, but in the end the persuasive delegate carried his point. The Secretary of State for India was petitioned for Pogson's services, and he was duly appointed Official Water Diviner to the Government of Bombay, at a substantial salary.

The responsibility for supplying water to the farms and villages in the three drought-stricken districts was placed directly on the shoulders of Major Pogson. According to accounts published at the time, his performance was nothing short of spectacular. The *Indian Journal of Engineering* reported that "Out of 49 wells which have been sunk upon spots indicated by Major Pogson only two have failed to produce water. It is a notable achievement." The article continues with this unexpected comment: "It is a somewhat bitter pill to engineers to be told by an evening contemporary that a major is better than machines, yet there is more than a mickle of justification for this clever newspaper head . . . Major Pogson can find water, it appears, when the machines specially designed for the purpose have failed. It is an interesting situation."

The first government report on Pogson's work in the district pointed out that "The majority of the bores have been sunk in localities not where normal boring by chance methods proves successful, but in places where bores sunk at random have little or no chance of striking water." To cap it all, ten months after his appointment, the government even "guaranteed the success of the water diviner to the extent that if water was not struck in any of the sites pointed out by him, a cultivator would be recompensed 50% of his expenses up to a sum of Rs. 400."

How does a dowser such as Major Pogson accomplish his task? The answer appears to be suspiciously simple. He cuts a forked branch from a healthy tree—usually a hazel or willow—trims off the twigs, and holds one end tightly in each hand with the fork extending outward and upward from his body. He then walks slowly over the land in question, covering practically every square foot of the area. At some point in his meanderings, the fork in his hand might suddenly dip toward the ground as if pulled by an unseen force—and at that spot, he places a stake. He may go on to check further by dowsing around the chosen area to discover exactly where the pull is strongest, since that would indicate where the water is most abundant and accessible. When he has found that spot, he insists with complete confidence that this is the place to dig for water.

In essence, this is the method which has been used for hundreds of years in all parts of the world. As might be expected, there are local variations on this process. Some use one type of branch, some another; while most diviners hold the palms upward, some hold them downward. And there are variations, too, in the name applied to this mysterious "gift." Water divining is common. Rhabdomancy (literally, magic with a rod) is uncommon, at least in this country. Water witching is the preferred term in the Midwest, South, and Southwest, and dowsing is the term most frequently used along the Eastern seaboard.

The practice has been traced by enthusiasts all the way back to Moses, who is said to have produced water in the wilderness by striking a rock with his staff (Numbers 20:9–11). Others associate it with the use of rods and pieces of wood in the divination practices of the ancient Scythians, Medes, Persians, and Greeks. But the first unambiguous account of the forked twig has been found in sixteenth-century Germany, where it was used in locating subterranean metallic ore in the Harz Mountains. During the regime of Queen Elizabeth I, German miners were brought to Cornwall to prospect for tin, and some brought divining rods with them. It was not long until the method was being used for locating water as well as ore deposits. The term "dowsing" is said to have been borrowed from a common Cornwall colloquialism meaning to "sink, as in dowsing or lowering a sail," because of the dipping action of the divining rod.

Any scientifically minded person is bound to raise questions about the authenticity of the practice. Certainly water does not appear to possess any special force which would exert an attraction upon a broken twig. And even granting that attraction, there is no apparent reason why the twig should suddenly and violently dip when held in the hands of a dowser and not in the hands of other individuals. It seems highly unlikely that dowsers possess an extraordinary gift denied to scientists and experienced laymen alike. On the face of it, then, water divining would appear to be a classic example of a fraud perpetrated on the gullible or a superstition harking back to an age of ignorance.

But we must judge by evidence, not appearance—and the first question to ask is, Just how successful is the dowser? Are his results actually superior to those of geologists, well diggers, and others who use instruments or cues from the terrain rather than divining rods?

It might be argued that dowsers would not be so plentiful, and reasonable individuals and governments would not use their services if they were not highly successful. Pogson is not the only dowser who has been called in when water was scarce, and the Indian Government is not alone in retaining a dowser on its staff. Official dowsers have been employed, among others, by the government of British Columbia, the government of Ceylon during World War II, and the Italian Army in Ethiopia. In this country alone the number of dowsers has been estimated at twenty-five thousand. Many of them practice the "art" as a hobby, offering their services as a favor;

others charge from five to fifty dollars and occasionally more. Well diggers, whose very livelihood depends on success in finding water, frequently employ the services of a dowser. Moreover, many water diviners are so sure of themselves that they work on a "no water, no pay" basis.

Nor should we overlook the opinions of geologists and physicists who have had experience in this matter. Most of them, of course, scoff at the whole idea. Nevertheless, F. N. Taylor, in his well-recognized treatise *Small Water Supplies* states, "When doubt exists as to whether sinking will yield water, or when great depths may have to be sunk, the services of a water-diviner are very useful. Water-divining is a gift; and very few practice this art and some of these are not reliable. On the whole, however, much reliance can be placed on a first-class man." Similarly, the celebrated British physicist Sir J. J. Thomson has stated, "There is no doubt of the reality of the dowsing effect. In fact, in many agricultural districts the dowser is the man they call in when they want to find the right place to dig the well, and he very often succeeds."

Statements of this kind, plus the apparently successful careers of many dowsers, strongly suggest that some kind of "dowsing effect" exists. At the same time, however, it must be recognized that some water diviners are out-and-out frauds, while others have made exaggerated claims for their ability, even to the point of infallibility. Moreover, dowsing has been surrounded by an aura of mystery and even magic that militates against acceptance in scientific circles. Although this attitude has sometimes been deliberately cultivated, it must be recognized that most diviners are honest, forthright individuals who are themselves mystified by their apparent ability.

The author recently interviewed a highly considered dowser in Putnam County, New York, who stated, "All I know is that I was watching one of these fellows 'way back when I was about fourteen, and I asked him to let me try it. He showed me just how to hold the branch, and I started walking over the land. Suddenly the thing dipped down all by itself. It went down so hard that my hands were sore! I have been doing it ever since as a favor to my friends, and I rarely miss. When I was having my own house built last year, I found lots of water at eighty feet while other people in the neighborhood were going down two hundred or more. I really can't tell how the thing works. People say it has something to do with electrical currents, but I don't know much about that."

E. Z. Vogt, an anthropologist, and R. Hyman, a psychologist, in their book *Water Witching, U.S.A.* quote a number of dowsers to the same effect. As an example, one of them said: "There's no trickery to it. You hold my hands and you'll see I don't move it . . . It works and wavers, works and wavers over water. Sometimes I can't hold it, and the bark comes off in my hands . . . I can't explain why. It's nothing in the body—no physical sensations—just the stick. I don't know why there is an affinity between me and water."

Such accounts can be duplicated in different parts of the country and abroad as well. Many people regard them as highly convincing evidence, since they are based on firsthand or eyewitness experiences. Yet in other fields such reports are notorious for their inaccuracy, especially when offered by "believers." Even though the individuals making them may be totally sincere and honorable, they may unconsciously distort the facts by overemphasizing successes and overlooking or underestimating failures.

We must therefore look for evidence that is better qualified on scientific grounds. Fortunately there have been a number of systematic studies and tests which are relatively conclusive in their results. The most extensive of these reports is a record kept by the New South Wales Water Conservation and Irrigation Commission for all wells drilled by private companies between 1918 and 1939. A total of 3,581 wells were dug during this period, approximately half of which were divined by dowsers and half not divined. It was found that 80.5 per cent of the divined wells and 89.1 per cent of the non-divined wells yielded serviceable water, and twice as many of the divined wells (14.7 per cent) as non-divined wells (7.5 per cent) were absolute failures. A less extensive study, reported by E. Z. Vogt for Fence Lake, New Mexico, yielded somewhat similar results: Of forty-nine successful wells sunk in 1933, twenty-four were divined and twenty-five not divined, but in this case the dowsers reported fewer dry holes (five) than the non-dowsers (seven).

Two outstanding field experiments have also been reported. L. A. Dale and his associates conducted a test in Maine in 1949, using a carefully chosen field which contained no obvious cues such as surface water or wells. They then pitted a total of twenty-seven diviners against two ground-water experts—a geologist and a water engineer. Each diviner selected the spot which he considered best for sinking a well, and the experts, as a control, made estimates of the depth and rate of flow of water at sixteen different points previously staked out on the field. Test wells were sunk at each of the spots assessed, and the depth and amount of water encounterd were measured in each case. Results showed that the experts did a good job of estimating the over-all depth of the water as well as the depth at specific points, but not in guessing the amount to be found at specific points (although the engineer made a close estimate on the over-all rate of flow). The diviners, on the other hand, were all complete failures in estimating both the depth and amount of water found in the spots they selected.

The other experiment, conducted by P. A. Ongley in 1948, involved seventy-five diviners, who were tested only on the type of detection in which they claimed to have a special ability: flowing water, still water, minerals, diseases, lost objects, etc. None of the water diviners performed significantly better than chance in a series of experiments that included locating an underground stream and returning to it with closed eyes; asking two or more dowsers to check one another on the location of underground water; asking the dowser to say whether a hidden bottle was full of water or empty; and asking two or more dowsers to determine the depth of water below the surface of the ground. The dowsers who were tested on detection of minerals, the discovery of owners of lost objects, detection of electrical fields, and medical diagnosis proved equally unreliable. As an example, seven health diviners found that a perfectly healthy individual was suffering from a total of twenty-five different ailments, and a blindfold diviner made a diagnosis of varicose veins on a man's wooden leg!

Some dowsers might object to the first experiment on the ground that they only claim to be able to detect the *presence* of water and not its depth or exact amount. Others might object to the second experiment on the additional ground that they can only detect the presence of water with their eyes open and under natural conditions, which would rule out the blindfold and bottle tests. (It would also rule out another type of test in which diviners have attempted, with no significant success, to locate water pipes in buildings or buried in the ground.) If these objections were granted, the dowsers might agree to fall back on the New South Wales and Fence Lake type of study. These reports do indicate that the diviners scored considerably better than chance, although no better than non-diviners who were using surface cues such as plants or rock formations, rather than the rod or pendulum.

Now for some crucial questions: How can an 80 per cent record of success be explained? What makes the rod dip and the pendulum swing? To what are they responding?

Before suggesting an answer to these questions, let us look briefly at an "explanation" which has been offered by many students and practitioners of dowsing in recent years: detection of radiation. Proponents of this point of view, such as J. C. Maby and T. B. Franklin who published a book entitled *The Physics of the Divining Rod*, claim that veins of water and minerals as well are surrounded by electromagnetic fields which send radiations to the surface of the ground. Certain individuals, they maintain, are by nature more sensitive than others to variations in the strength of these radiations and possess a special perceptual faculty which has been termed radiesthesia. They claim that the rod or pendulum merely picks up these radiations and transmits them to the human receiver. In many areas, particularly on the Continent, dowsers now call themselves radiesthetists.

A number of associations have been formed for the purpose of exchanging ideas on radiesthesia. Their members make extravagant claims not only for dowsing but for a variety of other feats. As D. H. Rawcliffe points out in *The Psychology of the Occult*, "With rod or pendulum they are able, as a perusal of their journals and literature will show, to forecast the future, dowse for water or minerals from plans and maps, sex eggs, diagnose and cure disease, detect thieves or missing persons, discover forces, fields, rays and beams galore, and explore the most intimate processes of the molecule and the atom with a degree of accuracy which must for long remain the envy of modern physical science." He characterizes this theory as a "naive blending of sympathetic magic with modern scientific ideas and terminology," and states that "to all those for whom the occult holds an irresistible appeal Radiesthesia is to be recommended; for here is magic with a difference, combining in wondrous fashion the psychic with the energy of the atom."

The radiesthesia theory of dowsing harks back to such long-discredited theories as Mesmer's "animal magnetism," and Grimes's "electrobiology," both of which proved to be variants of hypnotic suggestion. Another source appears to be the "aesthesiogenic agents" of Jean-Martin Charcot and Hippolyte-Marie Bernheim, noted French psychiatrists, who used metallic rods and magnets in treating hysterical patients. This effect, too, has been proved to be due to suggestion rather than electromagnetism.

The present-day claims of the radiesthetists have been under a double attack. First, scientists find no evidence for the existence of the waves which Maby and Franklin claim to exist. The following comment from a review of their work published in the scientific journal *Nature* is typical: "The theoretical section, by the second author, postulates some form of cosmic radiation resulting in electromagnetic waves of ten meters wave length. There seems to be no direct evidence for such waves, and the authors' discussion of their polarization cannot be justified on our present physical knowledge." Second, the practical applications of the theory have proven equally questionable. The diagnosis of disease by the swing of a pendulum has been disproved by many other tests than the one cited above. As to determining the sex of unhatched eggs, dowsers do not score better than chance for any length of time. There have been one or two widely publicized cases on the Continent in which missing mountain climbers were "located" by holding a pendulum over a map, but such cases have been adequately explained by showing that the radiesthetist knew the region thoroughly and used common sense mixed with a high proportion of luck.

More relevant for our purpose, tests have shown that map dowsing, either by rod or pendulum, is a thoroughly unreliable technique for finding water, except where it is so plentiful that it could be found in practically any part of the area in question. Some radiesthetists have claimed that in dowsing the land directly, the dipping of the rod ceases if they are completely insulated from the ground even if they know they are standing over water. This claim, however, has been disproved by tests in which the dowser was not aware of the insulation, as well as tests in which he was deceived into believing he was insulated and in fact was not. In the first case the rod continued to dip, and in the second it ceased!

If the dipping of the rod is not due to sensitivity to radiation, what *does* explain it? The answer appears to be that the dowser moves the forked stick in response to suggestion and expectation. He is right in claiming that he does not exert conscious control, and right also in insisting that a mysterious force is responsible for its dipping action. The reason for the mystery is that the stick's action is controlled by the power of suggestion operating on an unconscious level. This power causes the stick to move involuntarily and sometimes in spite of the dowser's conscious effort to control it.

The typical dowser usually learns the "art" by observing a veteran perform in an atmosphere of tension and expectation. In his first contact with the practice he is likely to be young and impressionable, and the dowser assures him that the stick will work if he concentrates hard enough on the task. Young people who respond to this suggestion and find that their rod moves usually continue on their own; those who do not respond to the suggestion shrug their shoulders and forget the whole business.

If a young person continues to dowse, his concentration probably increases to a point where he is in something resembling a trance state. This state is further reinforced by autosuggestion, and he begins to believe that he has a special gift. If he appears to be reasonably successful in locating water, many people applaud his so-called gift, and this recognition bolsters his expectation that the rod will dip like magic whenever it hovers over water.

Suggestion plays an even greater role in dowsing. The radiesthetist believes the rod or pendulum moves when he is in contact with radiations, and not when he is insulated from them. One dowser insists that willow works best for him, and another swears by cherry or peach. The believer in the radiation theory may prefer a pendulum made of metal on the theory that it transmits electromagnetism better than wood—and if he is also a devout believer in religion, he may find that it swings most effectively when attached to a Bible. Others believe their efforts will be most successful if they hold a related object in their hand or dangle it on the end of a piece of string as a pendulum. If they are prospecting for metal, they use a piece of the appropriate ore, and if they are trying to locate a missing person, they hold a piece of his clothing in their hand.

It seems evident, then, that unconscious suggestion plays a major role in dowsing. But more specifically, the suggestion is translated into the dipping of the branch or the swinging of the pendulum by *ideomotor action,* a process by which ideas or feelings automatically control movement. To be explicit, when the dowser arrives at a spot where he feels there is water beneath the surface, this feeling acts on the muscles of his arms and hands and, without realizing it, he contracts them in such a way that the branch suddenly dips. The contraction of muscles does not have to be very pronounced to move the branch, since his muscles are already under considerable tension. The same applies to the movement of the pendulum: Only slight extra tension is necessary to make it sway.

This interpretation has been increasingly accepted in recent years by those who are looking for a scientific explanation of the dowsing effect. Rawcliffe states, "The forked rod of the dowser serves to register and magnify automatic movements of the arm and wrist made independently of the conscious volition of the operator." The psychologist Joseph Jastrow used almost the same words in describing the *modus operandi* of dowsing in terms of "involuntary movements founded on subconsciously registered indications." Vogt makes a similar point: "It is plain that the witching stick dips in response to muscular contractions of the dowser that are due to some type of unconscious mental or psychic processes and *not* in response to the physical presence of underground water supplies."

Vogt and Hyman have elaborated the theory of ideomotor action by tracing the history of the concept and by presenting a number of examples in other fields than dowsing. The term originated with William B. Carpenter in 1852, who applied it to a wide variety of "automatic expressions of the ideas that may be dominant in our minds," as in speaking, writing, and tying our shoelaces. William James broadened the principle: "Wherever movement follows *unhesitatingly and immediately* the notion of it in the mind, we have ideo-motor action."

Among his examples are flicking dust off one's sleeve while talking, and tensing one's muscles while reading about a battle scene. The behaviorist John B. Watson went too far in this direction, maintaining that *all* thinking is "subvocal speech." The physiologist Edmund Jacobson was the first to measure the ideomotor effect. He attached electrodes to the arms of his subjects and proved that minute electrical currents activate the muscles when a person thinks of bending his arm or throwing a ball. It has also been shown that these action currents take place when watching *others* throw a ball, and undoubtedly the same thing occurs in watching the water diviner as his forked twig suddenly dips toward the ground. This gives the observer a start toward the ideomotor action, or "motor automatism," that is involved in dowsing.

This theory becomes even more convincing when dowsing is related to other dramatic examples of automatic behavior. Vogt and Hyman show that essentially the same process occurs when a person unconsciously moves the pointer of a Ouija board to the appropriate letters or numbers; when a "muscle reader" locates objects in a room by wandering around it with his hands lightly touching the arm or neck of an individual who knows where they are; when a group of "table turners" place their hands on a light table and concentrate on making it move "by itself" to the right or left; and when animals "solve" simple mathematical problems by perceiving involuntary movements made by their trainer. All these examples are based on the principle "when we think, we move," a principle that applies with equal force to dowsing.

Suggestion and ideomotor action are essential in explaining dowsing, but we still have to answer one crucial question: What are the ideas that translate themselves into the dipping of the stick? Granted that these ideas operate primarily on an unconscious level, we still have to ask exactly what they are. There is little doubt that they are basically surface cues to underground water encountered by the dowser as he roams over the land. Among these cues might be the growth and character of vegetation, the composition of the soil, outcroppings of rocks, and even in some cases the temperature of the surrounding air, the smell of damp earth, and slight sounds or vibrations produced by underground streams. These are the "subconsciously registered indications" to which Jastrow refers. But many others have made the same point. Sir William Barrett, who unfortunately embraced cryptesthesia, or clairvoyance, in his full explanation of dowsing, nevertheless recognized that "Underground water and metallic ores are often indicated by surface signs, imperceptible to the ordinary observer, but which become known to the experienced dowser. Such indications, even when not consciously perceived, may create a subconscious impression on the dowser that will excite the automatic motion of his rod." Vogt and Hyman also refer to surface indications, pointing out that "the diviner will unconsciously seize upon whatever cues are available when he is searching for underground water." Rawcliffe likewise recognizes these cues, and makes the further point that "It is a mistake to believe that the ignorant uneducated 'natural' dowser is the most successful. The fact is that most consistently successful dowsers are men or women of good education, with a good capacity for reasoned calculation. Many have a working knowledge of geology; and in all cases years of practical endeavor, with its inevitable sequence of successes and failures, constitute the background of their training."

The theory of unconscious response to surface cues explains why dowsers frequently perform as well as non-dowsers under natural conditions: They are using the same kind of observations! It also helps to explain the success of Major Pogson, an experienced operator who was long acquainted with the terrain of India. And it explains why diviners fail blindfold, bottle, and underground pipe tests. An amateur geologist—or indeed a professional—can hardly be expected to succeed under such conditions.

On the whole, then, we may conclude that while dowsers and non-dowsers share one important feature, they also differ in two major respects. First, dowsers have not merely learned to observe surface cues to underground water, but have learned to respond to these cues by automatically tensing the muscles that make the rod dip. The non-dowser also observes these cues, but translates his observations directly into words rather than into unconscious motor responses. Second, dowsers tend to put the search for water in the category of divination rather than common sense or scientific investigation. In so doing they are resorting to magic and superstition and are thereby turning the clock back instead of moving it forward.

In spite of the fact that science is revered in our society, dowsers are likely to be with us for a long time to come. The reason is that water is an essential commodity and homeowners are so anxious to find it that many of them will continue to turn to the man or woman who claims to have a special gift for locating it—especially since geologists and other water experts are not readily available. Moreover, as Vogt and Hyman point out, "The best geological knowledge of ground water resources that is currently available still leaves an area of uncertainty in the task of predicting the exact depth to water at any *given* location in a region with a variable ground water table. The water-witching pattern provides a reassuring note of response in this uncertain situation."

DECISION

"Doctor, I hope you don't mind my barging in like this, but I have a terrible problem. It's something I have to resolve and I can't seem to make any headway."

The doctor looked up and smiled. "I'll be glad to discuss it with you."

The young lady rushed on, hardly noticing his response. "For months now I've tried to come to a decision, but my thoughts seem to be blocked. A few weeks ago I became so anxious that all I could do was bury myself in my work to get it out of my mind. But that did not help because the problem would always come back to me at night and I would lie awake tossing and turning. I just can't go on like this. Will you help me?"

Dr. Milton H. Erickson was surprised that the agitated young woman came to him with a personal problem. Dr. Jane was a quiet, hard-working, intelligent intern at the hospital where he was teaching, and their contacts had been confined to guidance and instruction. Nevertheless he agreed at once to do what he could, and asked her to describe the nature of her problem.

"That's just the point. All I know is that I *have* a problem, but I really don't know what it is. But I *can* tell you what to do about it. Will you please—please—come to my apartment in the evening as soon as possible and hypnotize me. Now, don't ask me why, because I don't know. In fact, don't ask me any questions at all about my problem since I won't have any idea how to answer them!"

The request was a strange one, especially since the young woman had politely but firmly refused to participate in any of the hypnotic experiments which Dr. Erickson had been conducting at the hospital. Nevertheless, he nodded assent, and before he could say anything more, she continued: "After you hypnotize me I want you to be very emphatic about instructing my unconscious to think my problem through in a cool, unemotional fashion. I want my unconscious to discover what that problem is, and to look at it from every angle, to size it up, and then make some sort of a final formulation no matter what it is. Watching your subjects has impressed me with the way the unconscious can handle problems a person doesn't know he has. I know I have a problem that troubles me, makes me irritable and lose a lot of weight. I am just plain disagreeable in company. This can't go on. I've got to leave the hospital soon and I can't even make any plans. So I want my unconscious to straighten things out for me."

Then, to make sure that her professor would follow the procedure in detail, Dr. Jane repeated her instructions in these words: "This is what I want you to do. First, hypnotize me very soundly, and when I am in a deep trance tell my unconscious everything I have just told you, using the notes you have made so that you don't omit anything . . . You don't know what your instructions are going to result in and it is the same way with me. I don't know and you don't know what it is all about, but if you tell my unconscious everything I have told you, it will understand. Be sure to tell it that it must think the whole problem clear through. Be emphatic."

The young woman said she was sorry she didn't have any further information to give, and left the office as hastily as she had come in. During the following two days Dr. Erickson met her frequently in the hospital hallways, but she made no reference to the visit, On the third day he casually asked her if she had any plans for the evening. Apparently without seeing any special significance in this question, she replied that she was extremely fatigued and had planned to stay home and retire early.

At seven that evening Dr. Erickson knocked on her door, and she greeted him with evident astonishment. Nevertheless she invited him in, and they engaged in a typical social conversation, during which it became obvious that she had developed a complete amnesia for her visit to the office. She seemed extremely tired, yawned repeatedly, apologized for her seeming discourtesy, and explained that she had been suffering from insomnia. This gave her professor the opening he needed, and he suggested that hypnosis might be an excellent way to induce sleep. In contrast to her previous resistance, she immediately acquiesced and prepared herself by sitting in a comfortable position on the couch.

Dr. Jane responded quickly to the usual suggestions and was soon in a drowsy state of mind. She was then told to sleep deeply for a half hour in order to achieve a profound trance. After that stage was reached, Dr. Erickson commanded her to continue sleeping, and at once began to comment on the ability of the unconscious to take suggestions and to solve mental problems as well or even better than the conscious mind. He then reviewed in detail the conversation which had occurred in her visit to his office. During this entire recital, the young woman remained in the trance but at the same time listened with rapt attention.

As he concluded, Dr. Erickson asked, "Tell me, Dr. Jane, do you now understand the nature of your problem and are you willing to examine it and solve it?" With considerable show of emotion, she answered, "Yes, I know what it is. I understand. It is hard to decide but I have to do it and I suppose I might as well now." "And do you wish to talk it over with me?" "No, I don't want anyone to know about it—I want to solve it entirely by myself." "How long will that take?" "Come back in an hour and ask me if I am through, and I will tell you."

When Dr. Erickson returned and asked if it was time to awaken her, she said she was almost through, but it would take another half an hour. Promptly at the end of that time, she announced spontaneously, "I'm through. I've got it solved. You can awaken me any time you want to, but I think you had better tell me after I am awakened that it will be all right to know the answer." She was instructed to remain asleep a few minutes longer in order to be sure of everything, and then was told to awaken gently and easily.

When she came out of the trance, she apparently did not realize that she had been hypnotized, and was puzzled about the time that had elapsed, and equally puzzled about Dr. Erickson's visit. After twenty minutes of desultory conversation, it became evident that she was secretly wishing him to leave. As he got up, he looked at her intently and said (as she had requested during hypnosis), "It's all right for you to know the answer." She seemed utterly surprised by this remark, but when it was repeated, she responded with a bewildered look, and suddenly reacted with a startled flush and became tremulous and jerky in her movements and speech. With great anxiety she explained, "Won't you excuse me, please. I just found out something I was not prepared to know. I have to think about it right away so won't you please leave me alone. Please hurry."

The doctor made as graceful an exit as he could. He had followed his subject's instructions step by step as she had outlined them on her initial visit to his office, and apparently the hypnotic process had produced results. But what these results were remained a mystery.

During the days that followed, it seemed that Dr. Jane had an amnesia not only for the office visit but for the visit to her home, for she made no reference to either of them. However, her colleagues noticed a distinct change in her attitude and appearance. She seemed more relaxed, worked with greater ease, and was more outgoing. She also ate better and began to regain some of the weight she had lost.

So it went for a whole month after the hypnotic session. Then one day Dr. Erickson heard a knock on his office door, and in she walked holding up her left hand to display a wedding ring! Beaming with happiness, she exclaimed that she had been married the previous day, and wanted him to be the first to know since he had been so helpful in supervising her work on the wards. No mention was made of any other reason for breaking the news to him, and she seemed totally unaware that such a reason might exist. But when she revealed the name of her husband, he at once suspected the reasons for her indecision. Friends on the hospital staff, including Dr. Erickson, had known that the young man was greatly attracted to her, but were not aware that the attraction was reciprocated. To their knowledge, she had not been spending much time with him, and they assumed that she was not interested in him since, even though he was a worth-while person, he was decidedly her inferior both intellectually and culturally. Apparently the gap between them was responsible for her hesitation and for her attempt to seek help through hypnosis.

This suspicion was fully confirmed about three months later when Dr. Jane came into Dr. Erickson's office to thank him for his assistance. She revealed that she had suddenly become conscious of the entire episode as she lay in bed that morning thinking how successful her marriage had been, and wondering whether her happiness was deserved. "It was the first time I was consciously aware of what I was telling you that morning. But as soon as I left your office, I must have repressed it completely because I never thought of it again until this morning. When you came to my apartment to hypnotize me I was surprised to see you. I didn't know why you came. I just thought it was a social call. And when you suggested hypnosis to me, I was so tired that I didn't remember that I had always refused to be a subject for you . . . When I told you I had a problem and that I did not know what the problem was, I was telling you the truth. I just knew something was wrong. I was in love with John, but I didn't know it and I wouldn't have believed anybody that told me so. I tried not to go out with him very often, and I didn't, but just the same I was in love. There are many differences between John and me, as you know. Our family background is entirely different. John just plugs along and I was always at the head of my class. I have many interests—music, literature, art—that John hasn't. I repressed all my feelings for him the way I must have repressed that whole talk with you."

Dr. Jane went on to say that the experiments which she had watched Dr. Erickson perform had given her the idea that she could face her decision under hypnosis without revealing it to anyone—even to him—because "I had the feeling that my problem must be something I didn't want anybody to know or I wouldn't be keeping it from myself so completely." Since she had noticed that other subjects did not remember hypnotic experiences, she believed that she would be protected from revealing her secret, and therefore felt free to go ahead with her plan. At the end of the hypnotic session in her apartment, however, something strange had occurred. As soon as Dr. Erickson left, she had an experience resembling a hallucination. In her mind's eye she saw "a great long manuscript that slowly unrolled," and on it was written a long list of pros and cons about marrying John. Some of the items such as "industrious" and "lacking in imagination" were obvious to everyone, and she now mentioned them to the doctor, but others were too personal to reveal. At any rate, she had read and reread the items, and then proceeded to analyze them, reword them, and in some cases transfer them from one column to the other. Finally, she had counted them and found that the pros far outweighed the cons. "It seemed too good to believe," but she did believe the results, and "then I knew what my answer really was."

Why did Dr. Jane have an amnesia for the hypnotic experience? The answer seems to be that since she had observed that other subjects repressed such episodes, she expected to do the same. On the other hand, she did not have an amnesia for the decision itself since she had asked Dr. Erickson to tell her to be aware of the answer to her problem. At first, however, she could not understand what he meant when he said "It's all right to know the answer," because she was puzzled and distracted by the fact that it was so late and she could not account for the passage of time. "But when you repeated it, I suddenly knew that I loved John and would marry him if he asked me to. I was rather rude to you, but I did not know how that idea had come to my mind and I had to be alone to think about it. The more I thought about it, the more I knew I loved him. I went to bed happy for the first time in months, feeling as if I didn't have a problem in the world. The next morning I had thoughts about nothing except John. We became engaged and I wanted to tell you about it, but I couldn't figure out any reason for doing so. When we got married I wanted to tell you and the only reason that I could think of was the help you had given me in my work. That didn't seem to be a sufficient reason, but I used it anyway."

Two years later Dr. Erickson paid an unannounced visit to the couple and found them extremely happy. Taking him aside, Dr. Jane commented confidentially on the accuracy with which her unconscious had sized up the situation. As far as is known, she has never revealed to her husband the part that hypnosis had played in making her decision.

But why did the young woman resort to this circuitous route to the solution of her problem? It seems clear that she was suffering from a conflict between reason and emotion, between the head and the heart. She was well aware of John's limitations, and that according to the usual standards they were not well enough matched for marriage. Nevertheless she felt deeply in love with him —yet because of her conflict could not admit the truth to herself. But there was a conflict on the social level as well. As a highly regarded but rather insecure intern, she was concerned that her colleagues might criticize her for accepting a man who was far beneath her social and intellectual level. For this reason she kept her relationship as secret as possible.

Faced with this twofold conflict, she became confused and uncertain, and lacked the courage of her inner conviction. She then resorted to hypnosis for two reasons. First, it was a means of forcing herself to face her true feelings. There is little doubt that she already knew the "answer," but she adopted the device of the pro and con list in order to give the decision an air of rationality. (As a budding doctor, she felt compelled to put the problem on an analytical, intellectual plane!) Second, she was so insecure that additional reinforcement was required before she could make her final decision. By leaning on the hypnotist as an authority figure, she acquired the necessary strength—for even though Dr. Erickson did not make the decision for her, he was instructed to *order* her to make it, and to tell her it would be "all right" to know the answer. Unconsciously she had interpreted these commands as sanctioning or even ordering the marriage which she so deeply desired. The human mind works in devious ways!

In commenting on this unique case, Drs. Erickson and Hill state in an article in the *Psychoanalytic Quarterly,* "Since hypnosis can be induced and its manifestations elicited by suggestion, the unwarranted assumption is made that whatever develops from hypnosis must be completely a result of suggestion, and primarily an expression of it." Dr. Jane's case, however, demonstrates that subjects can do far more than respond to the commands of the hypnotist. They can, in some instances at least, think for themselves, come to terms with a problem, and make a weighty decision with greater insight and clarity than is possible during their waking life. As the authors state, "Hypnosis is, in fact, the induction of a peculiar psychological state which permits the subject to re-associate and reorganize his inner psychological complexities in a way suitable to the unique items of his own psychological experiences." This explains not only why Dr. Jane was able to become more fully aware of her love for John, but also why hypnosis has become an effective instrument in psychotherapy.

It also helps to explain an interesting sequel mentioned

by Dr. Erickson in a letter to this author. Twenty-five years after the events described in this chapter, Dr. Jane came up to him at a psychiatric meeting and identified herself as a practicing psychiatrist—and a proud grandmother. She then said that she had recently read his journal article on the hypnotic experience and felt that the awareness it helped her achieve had not only played a significant role in her practice, but had also contributed to the success of her marriage, in which satisfactory solutions "always seemed to happen for no apparent reason."

A Quartet of Prodigies

To most people nothing is more fascinating than the performance of prodigious feats. We like to talk about the records made by great athletes; we enjoy the breathless suspense of watching a circus performer on the flying trapeze; we marvel at the virtuosity of a Ruggiero Ricci who played violin concertos at the age of five. The reason for our fascination may be, in part, that the extraordinary takes us away from the humdrum of existence and gives us a thrill that makes life more exciting. And it may also be due, in part, to the fact that we unconsciously identify and empathize with the highest and best. Their glory becomes, in fantasy at least, our glory. But there is another reason as well. It is the feeling of wonder and awe at beholding behavior that seems to defy explanation. It is the mysterious element in these great feats that captures our imagination most of all.

There is no question, therefore, that case stories about prodigies belong in a book on the mysteries of the mind. But there is still another reason for including them. Ever since the study of human behavior became a science, psychologists have been interested in exploring the extremes of human ability. The first to make a systematic study of genius was the English scientist Francis Galton, who compared the genealogies of one thousand British leaders with the background of one thousand average citizens. His research revealed the fact that there were more distinguished relatives among the first group than the second, and he concluded that the difference was due to heredity. That conclusion would be regarded as extremely one-sided today since the geniuses tended to stem from culturally superior families who gave them advantages and opportunities which the average citizens did not enjoy. As a sidelight, it is interesting that Galton himself was a genuine child prodigy, for he could read at two and a half, write a letter at three, and read both Latin and French by five.

Another early explorer of the extremes of human ability, William James, demonstrated in his book *On Vital Reserves* that men and women possess huge reservoirs of energy, resourcefulness, and fortitude which ordinarily remain undiscovered and untapped. One of the examples he cites is a colonel in the British Army who existed almost wholly on brandy during the six-week siege of Delhi in 1857. Despite the fact that he was suffering from scurvy, constant diarrhea, and gangrene of the foot, he reported that "I certainly never found my intellect clearer or my nerves stronger in my life . . . It was only my wretched body that was weak."

Each of the case studies that follow deals with a different kind of prodigy, and each represents a different facet of the human mind: the effect of early training, the incredible speed of thought processes, a nearly perfect memory for sound, and that curious skill known as calendar calculation. In the course of these case studies, we will attempt to find answers to questions that are likely to be raised by everyone at one time or another: Do child prodigies tend to "peter out" when they grow older? How far can parents go in training and molding their children without doing them harm? And can a person be very bright in one respect and very stupid in everything else?

BREAKING POINT

On July 18, 1944, the proprietor of a small boarding house in the Brookline area of Boston called the Peter Bent Brigham Hospital to say that he had found one of his roomers in a state of coma. Within minutes an ambulance picked up the ailing man and took him to the emergency ward. Everything possible was done to save his life, but he had suffered a brain hemorrhage and expired within a few hours.

Thus ended, at forty-six years of age, the life of William Sidis, a man who years before had been hailed as a mathematical genius, an "infant prodigy" if there ever was one.

Why did William Sidis spend the prime of his life in a rooming house? Why was he alone and destitute? Why was his early promise never fulfilled? To answer these questions we must look to his father, Boris Sidis, a self-made Russian immigrant who earned both a Ph.D. and an M.D. degree, and who went on to become a professor of psychology at Harvard and a practicing psychiatrist with a sanitarium of his own in New Hampshire. At Harvard he worked closely with America's most famous psy-

chologist, William James, and named his son William
James Sidis out of admiration for his colleague.

Boris Sidis developed what he called the theory of
mental power. The mind, he maintained, differs fundamentally from the body in one major respect. All bodily
functions have a limit. We can't high jump ten feet un-
aided, or run a two-minute mile, or live two hundred
years. The mind, on the other hand, is unlimited in its
capacities; there is no end to the amount of knowledge we
can acquire, and there are no bounds to human creativity.
Much of the capacity of the mind, however, lies beneath
the surface: "Man possesses large stores of potential, subconscious reserve energy," but unfortunately this energy
is almost totally neglected and undeveloped. The reason,
he believed, is that our educational system is run by
businessmen, bureaucrats, and schoolmarms dedicated to
the single goal of mediocrity: "There is no place for genius in our schools because they stifle talent, they stupefy
the intellect, they suppress genius, they benumb the fac-
ulties of our children."

How can we rectify this sorry situation? According to
Sidis, anyone interested in "educating for genius" must
start the process at home, before the educational system
takes hold of the child and inhibits the development of
his capacities. In one of his works, he quotes Plato's statement that "in every work the *beginning* is the most important part, especially in dealing with anything young
and tender . . . for that is the time when any impression
which one may desire to communicate is most readily
stamped and taken." He then goes on to say that "for the
large majority the beginning of education is between the
second and third year. It is at that critical period that we
have to seize the opportunity to guide the child's form-
ative energies in the right channels. To delay is a mistake and a wrong to the child. We can at that early

period awaken a love of knowledge which will persist through life. The child will as eagerly play in the game of knowledge as he now spends most of his energy in meaningless games and objectless silly sports."

This, then, was the elder Sidis' point of view. But he was not content to state it as a theory; he put it to the test with his own son as his experimental subject. Practically from birth, Willie Sidis was subjected to stimulation designed to awaken his mind. Colored objects of varying shapes were dangled above his head as he lay in his crib, and soon these objects were replaced by blocks with raised letters embossed on their sides. As he was shown these letters, their names were repeated aloud so often that at a mere six months of age he had mastered the entire alphabet. Even before he learned to talk, he was able to pick out and point to any letter his parents called out. By the age of two he had learned to read and write, and by four he was typing not only English but French sentences. At five, he devised a formula by which he could determine instantly the day of the week on which any date in history fell. At six, he was taken to school for the first time and is said to have demonstrated by noon of the same day that he knew everything taught in the first three grades.

During the following half year, six-year-old Willie succeeded in completing a seven-year course in a Brookline public school. Numbers were particularly fascinating to him, and his teachers acknowledged that the precocious child handled fractions better than they did. In line with this interest, he began to memorize timetables during his seventh year and entertained friends of the family by reeling them off without error. At the age of eight, he demonstrated that his ability to handle numbers went far beyond rote memory, for he perfected a new logarithm table based on the number twelve. During this early period, his parents, both of whom were linguists, encouraged him to study both modern and classical languages, and before his eighth year was ended, he was able to speak as well as read Greek, Latin, Russian, French, and German.

At nine, young Sidis completed four years of high school work in less than a single year, and immediately applied for entrance to Harvard College. The admissions officers, however, felt that even though he could meet the academic requirements, he would feel out of place socially among the seventeen- and eighteen-year-olds in his class. They suggested that he wait two years, and his father arranged to have him attend Tufts in the interim. At eleven, he reapplied to Harvard and was accepted. A year later he suffered a breakdown and spent several months at his father's sanitarium. Returning to college, he specialized in mathematics, and at the age of fourteen delivered a paper on "Four-Dimensional Bodies" before an audience of leading professors at the Harvard Mathematics Club. The subject was so advanced that few of them could follow his reasoning, but those who understood his paper agreed with Professor Daniel F. Comstock of MIT who predicted that Sidis would become a mathematical genius and a leader in the scientific world.

A book written by William's father throws further light on his accomplishments. The work, *Philistine and Genius*, was written when William was twelve and contained not only the diatribe against the "Philistine" educational system of the time, as quoted above, but also a prize example of the way genius should be cultivated. That example, only thinly disguised, was his own son. In this book he argues not only against wasting time in "meaningless games and objectless silly sports," but against poisoning the child's mind with "fairy tales, myths, and fables." In their stead, he would bring the child up in "the love and enjoyment of knowledge for its own sake"—and in so doing, we should not be "afraid to strain his brain prematurely." If systematic efforts are made to introduce the child to learning, "by the tenth year without almost any effort the child will acquire the knowledge which at present the best college graduate obtains with infinite labor and pain . . . That this knowledge can be accomplished I can say with authority. I know it as a fact from my own experience with child-life, for at the age of twelve, when other children of his age are hardly able to read and spell, and drag a miserable mental existence at the apron strings of some antiquated school-dame, one of these boys . . . intensely enjoys courses in the highest branches of mathematics and astronomy at one of our foremost universities. The *Iliad* and the *Odyssey* are known to him by heart, and he is deeply interested in the advanced works of classical philology. He is able to read Herodotus, Aeschylus, Sophocles, Euripides, Aristophanes, Lucian, and other Greek writers with the same zest and ease as our schoolboy reads his Robinson Crusoe . . . He is well versed in Logic, Ancient History, American History and has a general insight into our politics and the groundwork of our constitution. At the same time he is of an extremely happy disposition, brimming over with humor and fun. His physical condition is splendid, his cheeks glow with health. Many a girl would envy his complexion. Being above five feet four he towers above the average boy of his age and looks like a boy of sixteen."

These are not idle boasts of a fond father, nor simply a justification for preconceived theories. Undoubtedly they were well intentioned and sincerely felt. But looking at them in the light of William's subsequent history, they have an ironic flavor. For it appears that at age twelve, when this glowing description was written, the boy had reached the peak of his powers, and from that time on decline set in. The first indication was his breakdown that same year, about which few details were ever divulged. But we also know that despite his size, the boy was extremely ungainly and self-conscious—certainly due, in part at least, to his sedentary life and his inability to participate in the games and sports his father derided. From more objective accounts of his life, we have also learned that he was socially awkward, scorned girls, and vowed never to marry. In addition, he deeply resented being called a "freak" and soon began to show a "marked distrust of people."

Willie's deterioration as a person was a gradual and painful affair. After his illness, he was able to continue his studies at Harvard, and graduated *cum laude* in 1914 at the age of sixteen. Newspaper reporters, aware of his early history, rushed to interview the "child prodigy" after commencement, but found him shy and retiring. The only statement he would make was "I want to live the perfect life. The only way to live the perfect life is to live it in seclusion. I have always hated crowds."

The young man remained at Harvard, and for the following three years attended the law school, graduating without distinction. He then returned to his original interest in numbers, and took a position at the Rice Institute in Texas as a mathematics instructor. By this time, however, he found it impossible to take any responsibility, and quit his position within a few months. A year later, in 1919, he participated in a Socialist demonstration at Roxbury, near Boston, and was arrested for shouting, "To hell with the American flag!" In court he denied the charge but admitted that he thought the Russian Revolution was a good idea, and was sentenced to eighteen months in the House of Correction. The sentence was appealed, and the case was dropped.

William's appearance in court was apparently a turning point in his life, for he resolved to take no more chances with publicity, and retired into complete obscurity. He also retired from the intellectual life, asserting that he was "tired of thinking"; and in 1924 took a $23-a-week job operating an adding machine in a Wall Street brokerage house. At about this time, too, he broke completely with his parents, who had prodded and pressured him into becoming a "genius." In 1926, when a friend informed him of his father's death, he berated him for wasting his time. That same year he returned to Boston and took a job as a clerk for the Massachusetts Unemployment Compensation Commission—this time at only $16 a week. At one point, he let himself go and made some suggestions for reorganizing the work, but when one of his associates urged him to bring his ideas to the attention of the administrators, he immediately withdrew, remarking, "Thinking is the boss's job. I just want to be told what to do."

Sidis continued working at one routine job after another. In his spare time he busied himself with his one consuming interest: collecting trolley transfers. Alone in his room, he would sort these transfers, map out the transportation system, and compile data on the trolley schedules—a hobby that recalls his early memorization of timetables. His labors eventually came to fruition in the form of a book, *Notes on the Collection of Transfers*. Written under the pseudonym Frank Folupa, this work was to become his only contribution to the sum of human knowledge.

In 1937, a *New Yorker* writer came across an account of Sidis' early history and decided that he would make an interesting subject for the series "Where Are They Now?" He therefore gathered all the information he could and even interviewed Sidis himself. The resulting article was not, on the whole, an unsympathetic account of his life, but it did point out his eccentricities, and it also claimed, quite mistakenly, that he skipped bail in the Roxbury affair. This offended Sidis, and acting as his own attorney, he promptly sued the magazine for libel and invasion of privacy. This was his only application of his training as a lawyer, but he lost the case on the technical ground that the article had not interfered with his livelihood, since he was still working.

To Sidis, *The New Yorker* article was final proof that he could only be harmed by publicity. He therefore retreated into the obscure existence that was to last for the remaining seven years of his life.

What conclusions can be drawn from the story of William Sidis? When he died in 1944, the press was quick to seize the opportunity, almost gleefully, to revive the old idea that after their initial flash of brilliance, prodigies are bound to peter out. Articles on Sidis therefore appeared under such titles as "Prodigious Failure" and "Burned-out Prodigy." But that idea has been challenged by case after case reported both before and since he lived. The list of prodigies who have "made good" covers many different fields, and includes chess experts such as Capablanca, Reshevsky, Evans, and Fischer; renowned composers such as Mendelssohn, Mozart, Franck, Berlioz, Brahms, Chopin, Liszt, and Haydn; eminent performers such as Heifetz, Menuhin, Rubinstein, Ricci, Schnabel, and Oistrakh; artistic geniuses such as Michelangelo and Van Dyck; famous philosophers such as Spinoza and John Stuart Mill; great writers such as Goethe, Macaulay, Tennyson, and Charlotte Brontë; and in the field of science, the mathematician Carl Friedrich Gauss, the astronomer T. H. Safford, and the physicist J. Robert Oppenheimer.

An especially relevant example of a mathematical prodigy who realized his early promise is Norbert Wiener. Like Sidis, Wiener was the son of a Russian immigrant who became a distinguished Harvard professor. He, too, was introduced to the world of learning at the earliest possible age. His father supervised his studies closely, and even during his high school years required him to recite his lessons to him every day. Like Sidis, too, young Wiener became nationally known as a child prodigy. He entered Tufts College at the age of eleven, graduated in three years, and at fourteen was enrolled as a graduate student at Harvard. There he befriended the shy, reticent Sidis, who was at that time three years younger and a freshman. In his autobiography, entitled *Ex-Prodigy*, he recalls attending the boy's lecture before the Mathematics Club and attests to the brilliance and originality of his presentation.

During the following years, when Sidis was beginning to decline, Wiener continued to advance and became not only a professor of mathematics at MIT, but was the originator of the science of cybernetics, a theory of communication and control which is the foundation stone of automation and computer technology. Yet even at the height of his career he did not forget his less fortunate friend, Sidis, and saw to it that he was given a job as a "human computer" at the Institute. As Wiener states in his autobiography, Sidis refused to take any job that entailed responsibility, but "he had a limited security in his work with us; we all knew his story and respected his privacy."

Wiener's comments on Sidis' breakdown are revealing. He states that "I have no doubt that even at the time I knew him at Harvard, competent psychoanalytic help of the sort that is generally available today could have saved young Sidis for a more useful and happier career. I am equally sure that his father, precisely because he was a psychiatrist and was busy reading the fine print of the psychological map, was unable to see the inscription written on it in the largest characters, stretching from one corner to the other. It was perfectly clear that the later collapse of Sidis was in large measure his father's making." In spite of this statement, Wiener refused to condemn the elder Sidis, but sought to understand his "follies." In his view, he was a victim of his own background as a Russian Jew who came here fresh from the persecutions of the time, tasted the success which the new land made it possible for him to achieve, and consequently strove in every possible way for the even greater success of his brilliant child.

Wiener's final comment is particularly significant: "Let those who choose to carve a human soul to their own measure be sure that they have a worthy image after which to carve it, and let them know that the power of molding an emerging intellect is a power of death as well as a power of life. A strong drug is a strong poison. The physician who ventures to use it must first be sure he knows the dosage."

To which we must add one all-important point: You have to know not only the dosage but the patient as well. Boris Sidis, a physician himself, ignored this simple fact. In his eagerness to prove his point, he forgot the child while remembering the genius. Deluded by his own academic achievements, his hatred of mediocrity, and his intellectual arrogance, he overlooked the fact that every child, prodigies included, needs games and sports, fun and exercise, and, above all, the companionship of his peers. Without fully realizing what he was doing, he encouraged his son to develop an unbalanced, lopsided personality, and denied him the opportunity to develop mature emotions and mature relationships. Moreover, he stood by, ironically admiring his handiwork, while the boy suffered the agonies of social rejection and the glaring light of publicity—until, ill equipped to handle these burdens, he reached his breaking point. Then, resenting the forces that made him what he was, he rebelled against his father, against thinking, and against his own capacities. His life was a failure, not because he was a prodigy, and not because he "burned out," but because he was forced to carry burdens which he was too immature, too one-sided, and too resentful to endure.

But why was Norbert Wiener able to carry burdens that appeared to be so similar in size and kind? The evidence is in his autobiography. Though his father came from the same type of background as Boris Sidis and had achieved similar status on his own, he was *both* a student and an outdoor man who preferred to live on his farm rather than in the city. Moreover, as his precocious son went through the awkward age, like other adolescents, both he and the boy's mother took pains to see that their son socialized with boys and girls of his own age—and as a result, he met an understanding young woman and achieved a happy, sustaining marriage.

Probably, too, there was a basic constitutional difference between the two. While Sidis was tall and appeared, to his father at least, to be sturdy, he actually did not have Wiener's stamina, and certainly not his emotional strength. Finally, though Wiener was labeled prodigy and received a good deal of publicity, he had an outgoing personality and was spared the jibes of the press. On the other hand, as he points out, "Sidis, who through his later life was a defeated—and honorably defeated—combatant in the battle for existence, was pilloried like a side-show freak for fools to gape at."

MAN VS. MACHINE

The scene is a big-city theater back in the thirties when vaudeville was still in its prime. Every seat is taken, and every eye is riveted on the performer standing beside a large blackboard. As an assistant wheels in a table containing a calculating machine, the performer announces: "Now I am going to race against the fastest thinking machine yet devised by man. There must be someone in the audience who is an expert at operating a rapid calculator. Who will volunteer?"

A young woman stands up, and he beckons her to the stage. "Fine," he says. "Now I want someone else to come up and write a column of 12 four-digit numbers such as 7643 and 9215, on this blackboard while the young lady and I have our backs turned." A number of hands go up, and he quickly selects a man, repeats his instructions, and asks him to cover the board with a large cloth when he has finished writing the numbers. He continues: "My assistant will signal when all is ready, and as soon as he removes the cloth, we will begin to add the numbers—you, my friend, on the machine, and I in my head."

The numbers are written, the cloth removed with a flourish, and the race begins. The machine clatters noisily while the performer glances at the column. It takes him only seconds to write his answer—but the machine clatters on and finally stops. The audience applauds, but the performer holds up his hand: "Wait! The mind was faster than the machine, but was it as accurate? Will you please read off your answer, miss?" She reads 81367 as he points to exactly the same number on his blackboard. Now the applause is deafening and the performer bows deeply.

There are two people in the audience, however, who do not join in the applause—two young men named W. A. Bousfield and H. Barry sitting together in the fourth row. They are too busy checking the stop watches in their hands and recording the time taken by the famous "lightning calculator." After a few moments they close their notebooks, leave their seats, and ask an usher how to get backstage. They follow his directions and are soon in the performer's dressing room. Introducing themselves, they congratulate him on his remarkable performance, and ask if they could take him to a nearby restaurant for a bite to eat. He is an affable man and agrees.

As soon as they are settled in the restaurant, the performer turns to his hosts, saying, "Well, now, what's this all about? Are you booking agents or what?" They smile and explain that they are not agents but psychologists with a particular interest in thinking processes. They had heard about his amazing feats of calculation and had come to see for themselves—in fact, they had attended all his performances for the past three days, and had recorded not only the problems he solved, but the exact time he took on each of them. In their estimation he was probably the fastest calculator appearing before the public. He beamed with pleasure and they asked the question that was uppermost in their minds: Would he come to their laboratory and permit them to study his mental feats more closely?

At first the performer refused on the ground that his success depended not only on the feats he performed, but on the air of mystery that surrounded them. Most people came to see him because they thought his gifts bordered on the supernatural, and if anyone were to explain his ability, he might lose his audience and his livelihood. This gave the psychologists the opening they needed. They asked if he himself could explain his phenomenal skill, and he at once confessed that he was almost as mystified as his audiences. After that it was relatively easy to get him to agree to the investigation, especially when they assured him that their findings, if any, would not be publicized in the newspapers, and even in professional journals he would be identified only by his initials S.F.

During the days that followed, S.F. spent many hours in the laboratory. The first few sessions were devoted to exploring his mathematical abilities as fully as possible, with an eye always open for possible explanations. The two investigators found that his skill was even more astounding than they had suspected. He could add a dozen two-digit numbers in a single second—about twenty-five times faster than the average individual. He could look at a square of digits composed of five rows of five digits each for a mere fifty seconds, and then repeat the numbers in any sequence whatsoever—vertically, horizontally, diagonally, right to left, left to right. He could rattle off the correct value of pi to 200 decimal places; whereas most people have trouble remembering the first four: .1416. He could give the logs of any number from one to 100 to seven places without hesitation. And he could glance at a lengthy number such as 27875145387941732 for a mere fraction of a second, and not only repeat it correctly immediately afterward, but twenty-four hours later. Most people can repeat only seven or eight numbers, and by the next day they are entirely forgotten.

During these demonstrations the psychologists not only observed S.F.'s behavior closely, but asked him question after question. By the time the tests were completed, they had arrived at not one, but three possible explanations of his astonishing skill.

First, they discovered that S.F., unlike the rest of us, lived almost wholly in a world of numbers, just as a composer lives in a world of notes and melodies and a botanist in a world of plants and flowers. In fact, he had become so preoccupied with numbers that practically any combination would immediately call to mind at least one meaningful association. Most of us remember a few dates or telephone numbers by association, but with S.F. these associations extended to hundreds of dates, all types of permutations and combinations, ascending and descending series, and an incalculable number of logs, powers, and roots. But here is an odd twist. Once in a great while a given number would *fail* to call up an association even in S.F.'s number-filled mind—but that made him remember it all the more, simply because it was so un-usual!

S.F. did not depend wholly on associations. Early in his life he had formed the odd habit of performing mathematical calculations in every spare moment. Extracting square roots was one of the many operations that occupied his mind. Let's take 9836 as an example: How many of us could reduce that number to the sum of the squares of 90, 40, 10, and 6? S.F. could do this in a matter of seconds—and he could do the same with any other four-place number the experimenters gave him.

And what about his remarkable ability to remember a long series of numbers such as the one mentioned above: 2787514538794l732? Bousfield and Barry found that he utilized both of the methods just outlined—association and manipulation. That long number registered in his mind in terms of a) the log of 1.9, b) the date of the fall of Constantinople, c) X's telephone number, and d) the square root of three!

To test this ability even further, they then picked a number at random—259—and found that it *immediately* called the following facts to S.F.'s mind: There are 259 propositions in the philosopher Spinoza's great work, the *Ethics*; 259 is divisible by 37; two raised to the fifth power (32) times 9 squared (81) equals 2592: and there are 2,592,000 seconds in a 30-day month!

The two psychologists became convinced that S.F.'s consuming interest in numbers was *one* answer to his astounding skill, but they felt it did not fully explain his ability to recall whole sequences of numbers many hours or days later, nor his ability to perform complex calculations faster than a machine. They therefore attempted to find out exactly what went on in his mind as he manipulated numbers—and they came up with an unexpected answer.

In brief, they discovered that every time S.F. was given a problem to solve, he would immediately form a remarkably clear and vivid image of the numbers involved. They would always appear as if written with white chalk on a blackboard in his own handwriting. Moreover, in working on the problem, he could make any group of numbers stand out from the others, move them about as he added, subtracted, or multiplied, and then integrate the results with the rest of the numbers on his mental blackboard. In addition, he could revive the entire blackboard after long periods of time, and *read off* the numbers and calculations at will.

To the investigators this meant one thing: S.F. possessed a highly unusual kind of visual imagery, one that goes far beyond our ordinary ability to see people, things, and numbers "in our mind's eye." This form of imagery, known to psychologists as "eidetic imagery," is found in 5 to 10 per cent of children, but is extremely rare in adults.

Eidetic imagery is the nearest thing to what is popularly called photographic memory. No one knows how or why it develops, but people who have this ability can look at any picture or object, including a set of numbers, then look away and see it as clearly and vividly as if it was still in front of their eyes. What is more, they can focus on any detail of the image, enlarge it at will, and even make out details they had not noticed when they looked at the original object. Finally, they can carry this image with them for several days, and evoke it at will, just as we might take a photograph out of our pocket and look at it.

The investigations of Bousfield and Barry go a long way toward explaining the mysterious ability of the lightning calculator. The important elements seem to be a preoccupation with numbers, assiduous practice, formation of innumerable associations, and an unusually vivid visual memory—plus, we may add, a naturally quick mind and the motivating factors of earning a good living and receiving the applause of thousands of people.

These explanations may not be complete, but they at least take this ability out of the realm of magic and mystery and into the realm of scientific research—and that is what psychology is all about. As Bousfield and Barry themselves point out, "When the operations involved in lightning calculation are analyzed, one is struck by their essential normality. Recognition of this fact should change our attitude from unreflecting wonder at a rare and mystifying 'gift' to an intelligent appreciation of the complexity to which certain familiar psychological processes may attain."

VIRTUOSO

It was a quiet, cloudless night at the Bethune plantation, and everyone had long since retired. As he lay in bed courting sleep, the colonel thought he heard the faint sounds of a piano coming from the drawing room on the first floor. Surely it couldn't be one of his daughters at this hour; they were only six and eight years old, and they must have been asleep for hours. He turned over, thinking to himself that it must have been a half dream.

But the music persisted. Finally, the colonel roused himself, muttered a soft curse, lit a candle, and went downstairs. When he opened the door of the drawing room, he found it in total darkness—but the sound of music continued. The light of his candle fell on the piano, and there he beheld—to his amazement—a small black boy sitting with his head thrown far back, flawlessly playing the Mozart sonata his older daughter had finally mastered after weeks of study.

This was Colonel Bethune's introduction to the prodigious talent of the boy he had named Thomas Greene Bethune. Tom was only four years old at the time of the midnight concert. He had become a member of the household at one year of age when the colonel bought his mother from Perry Oliver at a slave auction held in a nearby Georgia county. Oliver had kept the boy in hiding until the sale was made, then brought him out with a sly smile, saying, "Colonel, I forgot to tell you she has a boy. I'm throwing him in free." The reason was that Tom had been born stone-blind.

When he questioned his daughters the next day, Colonel Bethune learned that Tom, who had been given the run of the house, often listened to their practicing with rapt attention. He then discovered that not only music but sounds of all kinds held a peculiar fascination for the boy. He would sit for hours listening to the grating of a corn sheller or the dripping of rain on the roof. But he seemed irresistibly drawn to the piano, and the colonel gave him free access to the drawing room. Within a few years, he found that without any instruction whatever Tom had developed a totally unexpected ability. He could listen to a piece of music once, then sit down at the piano and play it through, note for note, accent for accent, precisely as it had been performed by his daughters or by a house guest who had played for the family after dinner.

Recognizing the boy's unique talent, the colonel decided to engage a professional teacher in nearby Columbus. After hearing him play, the musician is said to have refused to take him as a pupil, declaring, "That boy already knows more about music than I will ever know."

No other attempts were made to teach Tom, and he never attended school. The reason? He was found to be mentally defective and incapable of academic learning of any kind. Moreover, he was far too restless and explosive to adapt himself to any learning situation whether at home or in school. By modern standards he would be placed in the category of the moderately or severely retarded, for he had to live under constant supervision and never developed a vocabulary of more than a few hundred words.

Blind Tom continued to listen to music, and to play everything he heard, no matter how complex the composition. At around six years of age he revealed a gift of a different order: He could improvise as well as repeat. Proud of his ability, Tom was delighted when the colonel asked him to entertain his friends when they visited the mansion. So successful were these informal concerts that the colonel began to think in more practical terms: Perhaps he had a "gold mine" in his hands. He therefore decided to make an investment. He hired professional musicians to play for the child, and within a few months Tom had begun to build a repertoire of concert quality.

In 1857, when Tom had reached the age of seven, Colonel Bethune felt he was ready to make his debut, and rented an auditorium in Columbus. By that time, word of the "blind genius" had gotten around, and the concert was a sellout. It was also a musical triumph, and the newspaper reports were so enthusiastic that the colonel was encouraged to take his young protégé on a concert tour. This, too, was completely successful, and during the first year he is said to have made $100,000 on the boy. Tom and his mother saw little of this money, or of the vastly greater sums that flowed in during the years that followed.

As Tom continued to concertize in city after city, Colonel Bethune would feed his voracious memory by having outstanding musicians play for him. According to the accounts of the day, every note was indelibly imprinted on Tom's mind, and he was able to reproduce any piece of music he had heard from beginning to end without a moment's hesitation. His repertoire encompassed practically the full range of compositions played by virtuosos of the time, and included Beethoven, Mendelssohn, Bach, Chopin, Verdi, Rossini, Donizetti, Gounod, Meyerbeer, and many others. The program of one of his early concerts states: "Blind Tom can only play what he has heard or what he improvises. Until about two years ago a list of pieces that Tom heard was kept, numbering nearly 2000 pieces. Unfortunately this catalogue was lost. Since, he has heard perhaps 3000 pieces, and his repertoire now numbers upwards of 5000 entirely on his memory depending."

Tom's phenomenal auditory memory served him in more ways than one. A newspaper report of the day contained this passage: "His memory is so accurate that he can repeat, without the loss of a syllable, a discourse of 15 minutes length, of which he does not understand a word. Songs, too, in French or German, after a single hearing, he renders not only literally in words, but in notes, style and expression." Even allowing for journalistic exuberance, these are extraordinary feats for a person of limited mentality who scarcely knew his own native tongue.

Another contemporary report gives us a more intimate picture of one of his performances: "Blind Tom seated himself at last before the piano, a full half-yard distant, stretching out his arms full length, like an ape clawing his food; his feet when not on the pedals twisted incessantly; he answered some jokes of his master's with a loud 'Yha! Yha!'

"Nothing indexes the brain like a laugh; this was idiotic.

"'Now, Tom boy, something we like from Verdi!' the colonel commanded.

"The head fell further back, the claws began to work, and those of the composer's harmonies which you could have chosen as the purest exponents of passion began to float through the room. Selections from Weber, Beethoven and others whom I have forgotten followed. At the close of each piece, Tom, without waiting for the audience, would applaud himself violently, kicking, pounding his hands together, turning always to his master for the approving pat on the head."

Tom's fame spread, and in 1860 when he was eleven years old, he was invited to play at the White House before President James Buchanan. It was a full dress affair, and the boy's performance was most impressive. The following day, the Washington papers carried such a glowing account of his triumph that several musicians felt he had somehow tricked the public and the President. They visited Colonel Bethune at his hotel and asked if Tom would submit to a test. He agreed on behalf of his protégé, and they brought out two completely new compositions, one thirteen pages in length and the other twenty. Tom listened quietly as the first was played, then repeated it from beginning to end without effort. The second composition was then performed, and this Tom also played to perfection.

This was not the only time Tom's ability was tested by experts. In 1862, at the close of a long concert in Virginia, a man rushed to the stage with a sheaf of music in his hand. Before anyone could stop him, he announced that it was a fourteen-page *Fantasia* of his own—and challenged Tom, who was already very tired, to play a duet with him. The musician proposed to play the first, or treble, part while Tom would play the *secondo*. Since the boy could not read the music, which of course he had never heard before, this meant that he would have to improvise the entire second part in step with the musician's execution of the first part. According to a published report, "Tom's master refused to submit the boy's brain to so cruel a test; some of the audience even interfered; but the musician insisted, and took his place. Tom sat beside him—his head rolling nervously from side to side—struck the opening cadenzas, and then from the first note to the last, gave the *secondo* triumphantly.

"Jumping up, he fairly shoved the man from his seat,

and proceeded to play the treble with more brilliancy and power than its composer."

The report ends with these words: "To play *secondo* to music never heard or seen infers the comprehension of the full drift of the symphony in its current—a capacity to create, in short."

After the Civil War, Colonel Bethune took Tom on an extended tour of the concert halls of Europe. Everywhere he went, his concerts were hailed as artistic triumphs, and in London alone a series of performances netted his mentor an estimated $100,000.

During one of his Continental tours, the young man, then sixteen, was subjected to an ingenious test to determine whether he was one of those rare individuals who possess perfect, or absolute, pitch—the ability to identify and reproduce any note they hear. Three pianos were involved in the test. As Tom listened, two of the experimenters hammered noisily and haphazardly on two of the pianos, while a musician simultaneously performed a run of twenty notes on the third. The result was a bedlam of sound, yet when Tom was seated at one of the pianos immediately afterward, he was able to repeat the run of twenty notes perfectly. The fact that he could distinguish and reproduce these notes appeared to the experimenters to be proof positive that he possessed absolute pitch.

Following his European tour, Tom played to capacity audiences in a number of northern cities, including New York. The reports contained such phrases as "we know of no parallel case in musical history," and "the power of this boy is, so far as I know, unmatched in the development of any musical talent." In Philadelphia a committee of sixteen outstanding musicians examined him exhaustively, and at the conclusion signed a statement which read in part:

"Whether in his improvisations or performances of compositions by Gottschalk, Verdi and others; in fact, under every form of musical examination—and the experiments were too numerous to mention—he showed a capacity ranking him among the most wonderful phenomena in musical history."

Tom's virtuosity remained undiminished as he grew older, and he continued to appear on the concert stage until he was fifty-three years of age. At that time his public career came to a close due to the death of Colonel Bethune. He had become so dependent on his mentor that his urge to perform could not be maintained, and he sank into a sullen and belligerent state of mind. He lived his last years in Hoboken, New Jersey, and died in 1908, a lonely prodigy who had aroused the admiration and wonderment of hundreds of thousands of concertgoers and professional musicians both here and abroad.

Many attempts have been made to explain Tom's astonishing memory and even more astonishing mastery of the keyboard. Certainly a part of his ability can be traced to his absorption in the world of sound. This preoccupation probably stemmed from four sources. First, he had little to do, and listening to sounds of all kinds helped him to occupy his time. Second, he was deprived of normal visual stimulation (which accounts for about 85 per cent of what we learn about our world), and compensated for this lack by developing auditory sensitivity to the fullest possible degree. Third, he compensated further by developing the manual dexterity and co-ordination required for reproducing sounds on the piano. And fourth, he found at an early age that this ability elicited praise and amazement from people whom he had come to admire. The recognition and approval he received, plus the opportunities provided by the colonel, encouraged him to concentrate on his one outstanding ability to the exclusion of everything else in his life.

Absolute pitch also played a role in Tom's musical performances. Many people believe this is an inborn trait, but recent psychological experiments have demonstrated that when individuals who are weak in pitch discrimination are subjected to systematic training they almost invariably improve, and some even achieve absolute pitch. In Tom's case, it seems reasonable to suppose that he was born with a good, though perhaps not perfect, ear but developed his capacity further through persistent preoccupation with sound.

Tom's ability to improvise cannot be fully explained, but it is important to note that the type of music he was accustomed to hearing and playing tended to follow a certain order—for example, the a-b-a arrangement of the classic sonatas, and the "rules" for the resolution of chords. In other words, it is doubtful that the term "creative," as quoted above, can be literally applied to any of his performances. We must, however, admire his agility in improvising, especially during the remarkable duet he played with the musician who challenged him.

There is even less basis for an explanation of his astounding memory. We can cite case after case to show that tenacious retention is a prime characteristic of many "idiots savants" or "moronic geniuses"—but we are reduced to speculation when we try to advance a reason for this fact. Dr. Edward Podolsky, who reviews the case of Blind Tom in his *Encyclopedia of Aberrations,* ends his account with this comment: "There have been many mathematical and musical geniuses who have been devoid of all other ordinary mental abilities. Is it possible that one part of the brain develops to such an extent and degree that all other parts suffer and remain in a rudimentary state?" There is no anatomical evidence, as

Podolsky recognizes, that development of one area of the brain *inhibits* development of other areas. However, we do know that different functions tend to be localized in different parts of the brain, and that some areas may be defective while others are intact. In Tom's case this probably means that the brain cells which control hearing and auditory memory (in the temporal lobe) were not damaged or defective. This fact, coupled with his concentration on sound, and particularly on the sound of music, is just about all the "explanation" we can offer at present for his fantastic ability.

A FLAIR FOR DATES

It would be extremely unlikely for anyone, except perhaps a lawyer in a courtroom drama, to ask, "What day of the week did January 14, 1958, fall on?" And it would be even less likely for anyone to pose the same question about August 28, 1591, and expect to get an answer. But if you were to ask a young man named George the first question, he would almost instantly say, "Tuesday" —and to the second question he would answer, "Wednesday" after only a few moments' hesitation.

Checking the 1958 answer might take twenty or thirty minutes, but checking back to 1591 would take many hours—especially since you would have to figure an extra day for leap years. But in both cases you would find that George's answers were perfectly accurate.

George is what is known as a "calendar calculator,"

one of a select group of individuals who can identify practically any date with lightninglike rapidity. Even more extraordinary, George is not alone, for he has a double, an identical twin brother named Charles—and when you ask your question, the two of them are quite likely to give the answer in unison!

Calendar calculators have been reported in the psychological literature for many years, but never have they even approached the uncanny ability of these twin brothers. If you compare the two, you will find that George surpasses Charles in accuracy, particularly for dates before the present century. His range is also greater, for he will identify February 15, 2002, as rapidly and as correctly as that date in 1591—a span over six thousand years. Moreover, you can ask your question in other ways—for example, "In what years did April 21 fall on a Sunday?" They will both answer 1968, 1963, 1957, 1946, etc.—but George will continue all the way back to 1700. If you then ask George, "In what months of the year 2002 does the first fall on a Friday?" he will quickly answer, "February, March, and November." Or ask him the date of the fourth Monday in February 1993, and he will tell you in a few seconds that it will fall on the twenty-second.

One more outstanding fact about these twins, perhaps the most astonishing of all. They are both mentally retarded. In fact, they are so underdeveloped that they live in Letchworth Village, an institution for mental defectives.

In 1963, the directors of the Village agreed to have a group of psychiatrists at the New York State Psychiatric Institute make an exhaustive study of the twins, who were then twenty-four years of age. Their preliminary findings only served to compound the mystery, for they discovered that in spite of the boys' remarkable skill in calendar calculation, they were almost totally lacking in mathematical ability. Neither of them could add, subtract, multiply, or divide even simple digits like 3 and 7. Nevertheless, if you gave them your birth date, they would immediately tell you it was exactly twenty-nine weeks until your next birthday, or thirteen weeks since your last one. In fact, they often amused themselves by stopping a doctor friend in the hall, remarking, "Hello, Doctor, you're going to have a birthday in sixteen weeks!"

How did George and Charles acquire their phenomenal ability? And what accounts for the fact that their minds were undeveloped in all other respects?

A study of their case histories showed that the boys' mother had experienced a difficult pregnancy, and that she had hemorrhaged so severely at six months that a Caesarean section had to be performed. She actually gave birth to triplets, but the third child, a girl, did not live. The two boys were kept in incubators for two months, and both had convulsions when they were removed. These facts may help to explain their retardation, which was not diagnosed until their third year. After that, valiant but on the whole futile efforts were made to teach them letters and numbers. However, they were so restless and overactive that nothing would hold their attention for more than a few moments, and as they grew, they became so destructive that they had to be transferred to the institution.

One important event occurred before they were institutionalized. When he was six years old, George came across an almanac on the family bookshelf. One of its pages seemed to hold a peculiar fascination for him, the page that contained a perpetual calendar. He would spend hour after hour poring over it. The parents insist that they made no effort to teach him what it meant, yet somehow he learned to decipher it entirely by himself. Soon he became so adept at looking up dates that it became a family game. From the very beginning he never made an error—in fact, he was so quick and accurate that an aunt who served as a legal secretary would call to check dates on documents with him.

George's parents became convinced that his talent for dates was a God-given gift designed to compensate for his deficiencies. They praised him continually for his skill, and gave him a silver perpetual calendar as a prize. From that point on he spent even more time at the one activity that captured and held his interest.

When the two boys were placed in the institution, they became inseparable. Soon Charles, too, began playing the game of dates, but since he was a "late starter," he has always lagged behind his brother. In addition, though both twins are nearsighted and wear thick plastic glasses, Charles suffers from a more severe impairment of vision than George. Both boys, however, had approximately the same IQ when tested at the Village: in the 40 to 50 range. And both were extremely difficult and nearly unmanageable at times. But it is an interesting fact that during their stay at the Psychiatric Institute, when they received extra attention and acceptance from both the staff and the patients, their behavior improved markedly and their IQs rose a full 20 points.

In many ways George and Charles are typical idiots savants—individuals who, though clearly subnormal in general intelligence, show surprising skill in one specific area. (See "Virtuoso," above.) Many of them have amazing memories and remarkably quick minds in that area, but studies show that they can rarely handle abstractions. This was found to be true of the twins. For instance, they could subtract apples but not dollars. How, then, could they become so skillful at such a complex task as calendar calculation?

The usual explanation of this ability, which is not un-common among idiot savants, revolves around three points. First, since they cannot deal with abstractions and therefore cannot "figure things out" in the usual ways, they must simply memorize the calendars year by year, spurred on by the attention and praise they receive. Then, when they are asked about a given date, the appropriate calendar pops into their mind, and they "read off" the answer. Second, this process may be facilitated by a peculiar type of memory known as eidetic imagery, a rare and inexplicable ability to call up images that have the clarity and detail of a photograph. (See "Man vs. Machine," above.) Third, they somehow devise a me-chanical formula that takes into account leap year dates and enables them to calculate rapidly and accurately. (See "Breaking Point," above.)

The question is whether these explanations apply to George and Charles. And the answer is that they are totally inadequate! The investigators William A. Horwitz and his associates found that rote memory, even with the aid of eidetic imagery, could not fully account for the twins' ability since they could calculate dates far beyond the area where calendars were available: "They operate in a range of calendar calculation far before and beyond our usual 200–400-year perpetual calendar. The longest known perpetual calendar extends to about the year 2400 and one of the twins can reach beyond the year 7000. Furthermore, they calculate dates for which no formal calendar exists, such as the years in which a certain date in a certain month falls on a Sunday, etc., or which month in a certain year will the first fall on a Friday, etc." And as to utilizing a special formula, "They operate so rapidly that it is obvious they use no formula even if they were capable of learning one."

George and Charles were asked to give their own explanation, but they did not have the remotest idea. They merely shook their heads and said, "I just know," or "It's in my head." The investigators continued their efforts to find an explanation, but came to this reluctant conclusion: "After exploring their abilities with various people in different learned fields—psychiatrists, psychologists, internists and mathematicians, etc., we must candidly admit that we have no better explanation." This conclusion is shared by others who have commented on this extraordinary case. One of them, Dr. Arthur P. Holstein, states, "The importance, then, of the Idiot Savant lies in our inability to explain him; he stands as a landmark of our own ignorance . . . and as a challenge to our capabilities."

Here, then, is truly a first-class mystery of the mind.

Contagion

"No man is an island." This oft-quoted line of the poet John Donne might well be the motto of one of the fastest growing branches of psychology, the study of social behavior. We now realize more than ever before that man is basically a "political animal," as Aristotle pointed out long ago. If we are to understand human beings we must see them in relation to each other, not in isolation. We must watch them compete and co-operate, study them in groups large and small, discover how they interact in the family, in business, in organizations. This is the social dimension of human behavior, and no field of science is more important in a day when our most urgent problems involve our relationships to one another.

In recent years social psychology has encompassed an ever wider expanse: fads and crazes, riots and lynchings, propaganda and public opinion. Most of its findings are based on careful observation of people in real rather than laboratory situations, although in some cases there is experimental evidence to support these observations. The psychologist does not deliberately incite a riot to study its course and effects, but he might subject one group of people to a propaganda film in favor of nuclear testing and an equivalent group to a film in opposition, and compare the responses of the two groups on attitude tests given before and after the propaganda.

One of the major questions in social psychology is how crowd behavior differs from individual behavior. The best way to answer this question is to look at striking examples of the way people react to danger and disaster, mass suggestion, threatening rumors, and get-rich-quick schemes. The four case stories that follow were chosen to illustrate these facets of crowd behavior. Two of them took place several centuries ago; the other two are quite recent. Perhaps we will find that in spite of the passage of time, the crowds of today are likely to react in much the same way as those of the distant past. And in spite of our vaunted sophistication, hysteria and contagion may still be the rule rather than the exception.

THE DANCING PLAGUE

The town square in Apulia wore a gay and festive air. A band of musicians was playing a lively tune and groups of men and women whirled about in time to the music. Many of the dancers wore garlands on their heads, and practically all had decorated themselves with red ribbons. Though everyone danced vigorously, the women particularly were free and abandoned in their movements, raising their long skirts high and permitting their loose-fitting dresses to slip away from their shoulders.

When the piece was over, the hard-breathing dancers

sat—collapsed would be a better word—on the cobbled pavement, or rushed to the water trough to bathe their faces and arms. But the pause was brief, for within a few moments they began to shout, "Keep playing! Keep playing!"

What were the dancers celebrating? What festival was being held in this town in the heel of Italy? None at all! Despite the carnival atmosphere, despite the music and dancing, the citizens of Apulia were not on holiday. In fact, anyone who observed them closely would be almost bound to suspect that there was something more afoot than pleasure. The gaiety seemed a little too forced, the dancing too frenetic, the signs of exhaustion too obvious. And there was a compulsive quality about their insistence that the musicians keep playing with no more than a moment's pause.

The people of Apulia were dancing with one grim purpose in mind. They were trying to rid themselves of a disease that had attacked hundreds of men and women, a disease attributed to the bite of a spider, the tarantula, that infested their region. And the only effective remedy for the disease was music and dancing.

The period was early in the fifteenth century, and several experienced physicians of the time have recorded the details of the epidemic. Basing his description on these reports, a modern medical historian, H. E. Sigerist, has given us the following vivid account of this strange disorder: "The disease occurred at the height of the summer heat . . . People, asleep or awake, would suddenly jump up, feeling an acute pain like the sting of a bee. Some saw the spider, others did not, but they knew that it must be the tarantula. They ran out of the house into the street, to the market place, dancing in great excitement. Soon they were joined by others who like them had been bitten, or by people who had been stung in previous years . . . Thus, groups of patients would gather, dancing wildly in the queerest attire . . . Others would tear their clothes and show their nakedness, losing all sense of modesty . . . Some called for swords and acted like fencers, others for whips and beat each other. Women called for mirrors, sighed and howled, making indecent motions. Some of them had still stranger fancies, liked to be tossed in the air, dug holes in the ground, and rolled themselves in the dirt like swine. They all drank wine plentifully, and sang and talked like drunken people. And all the while they danced and danced wildly to the sound of the music."

The symptoms of the disease were not well defined, and in some cases they appeared even when there was no evidence of a spider bite. But where a bite had actually occurred, there was a small local wound surrounded by a swollen, discolored area. The principal complaints were headaches, difficulty in breathing, pains in the region of the heart, fainting, thirst, loss of appetite, and muscle pains. Many of the victims said they felt as if their bones had been broken—but, as Sigerist wryly remarks, the violent exercise which the patients went through during hour after hour of dancing was enough to explain these symptoms.

Physicians of the time, however, were convinced that the symptoms were due to the particular species of tarantula that infested the Apulian region during the hot summer months. They were also convinced that the spider infected its victims with a particularly virulent poison, since the disease appeared to be reactivated year after year, and some people were known to have relapsed every summer for as long as thirty years. A number of physicians offered explanations for both the cause and the cure of the disease that were in keeping with the medical concepts and language of the time. One of the most influential, Giorgio Baglivi, wrote a lengthy dissertation in which he declared: "This venom in respect of itself must consist in a high degree of exaltation; but with respect to the diversity of the constitutions of men, it produces various effects, among which the principal are condensation and coagulation, and an oppression of the spirits . . . nay, sometimes such is the agitation of the spirit that they degenerate into involuntary and purely spasmodic motions." These "motions" were undoubtedly the tremors and convulsions experienced by some of the victims during their frenzied dance.

Baglivi as well as other physicians experimented with many types of treatment for the disorder: lancing the wound, cupping to extract the poison, internal antidotes such as treacle or brandy. These treatments had little if any effect, and some of them could not be applied when there was no wound. The physicians also noted that the "tarantati," as the dancers were called, sweated profusely, and concluded that perspiration was the agent that drove out the poison. However, when they prescribed medications that made the victims perspire without dancing, the results were again negligible. Finally, they were forced to admit that music was the only remedy.

Here is the way Baglivi explained its effects: "It being manifest that music ravishes healthy persons into such actions as imitate the harmony they hear, we easily adjust our opinion of the effects of music in the cure of persons stung by a tarantula. It is probable that the very swift motion impressed upon the air by musical instruments, communicated by the air to the skin, and so to the spirits and blood, does in some measure dissolve and dispel their growing coagulation; and that the effects of the dissolution increase as the sound itself increases, until, at last the humours retrieve their primitive fluid state, by virtue of these repeated shakings and vibrations; upon which the patient revives gradually, moves his limbs, gets up on his legs, groans, jumps about with violence, till the sweat breaks and carries off the seeds of the poison." In a word, the cure is brought about by a mechanical process which breaks up the "coagulation" of the body fluids, much as one would shake a medicine bottle to distribute its contents evenly.

Music, then, was the only proven remedy. But it had to be music of a particular kind. Like the spider itself, which was believed to be a species indigenous to the locale, the music was characteristic of Apulia, and the melodies had to be endlessly repeated in the fastest possible tempo. Soon these tunes came to be known as the tarantella, a title that is frequently found in light concert programs to this day. During the summer months bands of musicians roamed the countryside playing these melodies on pipes, cithers, harps, timbrels, and small drums. In most cases vocalists accompanied the instruments, and the songs they sang had one common theme: love. Soon, however, a second theme developed—a longing for the sea, perhaps because the dancers felt that its serenity and broad expanse might soothe the "agitation of their spirits." Perhaps, too, water itself had a special lure for them because they perspired so much, and for this reason many of the victims carried tumblers of water as they danced. At any rate, it is said that the attraction of the sea became so strong that some of the tarantati actually flung themselves into the waves and perished.

One more curious fact about the "dancing plague" is worth noting. The dancing had to be continued to the point of exhaustion, and if the tarantati stopped and rested for any length of time, their spirits sank and they were at once overwhelmed by feelings of lassitude and depression. For this reason it was common for them to dance wildly for as many as four to six days straight. Baglivi reports that in many cases they kept to a regular schedule: "They frequently begin to dance about sunrising and so continue in it without intermission till towards eleven in the forenoon. There are, however, some stops made; not from any weariness, but because they observe the musical instruments to be out of tune; upon the discovery of which, one would not believe what vehement sighings and anguish at heart they are seized with and in this case they continue till the instrument is got into tune again, and the dance renews . . . About noon the exercise ceases, and they are covered up in a bed to force out the sweat. When this is done, and the sweat wiped off, they are refreshed with broth, or some such light food; for their extraordinary want of appetite will not allow them to feed higher. About one o'clock after noon, or two at farthest, they renew the exercise as before, and continue it in the manner above mentioned till the evening; then to bed they go again for another sweat. When this is over, and they have got a little refreshment, they lay themselves to sleep."

Tarantism was not a transient disorder—in fact, it reappeared year after year for almost four centuries, from approximately 1400 to 1800. Thousands upon thousands of people were affected, and many hundreds died each year of the affliction. The physicians of the time attributed these fatalities to the tarantula virus, but undoubtedly they were due to overexertion on the part of men and women who suffered from undiagnosed cardiac or respiratory disorders.

What was the true nature of the dancing plague? Why was it concentrated in a single locality? And why did it recur year after year?

The disorder was real, not imaginary. Even though the symptoms were somewhat indefinite and varied from victim to victim, they actually existed and produced great distress. This cannot be denied. But these symptoms were not produced by the bite of a spider; they were due to a psychological disturbance, a mass hysterical reaction. Here, in brief, is the evidence for this interpretation:

First, the fact that the symptoms varied from individual to individual indicates that they stemmed from emotional and not physical sources.

Second, the symptoms that occurred most frequently— fainting, headaches, loss of appetite—are typical of hysterical disorders.

Third, the bite of the tarantula is not poisonous and produces only a local and temporary skin irritation; and when the same spider bit people in other regions than Apulia, they did not become ill and did not have the urge to dance.

Fourth, many Apulians who did have this urge showed no evidence of having been bitten.

Fifth, the fact that the infection, when it did occur, responded only to music and dance and not to medical treatment is further evidence that the condition was psychogenic.

Sixth, the recurrence of the "disease" year after year indicates that a high degree of expectation was involved, and this is also characteristic of hysterical reactions.

Seventh, the fact that the dancers lapsed into a state of depression as soon as the music stopped indicates that the music served psychological rather than physical needs.

There is little doubt, then, that the dancing mania was a classic example of a psychological epidemic aroused by emotional needs and transmitted by the power of suggestion.

But what were the emotional needs behind this epidemic? There were probably many—otherwise tarantism would not have lasted so long or affected so many individuals. The frenzied dancing was undoubtedly a form

of emotional catharsis, for Europe was still in the grip
of anxiety generated by the plagues that took millions
of lives during the Middle Ages, and people had to find
some relief for the fears that beset them. As Charles
Mackay points out in his book *Extraordinary Popular
Delusions and the Madness of Crowds,* "Men's minds
were everywhere morbidly sensitive; and as it happens
with individuals whose senses, when they are suffering
under anxiety, become more irritable, so trifles are mag-
nified into objects of great alarm, and slight shocks, which
would scarcely affect the spirits when in health, give
rise in them to severe diseases, so it was with this whole
nation, at all times so alive to emotion, and at that
period so sorely pressed with the horrors of death . . . The
bite of venomous spiders, or rather the unreasonable fear
of its consequences, excited at such a juncture, though
it could not have done so at an earlier period, a violent
nervous disorder, which, like St. Vitus's dance in Germany,
spread by sympathy, increasing in severity as it took a
wider range, and still further extending its ravages from
its long continuance. Thus, from the middle of the fourteenth century, the furies of *the dance* brandished their
scourge over afflicted mortals; and music, for which the
inhabitants of Italy, now probably for the first time mani-
fested susceptibility and talent, became capable of exciting ecstatic attacks in those afflicted, and then furnished
magical means of exorcising their melancholy."

Besides affording relief from pent-up emotion, tarantism
served two other functions. Since it was a form of mass
hysteria, it provided the satisfactions of a shared experience—a feeling of togetherness in an anxious age,
group support in the face of a common though ill-defined
threat, and a new opportunity for exciting social relationships. It also served as a release for sexual impulses, for
everyone drank and danced with abandon; the women

were said to abstain from intercourse in order to dance more passionately; and the sentiments expressed in the songs were highly erotic and provocative. In a word, tarantism flourished for four centuries because it was based on three powerful drives: relief of anxiety, the social impulse, and sexual expression.

But why did this particular type of mass hysteria arise in Apulia? There appear to be two primary reasons. First, the people who lived in the heel of Italy were extremely volatile and temperamental, and emotional disturbance was common among them, due in part to their inherited make-up—and in part to the fact that their "emotional threshold" was lowered by the burning, unrelenting heat of the region. Baglivi's comments on this point are worth quoting: "The hot climate was matched by that of the inhabitants, for generally speaking they are of a hot, scorched constitution, with black hair and a brownish or palish skin, meagre, impatient, peevish, watchful, very quick in their way of apprehension, nimble in reasoning and extremely active. They are very subject to ardent fevers, frenzies, pleurisies, madness and other inflammatory disease. Nay, the heat is so excessive in that country that I have seen several of the inhabitants urged by it to the last degree of impatience and madness . . . There is a greater degree of melancholy and madness than in any other country of Italy . . . A further confirmation may be taken from the greater frequency of mad dogs, whose madness is justly attributed to the scorching heat of the air."

A second reason, and one that helps to explain the particular form of the hysteria, is historical and geographical in nature. The Apulians sought mass release from their anxieties and inhibitions in the dance because the region had been settled by Greeks hundreds of years before, and the tradition of the bacchantic orgies was still alive—orgies that revolved around music and dance, and served the same psychological purposes as tarantism. Sigerist makes some illuminating comments on this point: "Christianity came late to Apulia and found a primitive and conservative population in which ancient beliefs and customs were deeply rooted. In competition with paganism, Christianity had to adjust itself in many ways in order to win over the population. Ancient holidays were preserved and made to commemorate Christian events. Churches were erected on ancient sites of worship among the ruins of temples. Saints took over the functions and attributes of pagan deities. There were limits, however, that the Church could not well overstep. It could not assimilate the orgiastic rites of the cults of Dionysus (the god of wine and dance) but had to fight them. And yet these very rites that appealed to the most elementary instincts were the most deeply rooted. They persisted, and we can well imagine that people gathered secretly to perform the old dances and all that went with them. In doing so they sinned until one day—we do not know when, but it must have been during the Middle Ages— the meaning of the dances had changed. The old rites appeared as symptoms of a disease. The music, the dances, all that wild orgiastic behavior was legitimatized. The people who indulged in these exercises were no longer sinners but the poor victims of the tarantula."

As a mental epidemic, tarantism was unique in three respects: The reactions of the populace were attributed to a spider bite, the music was a special variety, and the wave of hysteria was primarily secular in nature. But it was not the only form of dancing mania, for two similar epidemics occurred in the fourteenth and fifteenth centuries, each with strong religious overtones. The first, St. John's dance, has been vividly described by Charles Mackay: "So early as the year 1374, assemblages of

men and women were seen at Aix-la-Chapelle who had
come out of Germany, and who, united by one common
delusion, exhibited to the public both in the streets and
in the churches the following strange spectacle. They
formed circles hand in hand, and appearing to have lost
all control over their senses, continued dancing, regard-
less of bystanders, for hours together in wild delirium, until at length they fell to the ground in a state of exhaustion." He goes on to say that "while dancing they neither
saw nor heard, being insensible to external impressions
through their senses, but were haunted by visions, their
fancies conjuring up spirits whose names they shrieked
out; and some of them afterwards asserted that they felt
as if they had been immersed in a stream of blood,
which obliged them to leap so high. Others, during that
paroxysm, saw the heavens open and the Savior enthroned
with the Virgin Mary, according as the religious notions
of the age were strangely and variously reflected in their
imaginations."

The contagion quickly spread through Germany, Bel-
gium, and the Netherlands. "Peasants left their plows,
mechanics their workshops, housewives their domestic
duties, to join the wild revels . . . Secret desires were
excited, and but too often found opportunities for wild
enjoyment . . . Gangs of idle vagabonds, who understood
how to imitate to the life the gestures and convulsions
of those already affected, roved from place to place
seeking maintenance and adventures, and thus, wherever
they went, spreading this disgusting spasmodic disease
like the plague; for in maladies of this kind the susceptible
are infected as easily by the appearance as by the reality."
The physicians of the time applied what treatment they
could, but to no avail, since the dancers were convinced
that they were possessed by a demon. They therefore
invaded the churches and sought relief in masses, hymns,

and exorcisms pronounced by the priests. According to Mackay, the "wild infatuation" began to die down within a few months either because the priests had a suggestive effect on the multitude, or because the hysteria burned itself out through sheer exhaustion.

Though the dancing mania subsided in the Rhenish cities, it reappeared from time to time in other localities for the next two centuries. Strasbourg was visited by this epidemic in 1418, and it had such an alarming effect on the populace that the town council itself brought the victims to the chapels of St. Vitus, where "many were, through the influence of devotion and the sanctity of the place, cured of this lamentable aberration." Because of this association with the chapels, the epidemic itself became known as St. Vitus's dance.

In commenting on the role played by religion in this epidemic, Mackay points out that "connected as it was, in the Middle Ages, with the pomp of processions, with public exercises of penance, and with innumerable practices which strangely excited the imaginations of its votaries, religion certainly brought the mind to a very favorable state for the reception of a nervous disorder." The mystical character of the religion, then, set the stage for St. Vitus's dance—but it is an equally interesting fact that the same religion provided one of the remedies for the condition, a remedy that worked through mass suggestion.

The history of music and dance in relation to mental disorder does not end with the mass epidemics of the fourteenth and fifteenth centuries. Today both of these arts are playing an increasing role in mental institutions throughout the United States. Trained specialists, who are usually members of the National Association of Music Therapy or the National Association for Dance Therapy, plan and carry out programs which are at once flexible and varied. Musical activities include concerts, music appreciation, group singing, and instruction. Dance therapy programs offer a similar variety: folk dancing, ballroom dancing, and rhythmic exercises.

In either case, the specialist co-operates with the psychologist and psychiatrist in selecting the activities and adapting the program to the interests and emotional needs of different groups of patients. For example, waltzes have been found particularly effective in encouraging listless or withdrawn patients to socialize with other people, and square dancing has been found to help tense or hostile patients to release pent-up feelings that stand in the way of normal, healthy relationships.

Music and dance do not cure mental disorders by themselves. They are supportive, adjunctive therapies which can be highly effective not only in calming the excited, arousing the depressed, and stimulating the stuporous, but also in providing pleasure and recreation in an institutional atmosphere that is too often cold and impersonal. Moreover, they have been found to make the patients more accessible to both group and individual psychotherapy. The skilled, sensitive dance or music specialist will closely observe the patients' reactions during these activities, and make suggestions which the psychologist or psychiatrist can utilize in the treatment process.

The flavor of dance and music therapy can best be conveyed by the following comments of Edith Stern on the work of Marian Chace, a pioneer in the field: "To break through the invisible walls with which all psychotics surround themselves to keep people away, she used primitive means of communication that go deeper than words—rhythm, movement and touch. Old and fundamental as humanity itself, simple and universal as mothers crooning and rocking their babies in their arms, these catch patients off guard, painlessly crumble their defenses, make them susceptible to other approaches. Over and over again she demonstrates that there is more strength in the mentally ill than most of us realize."

THE PHANTOM OF MATTOON

At about midnight on the first of September 1944, the telephone rang insistently in the police station at Mattoon, Illinois. Sergeant K sleepily picked up the receiver and heard a woman's voice scream, "Is that the police? I'm calling for a neighbor of mine, Mrs. A. She can't talk because she's been gassed!" "Gassed?" answered the sergeant. "What kind of gas?" "I don't know, but she's practically knocked out, and her daughter, too. Please send someone over right away—I'll give you the address."

Within a few moments the police car arrived at Mrs. A's house. The distraught woman was barely able to mumble that someone had opened the window in her bedroom and had sprayed her with a sweet-smelling gas which not only made her sick to her stomach but paralyzed her legs. The officers immediately searched the house and grounds, but found no evidence of an intruder. After trying to calm Mrs. A down, they cruised around the entire neighborhood and found the streets completely empty.

The officers concluded that the woman had probably eaten something that did not agree with her, and that the prowler story was just another false alarm. They returned to the station house—but two hours later they received another call, this time from Mrs. A's husband. He excitedly reported that he had come home a few minutes before, and had seen a man run from the window. Again the police rushed to the scene, and again they found nothing.

The following evening the Mattoon *Journal-Gazette* carried a front-page story on the "gas attack," under the headline "ANESTHETIC PROWLER ON LOOSE—MRS. A AND DAUGHTER FIRST VICTIMS." Early the next morning, a Mr. B called the police to report that in the middle of the night of August 31—the night *before* Mrs. A's attack—he had awakened sick and nauseous, had shaken his wife and asked her if the gas had been left on. She tried to go to the kitchen to check, but found that she was unable to walk. At about the same time a Mr. C, a night worker, called the newspaper office to say that he and his wife and daughter had experienced the same attack that was reported in the article. The daughter had awakened coughing violently, and when her mother got up to take care of her, she could hardly walk.

From there on the police and the paper were bombarded with calls. Between the first and the twelfth of September there were a total of twenty-four reports. The same general set of symptoms, except for one, occurred in every case: nausea, vomiting, palpitations, paralysis of the legs, dryness of the mouth. The exception was a woman who reported that she found a cloth on her porch, picked it up, smelled it—and the fumes burned her mouth and lips so badly that they bled. Most of the others described the gas as having a musty or "cheap perfume" odor. At least three insisted that the family dog must also have been gassed since he did not bark at the intruder.

The police were constantly in action. Every telephone call was followed up and every victim was immediately taken to the local hospital. In a few days the state police were called in to speed the search for the culprit, since they had modern radio equipment in their cars. As the chief of police put it, when a report was made, the house was surrounded "before the phone was back on the hook."

All attempts to catch the prowler in the act failed. The police tried to pin the deed on every "suspicious character" they rounded up, but these efforts also failed. The mystery deepened. Here, truly, was a "phantom on the loose," as the newspaper put it—a phantom who felled his victims seemingly without reason or motive, for no house was broken into, no money stolen, no woman molested. Only an ingenious fiend—a madman—could perform such acts.

The newspapers were as active as the police. The local paper's front-page article on the "anesthetic prowler" was followed by daily reports written in excited journalistic prose under such headlines as "MAD ANESTHETIST STRIKES AGAIN." Even on a day when no attacks were reported, the paper published an article with this opening paragraph:

Mattoon's "mad anesthetist" apparently took a respite from his maniacal forays Thursday night, and while many terror-stricken people were somewhat relieved, they were inclined to hold their breath and wonder when and where he might strike again.

They did not have long to wait, for that very night several new attacks were reported, and the following day a long article again appeared in the paper, under a banner headline almost an inch high.

On the sixth day of the reported attacks, out-of-town newspapers took up the story. Every day for almost two weeks, the Chicago *Daily Tribune* and the Chicago *Daily News,* both widely read in Mattoon, devoted from ten to thirty inches of space to accounts of the "mysterious marauder." The Chicago *Herald-American* gave the story even more space, and included a number of photographs of the homes where the phantom had struck. The opening paragraphs of one of its front-page stories were typical of its coverage:

Groggy as Londoners under protracted aerial blitzing, this town's bewildered citizens reeled today under the repeated attacks of a mad anesthetist who has sprayed a deadly nerve gas into 13 homes and has knocked out 27 victims.

Seventy others dashing to the area in response to the alarm, fell under the influence of the gas last night.

All skepticism has vanished and Mattoon grimly concedes it must fight haphazardly against a demented phantom adversary who has been seen only fleetingly and so far has evaded traps laid by city and state police and posses of townsmen.

That article appeared on September 10. On the eleventh, the *Herald-American* gave the story even more space under a one-and-one-half-inch headline reading "STATE HUNTS GAS MADMAN." On the twelfth; another front-page story appeared, this time illustrated with pictures of crying babies. Since no new cases were reported after the twelfth, the articles grew shorter and slightly skeptical, although they continued to speculate as to whether the "gasser" might be a woman, an apeman, and the like.

The story was carried by the press services and appeared in papers all over the United States. In New York, *P.M.* devoted a few inches to it, but the New York *Times* rejected it. Abroad, it reached as far as the London edition of *Stars and Stripes* and a weekly publication of the Persian Gulf Command—and a number of Mattoon servicemen anxiously wrote home to inquire about their wives and mothers. *Time* and *Newsweek* carried it and, though both were somewhat skeptical, neither drew any definite conclusions. As a result of the many articles, about three hundred letters and telegrams were received by town officials from all over the country. A sampling indicated that at least half of them offered suggestions for capturing the "menace," while the other half showed unmistakable evidence of mental aberrations. Paranoid trends were particularly prominent.

Among those who avidly followed these stories was a young psychologist at the University of Illinois, Donald M. Johnson. Deciding that the strange event deserved special study, he obtained the co-operation of the university's Research Board in carrying out an investigation. Starting in the middle of September, when the mystery was still fresh in every mind, he spent many weeks analyzing Police Department records and interviewing officials and residents involved in the extraordinary case. The account of his investigation, on which this case story is based, was later published in a psychological journal and has become a classic in the field of social psychology.

Johnson started his investigation with two questions in mind. First, could the symptoms experienced by the victims actually have been produced by a gas sprayed by an "ingenious fiend"—probably himself a paranoid case—who was able to elude every effort of the police? Or were the symptoms hysterical in nature, and if so, why did they spread so rapidly and affect so many people?

The "gasser" hypothesis ran into trouble from the start.

The symptoms were so fleeting and so devoid of after-effects that they were impossible to check. There was no doubt that vomiting did occur in some cases, but it could have been caused by dietary indiscretions or hysteria as readily as by inhalation of a gas. As to the gas itself, it seemed reasonable to suppose that any compound that would produce such immediate effects as nausea and paralysis would have to be very potent and very rapid in its action. Yet at the same time it would have to be so unstable that it would not affect others in the same room, and so weak that it would not leave any observable after-effects! The investigator made every attempt to find such a gas. He consulted the standard texts on anesthetics and war gases and conferred with colleagues at the university, but none of them could come up with a gas that would even remotely satisfy these contradictory demands.

And what about the phantom who was believed to have sprayed this mysterious gas? Could he have been completely fictitious? Here the answer seemed to be that people *did* see a prowler, at least in some cases—but there was no evidence that he was an "anesthetist." The fact is that prowlers were nothing new in Mattoon. They had been reported once or twice a week for several years. And even granting that such a person existed and diabolically sprayed his victims, what would be his motive? None could be found, for he made no assaults, did not enter the houses, and could hardly have obtained gratification from peeping, under the circumstances reported by the victims.

Evidence for the hysteria hypothesis appeared to be stronger from the start. A study of psychiatric literature indicated that the symptoms reported by the victims were all typical of a mild hysterical attack: choking sensations, heart palpitations, stomach distress, weakness in the legs.

Moreover, four of the victims had seen physicians, and in each case the condition had been diagnosed as hysteria. Johnson's own comment on this point is worth quoting: "The hypothesis of hysteria accounts for the rapid recovery of all the victims and the lack of aftereffects. It explains why no 'gasser' was found in spite of mobilization of local and state police and volunteers. It accounts for the fact that nothing was stolen and that dogs did not bark. The objections to the hypothesis of hysteria come from the victims themselves—quite naturally—and from others who do not realize the intensity and variety of effects which are produced by psychological forces."

This leaves us with the crucial question: What *were* the psychological forces that produced these hysterical reactions? They could be of two general kinds: inward, subjective tendencies; and outward, situational factors. The investigator was able to unearth considerably more information on the objective factors than the subjective factors, since the publicity surrounding the events had made the victims wary and unco-operative. He was unable to probe for possible unconscious motivations, but there were some indications of emotional instability since, when he questioned them about their health, an unusually high percentage used such phrases as "always been nervous," "never sleep much," and "doctoring for nerves." On the other hand, he could not determine whether any of them conformed to the standard picture of the "hysterical personality" which is defined as "a personality trait disturbance characterized by immature, self-centered behavior with frequent emotional outbursts and histrionic display . . . Studies indicate that they have usually been overprotected and spoiled in childhood, and their dramatic behavior is more or less consciously adopted to attract attention and get their way." (From *The Encyclopedia of Human Behavior*.)

Although we can only surmise about these internal tendencies, Johnson does not leave us in the dark about the more objective aspects of the situation. By examining the census reports for the period, he was able to compare the victims with the general population on certain critical points. First, he found that 93 per cent of his sample were women, as compared with 52 per cent in the general population. Second, 37 per cent were in the twenty-to-twenty-nine age bracket, as contrasted with 17 per cent. Third, 71 per cent had only attended grade school, as compared with a general average of 58 per cent. Fourth, various economic indices (electricity, radio, mechanical refrigerator, telephone) indicated that their homes were considerably below the general average. And fifth, the husbands (or wives) engaged in clerical, mechanical, sales, and other semiskilled or unskilled work, and none were in professional or semiprofessional categories.

These data were highly indicative since they conform quite closely to the patterns revealed by both case reports and laboratory studies—studies that show that women in general, particularly younger women, are considerably more prone to hysterical reactions than men, and that individuals on the lower educational, economic, and occupational levels are more suggestible than people on higher levels. The key factor is probably education, since the better educated are likely to be more critical than others about rumors and newspaper reports.

And as to those newspaper reports, certainly they played a major role in the entire sequence of events—especially since Johnson found that very few of the victims knew each other and less than one third had telephones. If Mrs. A's mild hysterical attack had not produced an equally dramatic, almost hysterical reaction from the local paper—which was usually conservative and unsensational in its treatment of the news—the "mental epidemic" would never have occurred. But, as it so happened, "the news spread, other people reported similar symptoms, more exciting stories were written, and so the affair snowballed." The entire episode is a commentary not only on human frailty but on the power of the press and the need for caution in writing for the public.

But there is one other factor that must not be overlooked, though the investigator omitted it in his report. It was the war. Many of the residents of Mattoon became "groggy as Londoners under protracted aerial blitzing," as the newspaper story put it, partly because that is exactly what had been happening in 1944. Even though the citizens of the inland city of Mattoon were not in fear of invasion, there had been talk of "nerve gas," and undoubtedly this had heightened their awareness of its paralyzing effects. Moreover, a world war itself produces a generalized anxiety, especially when local young men are directly involved. These anxieties set the stage for the wave of hysteria that engulfed Mattoon, and must surely have played a part in the acute though short-lived reactions of the more susceptible residents.

A BOOM IN TULIPS

Anyone who buys or raises tulips today would find it hard to believe that such an innocent, unpretentious flower could instigate one of the most dramatic examples of mass hysteria ever recorded. And anyone who knows the Dutch would find it equally hard to believe that these sober people were the principal victims of this wave of madness. Yet such was actually the case.

Though we associate the tulip with Holland, the flower actually originated in Turkey, and its name derives from the word "turban," which it vaguely resembles. In about 1550, the Viennese ambassador to Turkey brought the first tulip bulbs to western Europe, and the variegated blossoms immediately found favor among connoisseurs of exotic plants. Word of the new find got around quickly, and when an entire shipload of bulbs arrived from Constantinople in 1559, a new horticultural industry was born. Though the plants were greatly sought after in Austria, England, and France, they seemed particularly suited to the fertile lowlands of Holland—and, as it turned out, to the fertile imagination of the Dutch. Wealthy people in Amsterdam were soon sending directly to Constantinople for their own shipments, and the prices gradually inflated until, by 1610, a single bulb was valued at the cost of an entire dowry.

This, however, was only the beginning. According to Charles Mackay, who has vividly chronicled this event, "Until the year 1634 the tulip annually increased in reputation, until it was deemed a proof of bad taste in any man of fortune to be without a collection of them . . . The rage for possessing them soon caught the middle classes of society and merchants and shop keepers, even of modest means, began to vie with each other in the rarity of these flowers and the preposterous prices they paid for them." At first the bulbs were collected simply because of the beauty of the blossoms and the brilliance of their color—and it must be recognized that few if any species of flower can achieve greater diversity of shape, size, and hue through cultivation. But in 1634, the Dutch suddenly began to look upon the tulip more as an article of commerce than as an adornment for their homes and gardens, and within months, "the ordinary industry of the country was neglected, and the population, even to its lowest dregs, embarked in the tulip trade."

As more and more people devoted themselves to this trade, the law of supply and demand produced an explosive increase in prices. By 1635, a species known as Admiral Van Der Eyck brought 1260 florins, and the rare Semper Augustus was thought to be very cheap at 5500 florins, the equivalent of a house and lot. According to an author of the time, a single root of another rare species, the Viceroy, was delivered in exchange for "two lasts of wheat, four lasts of rye, four fat oxen, eight fat swine, twelve fat sheep, two hog's heads of wine, four tuns of beer, two tuns of butter, one thousand pounds of cheese, a complete bed, a suit of clothes, and a silver drinking-cup."

One story of the period indicates the value of the bulbs even more strikingly. A sailor brought a rich merchant news that a valuable consignment of merchandise had arrived from the Levant, and was munificently rewarded for his trouble with the gift of a single red herring. On his way out of the merchant's storehouse, he noticed what he thought to be an onion on the counter, and slipped it into his pocket as a relish for the herring. A little later, the merchant noticed that his favorite bulb, a Semper Augustus, was missing. After searching high and low he finally thought of the sailor, and his entire household took after the poor man—only to find him munching the last morsel of his onion with his last bite of herring, "a breakfast whose cost might have regaled a whole ship's crew for a twelvemonth." The sailor was immediately taken to court, convicted of felony, and sentenced to several months in prison.

By 1636, the demand for tulips had mounted to a point where regular marts for their sale were established on the stock exchanges in Amsterdam, Rotterdam, Haarlem, Leyden, and other cities. From then on, gambling fever took hold of the populace, and tulip jobbers made huge profits by manipulating the prices, buying when the prices fell and selling when they rose. At first, when confidence was at its height, everyone gained and many ordinary individuals grew suddenly rich: "A golden bait hung temptingly out before the people, and one after another, they rushed to the tulip-marts, like flies around the honey pot." Fantasy fed on fantasy, and soon the entire country was deluded into believing that the passion for tulips would last forever, and that people from all over the world would pay whatever prices were asked for them. They convinced themselves further that "the riches of Europe would be concentrated on the shores of the Zuyder Zee, and poverty banished from the favored clime of Holland. Nobles, citizens, farmers, mechanics, seamen, footmen, maid-servants, even chimney-sweeps and old-clothes women dabbled in tulips."

Everywhere people converted whatever property they had into cash at ruinously low prices, and the proceeds were invested in bulbs. During the first few months, true to prediction, hundreds of people in other countries were caught up in the "tulip mania" and huge sums of money poured into Holland from all directions. This sudden influx of funds produced an inflation in the value of houses, land, and other property, and further convinced the populace that the economic millennium had arrived.

Within a year, however, a few astute merchants began to recognize that the sudden wave of prosperity was built upon speculation alone. People were only buying tulips to sell to others at exorbitant profits—which meant that somebody would be caught short and lose disastrously in the end. As this conviction spread, confidence was weakened and prices began to fall. This effect spi-

raled, like the mania itself, and the population was soon
in the grip of panic. For a time there was still buying
and selling, but the market fell so rapidly that a buyer
who had agreed to pay 2000 florins each for a dozen
bulbs would find that by the time they were ready for
delivery they would be worth only 200 florins. Consequently, these buyers defaulted on their contracts: "Hundreds who, a few months previously, had begun to doubt
that there was such a thing as poverty in the land,
suddenly found themselves the possessors of a few bulbs
which nobody would buy, even though they offered them
for one quarter of the sums they had paid for them."

Meeting after meeting was held all over the country to
devise measures that would ease the hardship and restore
public credit, but no practical remedies could be found.
Even the Provincial Council at The Hague could offer
nothing more than the suggestion that when the contracted price had changed, the tulips should be sold at
auction and the original contractor should be responsible
for the difference. But this was no solution because every
judge in the country refused to enforce payment on the
ground that the original transaction was a gamble, and
debts contracted in gambling were not recognized by law.

A few investors, anticipating the crash, sold out before
the panic set in and invested the money in foreign mar-
kets. But the vast majority suffered irreparably from their
losses: "The cry of distress was everywhere, and each
man accused his neighbor." As always, the common man,
who had at last seen an end to his struggles, suffered the
most; but many substantial merchants and great noble-
men were also ruined beyond redemption. So widespread
were the losses that Holland's entire economy suffered a
shock from which it did not recover for years to come.

Why did the tulip craze take place? Mackay gives
some but not all the answers in recognizing that greed

and the desire to make a killing were major motivations. But there are other considerations as well. First, communication played an important role. Studies of crowd behavior have shown that social contagion is most likely to occur when people are in close contact with each other. One reason the tulip mania swept through the land with lightning speed was the fact that Holland is a small country where communication was relatively easy and swift.

Second, status also figured prominently. The craze started among wealthy people who could afford the rarest bulbs; but the man in the street found he could emulate his "superiors" by buying one or two fairly expensive bulbs and others of lesser worth. While the average person could not afford a stable of horses he could at least own a few rather valuable bulbs. Also, since the rich were so interested in acquiring bulbs for resale, the less privileged felt they were on secure ground in purchasing all they could afford—and more. There appeared to be no risk at all because the tulip trade had the stamp of approval of the high and mighty.

Third, competition arrived on the scene early in the game and became increasingly intense. The boatloads of bulbs arrived infrequently, and the demand therefore became greater than the supply. This not only raised prices but also made the bulbs appear more and more desirable—which for a time was proven by the fact that they could be sold both inside and outside the country at still higher prices. People therefore began vying with each other for the available bulbs, and often mortgaged their entire future in order to buy as many as possible.

All these factors taken together served to blind both the poor and the rich to their folly. Then suddenly some of the wealthier purchasers started to unload their wares, and the whole flimsy structure began to collapse—like the

South Sea bubble of eighteenth-century England, the Florida land boom of the 1920s, as well as runs on banks which occur when a single bank fails. As Roger Brown says in his discussion of "acquisitive panics," "For a time it seemed that the demand for tulips would hold forever; wealthy people the world over were expected to find the flowers irresistible and so to be willing to pay any price for them to the merchants of Holland. Eventually, however, the Dutch could not fail to see that the appeal was largely limited to Holland, and in Holland most people were buying bulbs only to sell them again. Even the rich were not planting the rarer bulbs but seemed only to be interested in selling at a profit. As in the game of musical chairs somebody must eventually be left standing, so it began to appear that someone was going to be left holding tulips that nobody else wanted any more. To recognize this outcome as inevitable was, of course, to bring it about. And so the panic came and the price of tulips fell to a reasonable sort of value and very many people were very much poorer."

STAMPEDE

The weather was crisp and clear on Saturday night, November 28, 1942. The Thanksgiving holiday was in full swing, and the football season had climaxed that afternoon with the unexpected victory of Holy Cross over Boston College. To celebrate, or to drown out disappointment, over 850 patrons were crowded into the city's most popular night club, the Cocoanut Grove. The mood was gay and carefree, the liquor was flowing freely, and exuberant conversation combined with lively dance music to raise the sound level to almost deafening proportions.

Suddenly a piercing cry rose above the din in the Melody Lounge on the basement floor: "Fire! Fire!" All eyes turned in the direction of the shrieking woman rushing across the floor with her hair ablaze. A momentary silence gripped the onlookers as they gasped in horror. Then horror gave way to terror as they saw flames shooting up from one of the artificial palm trees that decorated the club. Finally a few people regained their voices and shouted "Get a fire extinguisher!" "Call the manager!" "Keep calm!" But as the flames mounted and began to spread along the ceiling and walls with lightning speed, their voices were drowned out by panic-stricken cries: "Let's get out of here!" Then, almost to a person, they rose to their feet and surged wildly toward the steps leading up to the main floor where seven hundred people were dining and dancing.

The Cocoanut Grove had at least eight exits, and a few patrons escaped through rear or side doors or through a window in the Melody Lounge. Others tried a "panic door" in the back and were trapped inside when they found it was bolted. But as the flames and smoke swirled through the building, the great majority rushed toward the main entrance and tried to get out through the revolving doors. Again a few managed to escape, but almost at once the stampeding mob began to push both sides of the doors at the same time, and they immediately jammed. Some tried to force the crowd back long enough to free the doors, but this was impossible due to the enormous pressure exerted by those in the rear. Others tried to break down the doors but could not because they were made of heavy plate glass and metal. Still others tried to turn and seek another exit, but the bodies of suffocating patrons had already begun to pile up, and the mass was immovable.

The scene in the club became a veritable nightmare. As one account put it, "Blazing draperies fell, setting women's evening gowns and hair on fire. Patrons were hurled under tables and trampled to death. Others tripped and choked the six-foot-wide stairway up from the Melody Lounge. Those behind swarmed over them and piled up in layers upon layers of corpses."

The fire department was summoned immediately, and brought the blaze under control a scant half hour after it had started. But in that short space of time incredible damage had been done to human life. Only one hundred people out of the approximately nine hundred patrons and employees escaped unhurt. Many of the survivors were severely burned and a large number developed psychiatric complications. But the most tragic result was the enormous death toll, which the investigations revealed to be due primarily to inhalation of noxious fumes from the decorations and leatherette upholstery. Nearly 450 people lost their lives during or soon after the fire, and the number rose to 492 in the weeks and months that followed. One man was so stricken with feelings of grief and guilt over the death of his wife, whom he had tried to save, that he committed suicide in the hospital where he was confined.

The Cocoanut Grove disaster produced a shock wave of huge proportions not only in Boston but throughout the country. Everywhere people were asking, How could a catastrophe of this magnitude be "allowed" to occur in the twentieth century? Who was to blame? What made the patrons lose their heads? How could the panic have been prevented? And what could have been done to control it once it had started?

During the days that followed the holocaust, the Boston newspapers devoted over half of their news space to articles on the fire, and almost immediately psychologists, psychiatrists, and other social scientists began gathering data, formulating theories, and suggesting preventive measures. Before looking at these two approaches, the journalistic and the scientific, it might be useful to recall another catastrophe that occurred at the very beginning of this century, one that bore a remarkably close resemblance to the Cocoanut Grove disaster.

The event in question was the Iroquois Theatre fire which took place in Chicago in 1903. The house was filled to capacity and the famous comedian Eddie Foy was on stage at the time. Suddenly smoke was seen to rise from the backstage scenery, and, as Foy expressed it in his autobiography, "As I ran around back of the rear drop, somebody had, of course, yelled 'Fire!' There is almost always a fool of that species in an audience; and there are always hundreds of people who go crazy the moment they hear the word." He goes on to describe his own efforts to calm the audience and prevent panic, but these attempts were futile and pandemonium took over within seconds. His account is so vivid and so instructive that it deserves to be quoted in full:

"I began shouting at the top of my voice, 'Don't get excited. There's no danger. Take it easy!'—and to Dillea, the orchestra leader, 'Play! Start an overture—anything! But play!' Some of his musicians were fleeing, but a few, and especially a fat German violinist, stuck nobly.

"I stood perfectly still, and when addressing the audience spoke slowly, knowing that these signs of self-possession have an equally calming effect on a crowd. Those on the lower floor heard me and seemed to be reassured a little, but up above and especially in the gallery, self-possession had fled; they had gone mad . . .

"As I left the stage the last of the ropes holding up the drops burned through, and with them the whole loft collapsed with a terrifying crash, bringing down tons of burning material—and with that, all the lights in the house went out and another great balloon of fire leaped out into the auditorium, licking even the ceiling and killing scores who had not yet succeeded in escaping from the gallery.

"The horror in the auditorium was beyond all description. There were thirty exits but few of them were marked by lights, some even had heavy portieres over the doors, and some of the doors were locked . . .

"They were finally burst open, but meanwhile precious moments had been lost . . . The fire escape ladders could not accommodate the crowd and many fell or jumped to death on the pavement below . . .

"But it was inside the house that the greatest loss of life occurred, especially on the stairway leading down from the second balcony. Here most of the dead were trampled or smothered, though many jumped or fell over the balustrade to the floor of the foyer. In places on the stairways, particularly where a turn caused a jam, the bodies were piled seven or eight feet deep . . . The heel prints on the dead faces mutely testified to the cruel fact that human animals stricken by terror are as mad and ruthless as stampeding cattle . . .

"Never elsewhere did a great fire disaster occur so quickly. It is said that from the start of the fire until all the audience were either escaped or killed or lying maimed in the halls and alleys the time was just eight minutes. In that eight minutes more than five hundred lives went out. The fire department arrived quickly after the alarm and extinguished the fire in the auditorium so promptly that no more than the plush upholstery was burned off the seats."

The parallel between the disasters at the Iroquois Theatre and the Cocoanut Grove is a striking one. In each
case the scream of a single individual focused attention
on the danger and produced an immediate terror reaction. Despite efforts to preserve calm—more in the case
of the theater than the night club—the patrons made no
real attempt to deal with the emergency in an orderly,
rational way. In both cases the sight of the flames trig-
gered one overriding response—a mad scramble to get
out. This unthinking response crowded out of their minds
any possible thought that they might block the exits and
actually prevent themselves from escaping. It was as if
the sudden threat to life had paralyzed their brains and
released only the primitive instinct for survival.

In each case, two additional factors brought the panic
and loss of life to an agonizing peak. First, a large mass
of people became completely hysterical and cut off any
possibility of escape for themselves and many others. In
the Iroquois fire, it was the entire gallery, who were
beyond reach of Foy's voice because of the deafening
din, and who felt trapped in the upper regions of the
theater. Many of them either fell or jumped or blocked
the stairways. At the Cocoanut Grove, the crowd in the
downstairs Melody Lounge felt equally trapped, and
practically all of them attempted to rush up the stairway
at once. As a result, some of the people ahead tripped and
fell, and others trampled them underfoot or fell on top
of them.

A second factor was the insufficient number of available
exits. At the Cocoanut Grove, two of the main doors had
been closed and locked because it was a cold night
and the manager wanted the crowd to use only the revolving doors. Another door opened inward, but the pressure of the crowd kept it closed. Similarly, a number of
the doors at the Iroquois Theatre were either locked,

frozen, rusted, or hidden by portieres, and valuable time was lost in forcing them open. In both instances, the fire and the panic spread so rapidly that scores of patrons were burned, trampled, or suffocated, and their bodies blocked the escape of others.

These two disasters, though forty years apart, have helped psychologists to define the true nature of panic. In its broadest terms, it has been described by one of the major investigators, D. P. Schultz, as "Fear-induced flight behavior that is non-social, non-rational, and non-adaptive from the standpoint of total group survival because it reduces the survival possibilities of the group as a whole." It is non-social because it is every man for himself, and there is therefore a minimum of organized behavior. It is non-rational because the emotions of terror and anxiety take over and block the crowd's normal processes of thought which might help them find a sensible way of meeting the threat. But instead of pausing to think, they respond to mass suggestion and flock to the same exit. It is non-adaptive because their behavior is egocentric, inflexible, and single-minded, and they therefore do not try alternative solutions or co-operate with others in finding a solution. When they block out reason, fail to communicate with others, and concentrate on their own escape without taking others into account, they inevitably cut each other off, interfere with each other's efforts, and lose the opportunity to change their course of action. All this may be described as self-defeating behavior, for panic-stricken people are not only reducing the survival possibilities of others but of themselves as well.

These points are clearly stated by the psychologist J. C. Coleman in his comments on these two disasters: "Panic behavior usually takes place in the face of a sudden, overwhelming danger in which immediate escape seems to offer the only hope of safety. If escape routes are either limited or blocked altogether, ordinary social controls tend to give way to blind fear and desperate attempts at personal survival. The frantic, irrational behavior of a crowd in panic usually increases the original danger." And as another investigator, C. E. Fritz, has pointed out, "An instantaneous disaster—i.e., one in which there is no forewarning—tends to produce the maximum in social and psychological disruption. If persons are given sufficient forewarning to prepare psychological and social defenses, the traumatic effects of the disaster will be minimized." Certainly these two disasters were "instantaneous"—particularly the one at the Cocoanut Grove, since the fire was not on a stage, away from the audience, but struck one of the patrons immediately and then quickly spread along the walls and ceiling. And certainly we must recognize that the cards were stacked against the guests, not only because of the locked doors but because of the overcrowding, the inflammable decorations, and possibly the heavy consumption of alcohol, which notoriously reduces rational thinking and releases primitive urges.

Panic behavior, then, is most likely to occur when a threat is sudden and overwhelming, and there is no time to plan or prepare for the danger. In contrast, the entire city of London was organized in anticipation of the air raids during World War II. The morale of the populace was maintained at a high level by assigning everyone an active duty such as serving food or cleaning the shelters, and by convincing them that unity and solidarity alone would save their native land. As part of the preparation, clinics were established throughout the city, and psychiatrists were required to be in attendance around the clock. But it is an interesting fact that they usually waited in vain for patients, even after the heaviest air raids. In fact, there is evidence that fewer breakdowns occurred than in normal times, since even the most unstable individuals gained strength, purpose, and group support from their last-ditch efforts.

The social psychologist Roger Brown stresses another aspect of panic, one which is actually implicit in what we have said above. He points out that this term never applies to orderly escape behavior, but is reserved for "cases like the Iroquois Theatre fire and the Cocoanut Grove fire in Boston when the 'social contract' is thrown away and each man single-mindedly attempts to save his own life at whatever cost to others." But why do people behave like terror-stricken animals? It is not the danger alone, nor the fear it arouses—"there must be the possibility of escape and also the possibility of entrapment. When escape routes are completely closed, as in mine disasters and submarine accidents, no panic occurs. When escape routes are completely open panic also does not occur." It is only when people are face to face with the possibility of being trapped that they lose their heads, especially when this possibility occurs suddenly and unexpectedly.

But is panic *inevitable*? Could something have been done at the Cocoanut Grove to control the situation and at least minimize the loss of life? Looking back, we can only speculate. Men in the room where the fire started might have tried to smother the flames with their jackets. The draperies might have been torn from the windows to trample out the fire or prevent it from spreading. The servicemen who were there (World War II was in progress) might have taken over and issued sharp commands to file out slowly or to stay seated until fire extinguishers could be brought. In addition, an employee or guest might have used the band's mike to calm the crowd or direct them to the kitchen or side exits; and the management or waiters might have checked and opened all doors before the rush began. All these suggestions are mere afterthoughts, and it may be that some of them were actually attempted. The lightninglike spread of the flames, as well as the sudden panic, may well have annulled these efforts.

More to the point, perhaps, is a summary of preventive measures which could be applied in all situations where crowds gather and panic might develop. Many organizations, agencies, and students of crowd behavior have suggested such measures, and some of them have been carried out on a more or less wide scale. Fire departments are more alert to the problem of overcrowding, and conspicuous signs are posted in many public places stating the maximum number of occupants permitted. Public address systems are almost universal, and in some establishments martial music and prepared announcements are available for instant use. Stricter regulations on exit doors, exit signs, and lights are now in force. Sprinkler systems have been installed in many buildings, and fire extinguishers are more carefully and frequently checked. New flameproofing chemicals have been developed, and fireproof materials such as fiberglass are often required by law.

These provisions have reduced the likelihood of fire and have increased the chances of escape should a blaze occur. But they do not solve the psychological problem of preventing panic reactions. Along this line, the suggestion has been made that each establishment select one or more employees (by psychological test if possible) who has leadership qualities, and that these persons be given special instruction on handling emergencies of any kind. Unfortunately, not many establishments have taken this suggestion. More basic, however, is the need for developing a panic-proof population. School fire drills are essential, and should be supplemented by classroom discussions and films that depict effective and ineffective behavior in emergencies.

But the strongest line of defense is a stable, resourceful personality. This can only be achieved by establishing a sound emotional foundation of acceptance and approval, by graduated experiences that involve mild risk and danger (from the jungle gym to a night in the woods), by co-operative activities in which each individual contributes to the advancement of the group, by games that involve rapid decision-making, and by practice in taking leadership. Training of this kind will prepare the individual for meeting emergencies of any type with a cool and level head.

But we have yet to face two questions raised at the beginning of this account: Who was responsible for the Cocoanut Grove fire itself, and who was responsible for the situation that seemed tailor-made for panic and disaster? Those were the questions uppermost in the minds of the journalists who covered the Cocoanut Grove story —and largely because of their efforts, they were the questions on which the public focused most of its attention in the days and weeks that followed the fire. In a word, the press and the public were searching for a *scapegoat* as a means of fixing blame for the frightful loss of life.

Fortunately, we have an excellent account of this scapegoat process, published by two Harvard psychologists, H. R. Veltfort and G. E. Lee, a few months after the fire. This account, based upon articles and letters to the editor printed in the Boston *Traveler*, the Boston *Globe*, and other local newspapers, shows that a series of individuals and government agencies were blamed for the catastrophe, one after the other.

The first target of public wrath was a bus boy employed

by the Cocoanut Grove during weekend rushes. As the papers put it, this "offender confessed" that he had struck a match to replace a light bulb removed by a prankster, and in so doing had accidentally set fire to one of the decorative palm trees. He served as a scapegoat only briefly, for the public, in their letters to the editor, soon accused the papers of persecuting the boy who so straightforwardly admitted setting the fire. And when investigation revealed that his teachers and friends regarded him as a model young man, and that the family was impoverished and his mother seriously ill, he became almost a public hero and received many fan letters, including one with a check for twenty-five dollars.

But the main reason for exonerating the bus boy was the feeling that even though he started the fire, he was not actually responsible for it. That responsibility was soon shifted to the prankster—but only briefly. Since he was not legally culpable, and since his identity was never discovered, and he may have died in the fire, the press and public looked for a more satisfying scapegoat. That post was filled by public officials when, on the Monday following the fire, it was discovered that the city fire department had approved the club just eight days before it burned. The immediate target was the fire inspector, and the text of his inspection report, in which he pronounced the exits and extinguishers "safe" and the general condition of the club "good," was printed in every paper. His testimony at the inquiry, to the effect that he had tested the inflammability of the palm trees and found them "treated to my satisfaction" (with flameproof liquid), was ridiculed. The fire commissioner was also attacked on the ground that he was responsible for his subordinate's performance of duty.

Though the fire department bore the brunt of journalistic censure, other officials and departments also came

in for their share of the blame. The press discovered that
a police captain was in the club at the time of the fire,
allegedly engaged in routine inspection—but that he did
not enforce the laws against overcrowding or employ-
ment of underage workers such as the bus boy. No
mention was made of any effort on his part to stem
the panic, and the general implication was that since he
was dressed in plainclothes, his visit to the club was
probably more social than professional. His superior, the
police commissioner, was also accused of mismanagement
and negligent supervision.

The wave of criticism rose even higher in city government when the *Globe* revealed that the building code,
similar to those enforced in other cities, had been in the
hands of the City Council for a full four years without
action. The press then pointed out that the mayor had
not urged the council to adopt the code and that he was
also ultimately responsible for the fire and police activities since he had appointed the heads of these departments. He became the target of even more public rage
and journalistic innuendo when the press quoted an
alleged statement made some time before the fire by
Barnett Welansky, owner of the Cocoanut Grove, to the
effect that "the mayor and I fit." Another interesting
feature of the attacks on public officials was "blanket
scapegoating"—i.e., the wholesale denunciation of the
city government—which indicated, as the investigators
put it, "a deep-rooted, perhaps unrecognized hostility
toward all political authority, toward those 'higher up.'"

The press also heaped abuse upon the owner and oper-
ators of the night club, though Welansky himself was
seldom mentioned by name since he was confined to
the hospital with a serious illness at the time of the fire.
The owner was accused of greed for admitting over
850 guests when his license specified that the Cocoanut

Grove had only 460 seats. Article after article implied that the club was in the hands of a secret syndicate; that the owner was a cheap profiteer who furnished the club with "imitation leather" and "flimsy, tinsel-like" decorations; that the liquor was better protected than the patrons since it was stored in a fireproof vault; that an unlicensed electrician had done the wiring for a nominal wage; that an underage bus boy was employed; and that the decorations were not adequately fireproofed. The papers not only accused the owner of "greed and cupidity," but implied that he "took care of" the right public officials. They also attempted to associate his name with racketeers, bootleggers, and a "lord of the underworld." Though these implications were never proved, most of the public accepted them as fact.

The effect of all these charges was to provide ammunition to the critics of the city administration, to inflame the public against so-called "money czars" and "political bigwigs," and to revive the smoldering anti-Semitism which Father Coughlin's followers had been spreading in Boston. This is not to assert that all the charges were groundless. Certainly there was legitimate reason to criticize the club management for permitting the overcrowding, installing flammable decorations on the ceiling after the club had been inspected, and allowing the exit doors to be locked. (Months later, the owner Barnett Welansky was tried and sentenced to twelve to fifteen years in state prison for manslaughter. The fire inspector and building commissioner were tried and acquitted.) The accusations, however, went beyond all bounds of reason and justice, and testified to the fact that the panic was not confined to the Cocoanut Grove but actually spread to large segments of the Boston populace itself. They were frightened by the possibility that a similar catastrophe might befall them. They were angry and frustrated when they could not explain how such a disaster could occur. And they also felt vaguely guilty that it could happen in their own city.

In response to this combination of fear, frustration, and guilt, the public struck out wildly against anyone on whom they could pin responsibility for the tragedy. At the same time they unconsciously used this opportunity as an excuse for releasing stored-up aggression against the government and against the rich and successful as well. As Veltfort and Lee say in their summary, "Frustrations and fears aroused by the Cocoanut Grove holocaust created a desperate desire on the part of the people of Boston to fix the blame and punish those responsible for the catastrophe. There resulted violent accusations, if not unwarranted, at least out of proportion to the possible guilt of the accused. The scapegoating was most intense against the owners of the Grove and against the public officials responsible for the safety of Boston's citizens. Officials and owners were especially satisfying scapegoats since the tragedy permitted the releasing of much latent aggression. It is when such latent hostility is present that scapegoating is most dangerous."

The significant fact is that by focusing attention on blameworthy individuals, the people and the press overlooked two important factors in the situation. First, all but a few people ignored the fact that the public itself was ultimately responsible for the election of public officials and for the lax laws that prevailed at the time. And second, they failed to recognize the psychological fact that panic behavior was largely responsible for the great loss of life. As the Committee for National Morale stated shortly after the catastrophe, "The Boston tragedy was due in part to a psychological collapse."

In Twos and Threes

To the man in the street a pair of identical twins is simply a passing curiosity. He may merely turn his head to look at them again and perhaps mutter something like "I wonder if their mother can tell them apart." To the psychologist, however, look-alikes are not objects of wonder but subjects for study and experimentation. We have learned a good deal about human development from them. We now know, for example, that they are more prone to be miscarried or premature than singletons. We know, too, that fraternal twins may be fairly similar in appearance, or may be as different as day and night. Identicals, on the other hand, maintain a striking resemblance throughout life, and in old age there is great similarity in the graying of their hair, the formation of wrinkles, and the pattern of tooth defects. These facts argue for the tremendous effect of heredity since identical or one-egg twins stem from identical genes while fraternals originate from two different fertilized eggs.

Scientists have sought to settle a number of crucial problems by studying twins. The problem we'll be looking at in the first two stories of doubles is the relative influence of heredity and environment on intelligence. The other two will deal with rare disorders in which resemblance of one kind or another is a dominant factor. One is a case in which a woman had a brief and near-tragic encounter with her double. The other is an equally unusual case in which three people became as alike as triplets in their madness if not in their looks.

DOUBLES NUMBER ONE AND TWO

NUMBER ONE

A strapping young man of twenty-two was busily at work in the repair center of the local telephone company. Deep in concentration, he did not notice that another young man, apparently a new employee, was being shown around the department. As the newcomer passed his work bench, he stopped short, did a double take, and exclaimed, "Fred! Imagine finding you here! How's tricks?" Failing to note the puzzled expression on the worker's face, the newcomer continued, "Now that's a first-class coincidence if there ever was one—*both* of us transferred all the way out to Iowa!"

The man at the bench flushed and managed to stammer out, "You've got your wires crossed, buddy. I never laid eyes on you in my life. And besides, I haven't been transferred. Been here for years."

"C'mon now, Fred, quit your kidding. You and I were buddies back in Omaha."

"But I'm not kidding, believe me. I've never been in Omaha in my life, and what's more, my name isn't Fred, it's Ed!"

So began one of the strangest of all cases unearthed by behavioral science in recent years. Ed shrugged off the curious incident, perhaps thinking to himself that there may be some truth in the old idea that every one of us has a double somewhere in the world. But when another transferred repairman mistook him for Fred a year later, he was so mystified that he decided to tell his parents about his two odd experiences.

Ed's parents listened intently to his story and at first merely expressed surprise. But after discussing the matter in private, they concluded that it was time to reveal a situation that had remained hidden for years. With understandable trepidation, they confessed to Ed that he was not their own child, and that he had a twin brother who was adopted by another family at a very early age. They felt that the young man he had been mistaken for —Fred—was undoubtedly his brother.

Ed was mature enough to take this double revelation with equanimity and curiosity. He was eager to meet his twin, not merely because they both worked for the telephone company, but because from early boyhood he had been obsessed with the idea that he had a brother who had died. He lost no time in getting in touch with Fred, via the telephone company, and since Fred was out of work at the time, he came to visit Ed in Iowa. One of the first things Fred said was, "You know, I've always had a haunting feeling that I once had a brother, but that he died. I'm glad to see you're still around!"

After recovering from the initial shock of finding their double, they asked Ed's parents to tell them as much as they could about their early life. Gradually the story came out. They learned that they had been orphaned in early infancy and had been adopted by different families who lived for a time in the same New England town. Both couples were childless and in both cases the boys had been raised as only children. The two families lived on about the same social and economic level, but were not acquainted with each other. However—and this was most surprising—the adopted sons had attended the same school for a short time but were never close companions. At this point the two young men suddenly recalled that they had noticed how much they resembled each other, but had never suspected that they were twin brothers.

Ed and Fred then learned that when they were eight years of age their families had moved to different cities, one in Michigan and the other in Iowa. Up to that time their lives had been similar in many important respects, but these similarities were far more understandable than the parallels that revealed themselves when they began to compare notes on the intervening years.

They started with their work for different branches of the telephone company, a fact that was startling enough in itself. But they also found that they performed virtually the same type of job—electrical repairing. When they got into the reasons for choosing this work, they discovered that both had developed a consuming interest in electricity at an early age. As they went on to compare their academic lives, both had to admit that they were poor students and had dropped out of high school—though Fred had completed three years and Ed only one. After this they began to compare their personal lives, and the similarities that came out were nothing short of astonishing. They found that they had been married the same year to young women who were not only the same age, but remarkably alike in personality and appearance. What is more, each had a four-year-old son—and each owned a fox terrier named Trixie!

These, then, are the highlights of the lives of Ed and Fred—identical twins who not only looked alike but lived alike in spite of twenty-five years and one thousand miles of separation. But it is only the first chapter of their story. The rest is scientific history of the first order, for this pair of twins has contributed immeasurably to the solution of one of psychology's most formidable problems.

The second chapter begins at the Quadrangle Club of the University of Chicago. In the club's dining room is a famous table known as the "Round Table," where informal discussions are held over luncheon every day in the week. One day, back in 1926, the talk centered around the age-old question of heredity vs. environment, and in the course of the discussion someone suggested that a new attack on the problem might be made by studying twins. Three of the professors who were gathered around the table—F. N. Freeman, a psychologist, Karl H. Holzinger, a statistician, and H. H. Newman, a biologist—decided to pool their resources and collect all the data they could about two types of twins: identical, or one-egg, twins, who develop from the same sperm and ovum; and fraternal, or two-egg, twins, who come from different germ cells and therefore have different heredity.

Within a year the three collaborators had collected detailed data on fifty twins of each variety from the city schools. As a whole, they found remarkable similarities between identical twins, but far less similarity between fraternal twins in all major areas: intelligence, motor skills, social development, personality, and temperament. Since each set of twins had been brought up in the same family, it seemed reasonable to conclude that the over-all differences between the two groups were primarily due to hereditary rather than environmental factors. However, at this point one of the investigators came across a case of one-egg twins who had been reared *apart*, one in England and the other in Canada. A study of this case suggested a new and crucial question: If identical twins are brought up separately, will they still be alike, or will their different environments make them different?

The problem was how to find a sufficiently large number of identical twins who had been reared apart. A few cases were gathered through newspaper and radio appeals, but not enough. Finally they hit on the idea of offering a free trip to the Chicago Century of Progress Fair of 1933 as an inducement, in exchange for two full days devoted to laboratory study. The idea worked—and that is where Ed and Fred and nine other pairs of separated twins came into the picture.

Ed and Fred had the time of their lives at the Fair, especially since they met another set of twins invited by the professors, Ethel and Esther. Everywhere the two couples went, they attracted attention—in fact, even when they visited the Siamese twin exhibit, they stole the show!

Then came the two days of tests and interviews. The results were most revealing. Though Ed and Fred were now twenty-five years of age and had been brought up in different families, they were so similar in general appearance that the investigators kept mistaking one for the other. Both were decidedly healthy, and neither had suffered any serious illnesses in the past. They were within a half inch of each other in height and only a pound and a half apart in weight. Their head measurements were practically the same, and their hair, eye color, and complexion were identical. Their teeth showed the same degree of irregularity and were in equally good condition. Each of them had an extra upper canine high in the gum (Ed's had been extracted), but it was on the right side in Ed and the left in Fred—an example of the "mirror imaging" frequently found in identical twins. Their palm prints were practically identical for their right hands (a little less so for the left), and their finger-prints had precisely the same number of ridges for each hand.

Tests of ability and personality showed some slight differences. On two IQ tests their scores were equal, but on two others Ed was slightly superior. In educational achievement (reading, literature, arithmetic, etc.) their general average was the same, though there was some divergence on specific areas such as spelling, but these differences could be readily explained by differences in interest and educational opportunity. The same was true for the tests of temperament and personality: There was a marked similarity on general characteristics such as emotional balance, speed of movement, and interest in detail, with some differences on such specifics as speed of decision and flexibility of movement. There was, how-ever, one general difference in personality: In conversa-tion as well as on the tests, Ed appeared to be some-what more emotional and vivacious than Fred. The investigators concluded that this difference was not significant since many studies have shown that adult identical twins differ more in personality than in phys-ical and intellectual characteristics.

In spite of their long separation, then, Ed and Fred were found to be, on the whole, as much alike as almost any pair of one-egg twins brought up together. But what about those startling similarities revealed when they com-pared their intervening lives? Were they simply due to coincidence, or are there logical explanations?

Let's take them one at a time. First, their mutual feel-ing that they once had a brother who died. Three possible bases for this feeling come to mind: a "psychic affinity," which is often alleged to exist between a one-egg twin and his "other half"; an actual memory harking back to the short period when they were together as infants;

and a feeling of brotherhood that originated during the time when they were pupils at the same school. The first theory is supported by the fact that identical twins frequently anticipate each other's thoughts, use identical expressions, and even develop a shorthand language of their own which others do not understand. But this kind of behavior occurs only because they spend so much time together, and cannot be expected when they are raised apart, as with Ed and Fred.

The early-memory theory gains some support from psychoanalysts who claim to have elicited memories dating back to the first few months of life. While this explanation cannot be ruled out completely, it seems far more likely that the idea was generated when the boys were at school together and noticed their resemblance to each other. Since they were brought up in different families and had no reason to suspect that they were actually brothers, we can conjecture that they *unconsciously* translated the idea of brotherhood into the notion that they had *lost* a brother. This type of fantasy is not uncommon among children.

As for the other parallels, the fact that both became interested in repair work can be at least partially explained by their limited education and the semiskilled economic level on which their families lived. The fact that they both worked for the telephone company, however, must be attributed to coincidence. The same for the dates of their marriage and their four-year-old sons. The similarities between their wives is not too surprising in view of their similar personalities. And the two fox terriers named Trixie? Well, we could speculate that people with the same type of personality are likely to choose the same type of dog, but that idea has not been scientifically established. At any rate, we do know that fox terriers were popular at the time and were frequently owned by families with small sons. And Trixie was not only a common name, but was considered particularly fitting for this breed of dog.

All these facts, plus an ample amount of coincidence, should be enough to keep us from resorting to more esoteric explanations such as telepathy or other psychic relationships.

NUMBER TWO

As one of the investigators, H. H. Newman, points out, the case of Ed and Fred goes far toward proving that when identical heredity and closely similar environments collaborate, they produce almost identical results. But what would happen to separated twins brought up in *dissimilar* environments? Would their common heredity keep them alike, or would their contrasting environments make them different? Or, to put it in another way, would nature triumph over nurture, or nurture over nature?

Another of the Chicago Fair cases, that of Gladys and Helen, throws a good deal of light on these questions. In barest outline, these two sisters had been separated at eighteen months of age and did not meet again until they were twenty-eight. Unlike Ed and Fred, each of them knew she had a twin sister somewhere—but like those young men, they discovered one another as a result of mistaken identity. Unknown to each other, they had moved—surprisingly—to the same city, Detroit, where Helen was a schoolteacher and Gladys an employee in a printing firm. One evening a favorite pupil of Helen's attended a concert in a distant part of the city and noticed her teacher sitting in a nearby row. But when she tried to speak to her, she was greeted by a cold look. The next day Helen noticed that her pupil was less cordial than usual, and asked her why. When the girl explained what had happened, Helen immediately suspected that the other woman was her long-lost sister. Through inquiries made in the part of the city where the concert had been held, she was finally able to locate her sister, and the two had an excited and memorable reunion.

Some years later Gladys and Helen, now thirty-five, came to the Fair in response to the appeal for identical twins who had lived separate lives. The first finding of the interviewers was that those lives had been just about as different as could be imagined. Helen had been brought up by a childless farmer and his wife, a relatively uneducated woman who was determined to give her adopted daughter the best possible education. She did extremely well in school and had been graduated from a well-known Michigan college. In the course of her education she had developed into a young woman of great poise, polish, and charm. At the time of the interview, she was married to a cabinetmaker, was quite well off, and had one child.

Gladys' lot had been different in every respect. She had been adopted by a Canadian railroad conductor who was stricken with tuberculosis when she was in the third grade. To promote his recuperation, the company sent him and his family to an isolated part of the Canadian Rockies, where there were no schools. When they finally returned to Ontario, Gladys was too old to associate with third-graders, and received no more schooling. In addition, her mother was strongly opposed to education for women, and her daughter merely helped around the house. When she was old enough she got a job in a knitting mill, then in stores as a salesgirl. At nineteen she moved to Detroit and began working in the printing establishment. After marrying a mechanic at twenty-one, she kept her job, and within a few years was advanced to assistant to the proprietor. In the course of her working life she had become businesslike and somewhat mannish, and had acquired none of the social ease and polish of her sister.

The psychological and biological tests revealed that these long-separated twins were markedly alike in physical measurements and general appearance, though Helen's expression was softer and less determined than Gladys'. She was also more graceful, better groomed, and looked younger than her sister. They were now in equally good health, but Helen had always been healthy, while Gladys had suffered several serious and almost fatal illnesses as a child. Gladys, who had received a minimal academic education, was considerably inferior in intellectual development. Her IQ was near the bottom of the normal range (92), while Helen's was close to the superior range (116), a difference of 24 points.

The differences revealed by the behavior and personality tests were only slightly less marked. Helen made considerably higher scores on tests of speed, flexibility, and control of responses, but the two women were practically equal in aggressiveness, probably because Helen had developed more social confidence and Gladys had to overcome more difficult situations in her life. One of the tests showed that they were about equally disposed to neurotic behavior, possibly because there had been a considerable degree of friction with the foster mother in both cases. Other results on this point were mixed. Helen's handwriting was decidedly neater, more beautiful, and more mature than Gladys', whose writing was comparable to a fourteen-year-old's in spite of the fact that she had to do a good deal of writing in her occupation.

In general, the investigators concluded that the close similarities in physical characteristics were due to identical heredity, while the differences in personality could be attributed to extreme differences in life experience. As to intelligence level, we can assume that the twins, being identical, started out in life with the same intellectual potential, but "The differences in test intelligence are greater for this pair than for any other pair of separated twins, and, strikingly enough, this largest difference is correlated with the largest difference in educational experience."

Here, then, is compelling evidence that environment can have a pronounced effect on hereditary tendencies.

STRANGE ENCOUNTER

Now for a totally different type of twin case from those presented in "Doubles Number One and Two." But first a word of introduction is needed.

One of the most ancient and persistent of all human beliefs is the notion that "every man has a double." The idea probably originated before the dawn of history, for it is still prevalent among primitive people in many parts of the world. Some trace it to the fact that early man encountered his own likeness in dreams, shadows, and reflections in water—and failed to distinguish between image and reality. According to Otto Rank, one of Freud's most gifted followers, these mysterious experiences explain why actual doubles (i.e., twins) were often regarded with awe, and even endowed with special creative powers, as in the myth that Rome was founded by Romulus and Remus.

A wide variety of other beliefs has been attributed to the idea of the double, ranging from ghosts to "astral projections" to the soul and its immortality. And despite its long history, it keeps cropping up in new places. Of these, one of the most significant is the psychological novel in which the double, or alter ego, represents the unconscious wishes and impulses of the protagonist. Among the authors who have employed variations on this theme are Oscar Wilde, Joseph Conrad, Herman Melville, Thomas Mann, Guy de Maupassant, Vladimir Nabokov, William Faulkner, and, above all, Fëdor Dostoevski.

The case that follows suggests that *some* doubles, at least, might originate in a way that is not recognized by either the students of primitive culture or the writers of modern novels.

In the early 1960s, a twenty-seven-year-old Okinawan woman, Mrs. F, was admitted to a hospital in the United States in desperate condition. Her face was swollen and congested. Her neck showed clear evidence of strangulation, and she was covered with blood from a jagged cut in the anterior part of her tongue. When she had recovered sufficiently to be questioned, she told a story that went roughly as follows:

> Yesterday, when I was shopping in a store, I noticed a woman looking sharply at me, with a serious expression on her face. I felt uncomfortable, of course, but the thing that disturbed me most was that she looked exactly like me, and wore exactly the same clothes!
>
> I had been carrying two packages, but I was so upset and confused that I put them on the counter—and when I returned a few minutes later, one of them was missing. I looked all around, but it was nowhere to be found. Finally I returned home without it—and guess

what happened! I opened our apartment door, and there it was. There seemed to be only one explanation: The woman who stared at me in the store must have brought it there. The whole experience made me so overwrought that I couldn't sleep a wink last night.

This morning I called my husband at work and asked him not to telephone me at noon, as he always did, because I was very tired and wanted to take a long nap. After the call, I started to feed our six-month-old baby, and heard someone knocking at the door. Before I had time to open it, I found the woman standing inside—the very same woman I had seen the day before, wearing exactly the same clothes and carrying the same kind of brown bag I had brought from Okinawa. She had not spoken to me in the store, but this time she said, in rather poor Japanese, "Let us go inside." I understood what she was saying because I knew Japanese and spoke it much better than she did.

I felt terribly frightened by the whole thing but said, "OK" and took my baby to a neighbor's house without telling her about my strange visitor. When I returned, the woman was still standing just inside the door of my apartment. She ordered me to wrap up the apartment key and put it in the mailbox. For some reason I can't understand, I had to do what she commanded. I felt as if I was being drugged or under some kind of spell, because an eerie light seemed to be streaming from her eyes, and I thought I smelled ether.

I don't know what happened right after that, but I found myself in a dark place with this woman, who was speaking in a voice that sounded just like mine. And while she was talking, she was putting a rope or belt around my neck and was trying to tighten it. She even asked me to help her, and I felt sure I was being killed.

Naturally I was terrified and cried, but nevertheless I held the belt for her, though I would not draw it tighter around my neck. I didn't want to die, but I was powerless to resist this woman who was trying to strangle me. Then I passed out, and when I woke up, she had a pair of scissors in her hand and was trying to cut my tongue off! The pain was unbearable, and I must have passed out again.

When I finally came to, the woman had disappeared. I looked around and was amazed to find that I was in my own closet. Though I was frightfully weak, I managed to open the door and crawl to the kitchen for water. When my husband came home, he was shocked to find me lying on the floor asleep in this terrible condition. He brought me to the hospital as quickly as he could.

Several doctors attempted to elicit more details by asking questions, but Mrs. F's answers failed to throw much additional light on her harrowing experience. Here are some of the questions and answers:

Q: Why did the woman want to hurt you?

A: I don't know. I didn't know her. If I ever meet her again, I shall ask her.

Q: Was she exactly like you?

A: Yes, but I smile and have kind eyes. She had no smile and sharp eyes.

Q: Why did you take your baby to the neighbor?

A: I was afraid maybe she would hurt the baby.

Q: Why didn't you tell your neighbor?

A: I don't know. I was very much afraid.

Q: Why did you put your key in the mailbox?

A: I don't know. I did as she told me.

The police were notified, and the Homicide Squad

rushed to the apartment to investigate. Everything appeared to be in order, and there was no sign of a struggle. They then went through all the closets, and finally found one in the back of the apartment which was so small that only one person could stand in it at a time. It was spattered with blood, and on the floor was a black leather belt, a pair of bloody scissors, and a piece of cut-off tongue. They then looked in the mailbox and found the key wrapped in paper, just as Mrs. F had said. In a word, every detail of her story was corroborated—except one. There was no evidence that a second person had been in the apartment with her, and they therefore concluded that she had made a serious attempt to commit suicide.

During her hospitalization Mrs. F was carefully observed, and several types of tests and examinations were administered. A report of her case by C. B. Bakker and S. E. Murphy describes her as a "fairly attractive Okinawan woman who was anxious and depressed, but well oriented." She insisted that she was not ill, but stayed by herself and frequently cried, especially when her husband visited her in the hospital. Psychological tests confirmed the fact that she was anxious and depressed, but also revealed that she was a passive, immature, dependent personality who used withdrawal and denial of illness as defense mechanisms. During the first few days she was afraid that the identical woman might come back, but her fear gradually subsided when this did not occur.

Mrs. F kept insisting that her story was true, and became angry when anyone appeared to doubt it. She was interviewed three times under sodium amytal, a drug that has been called a "truth serum," and in each case she repeated essentially the same details. Neurological examinations revealed no abnormality, but an electroencephalograph, or brain wave test, indicated a moderate, diffuse disturbance of brain function. There was no evidence of a convulsive (epileptic) disorder. The cause of the EEG changes could not be determined, but the readings gradually came back to normal during her stay in the hospital. She also became less anxious and depressed, and was discharged after forty-seven days.

Three months later Mrs. F was asked to return for a follow-up examination, which showed that she had made a good adjustment at home. When questioned about her "accident," as she called it, her account remained unchanged.

That, in essence, is the case of Mrs. F—except for some important questions. Who was the identical woman —the "double"—who, she insisted, took her package, followed her home, and nearly killed her? What did the psychiatrists think of the idea that she had attempted suicide? What was their final diagnosis, and what explanation did they offer for these strange events?

After extended observation and examination, the doctors came to the conclusion that Mrs. F's "double" was not a real person at all but a figment of her imagination. She had experienced what is called an "autoscopic hallucination." In simplest terms, this means that she had projected her own body image into external space—which explains why her "double" looked exactly like herself and wore the same clothes. The term "autoscopy" means, quite literally, "to look at one's self," and a hallucination is a fictional perception originating entirely in the brain. The usual examples of hallucinations are the drunken person who sees pink elephants or the mentally disturbed individual who experiences unreal visions.

But Mrs. F's case was far from usual, for autoscopy is itself an unusual disorder, and the particular form it took with her was even more rare. In fact, it was the first case of its kind reported in the literature, and for this reason Bakker and Murphy entitled their report "An Unusual Case of Autoscopic Hallucination."

Mrs. F's experience was essentially different from previous cases in two major ways. In the first place, most individuals who have these hallucinations feel that the double is not a completely independent person, but is somehow part of themselves. In some instances they even maintain that they can experience the double's feelings without communicating in words. But, as the authors state, "Our patient, in contrast, encountered her double as a stranger who was identical to herself only in all superficial characteristics. The double appeared angry, aggressive, and hostile—qualities which the subject denied possessing herself. Also, the double spoke in a manner for which our patient seemed to have contempt, as the patient prides herself on the ability to speak very proper Japanese. In addition, it was inconceivable to the patient that she could ever indulge in the aggressive actions which the double displayed."

In the second place, no one had ever reported a case in which the double had attacked the subject—in fact, as noted in *The Encyclopedia of Human Behavior,* "The double usually appears fleetingly, and acts, if he acts at all, exactly like himself, and then vanishes." This description is borne out by an article published by C. W. Lippman, in which he cited a number of first-person accounts of "hallucinations of physical duality" which occurred just before, during or after migraine attacks. One of these accounts reads, in part, "Just after a headache I would be walking down the street. Suddenly I would become aware of a 'second self,' vaguer and more tenuous than the original 'me.' I felt just like a double exposure looks. The 'second self' quivered and wavered. It came and went every few seconds for a minute or so. Then, just as suddenly I came back into focus, and I was one again. There was no sensation when two became one."

Mrs. F's double appeared to be far more vivid, active, and disturbing. Moreover, its personality characteristics and behavior contrasted sharply with those she ordinarily displayed. For these reasons the doctors were reminded of cases of multiple personality, in which the secondary self is usually the very opposite of the primary self. In the celebrated case of Christine Beauchamp, described by Morton Prince in his classic work, *The Dissociation of a Personality*, the patient was prim, proper, and reserved, but one of her secondary selves, who called herself Sally, was the very opposite. This personality (of which Miss Beauchamp was totally unaware) was completely uninhibited and played any number of tricks on her, such as charging extravagant purchases to her account in department stores, repeatedly unraveling her knitting, frightening her out of her wits by sending her a package of spiders, and taking her for long, fatiguing hikes in the woods (which she hated), and then deliberately turning into Miss Beauchamp to make her find her way back. Similarly, in the case treated by Thigpen and Cleckley and dramatized in the film *The Three Faces of Eve*, mischievous Eve Black played pranks on the controlled, well-behaved Eve White. For example, as she herself put it to the therapist, "When I go out and get drunk, *she* wakes up with the hangover. She wonders what in the hell's made her so sick."

In view of these cases and the fact that Mrs. F's personality had much in common with the patients they involved (all of whom tended to be dependent, immature and repressed), the authors concluded that Mrs. F was probably suffering not only from autoscopy but from at least a tendency toward dual personality. They also became convinced that due to her disturbed state of mind she had made an actual attempt at suicide, and on this point they agreed with the verdict of the police.

But why was this attempt made, and why did Mrs. F develop an autoscopic hallucination? The reasons—as far as they can be determined—appear to be based on a combination of physical and psychological factors. On the physical level, there was no doubt that she had suffered a temporary brain disturbance, which other investigators have found to be an important prerequisite for the perception of the double. Definite evidence of this disturbance was found not only in the brain wave tracings but in Mrs. F's confused state of mind when she lost her package, as well as her hazy recollection of her double in the store and its sudden appearance inside her apartment. Her loss of consciousness just prior to the "attack," and the etherlike smell also seemed to indicate a brain disturbance, even though the specific cause of this abnormality was not apparent.

The factors that contributed to Mrs. F's anxiety and depression were much clearer. She had been brought up in Okinawa by doting, overprotective parents who granted her every wish but discouraged any expression of anger. After graduating from college, she married into a very proud family, and her husband insisted on living in his family's home. His parents were so demanding and subjected Mrs. F to so much criticism that she frequently became ill, and lost considerable weight. She also had a miscarriage, for which she was blamed. Shortly afterward her husband went to the United States to study, and she moved back to her own family for a few months. When she rejoined him, she became afraid of Americans and had difficulty making friends. Nevertheless, her husband left her alone a great deal, and after a child was born, paid far more attention to the baby than to her. Like his parents, he became overcritical, but, like hers, strongly disapproved of any open expression of anger or frustration on her part. As a result, Mrs. F became increasingly homesick, lost twenty pounds, and suffered insomnia. On the night before her "accident," she had slept poorly and was extremely depressed—a symptom found in many patients who experience autoscopic hallucinations.

On the basis of all these facts, the doctors formulated a tentative interpretation. In brief, they were convinced that she had not fabricated the story of the double, but had actually experienced a "dreamlike" hallucination. The fact that the double was far more aggressive than Mrs. F indicated that she had been storing up feelings of resentment toward her husband and probably toward her baby as well, since it deprived her of his attention. As a result of her upbringing and her husband's attitude, she was unable to express these feelings openly, and felt extremely guilty for harboring them. Then, when her level of consciousness was lowered due to the brain disturbance and insomnia, she unconsciously created a "double" on whom she could project her "intolerable destructive impulses" not only toward others but toward herself as well. The double served the purpose of enabling her to release and act out these impulses without assuming the "burden of responsibility" for her behavior.

To this analysis we might add the further speculation that these impulses created such an unbearable feeling of guilt that her attempted suicide took the form of strangulation and cutting her tongue, in order to prevent expression of her feelings in words. Perhaps, too, her suicide attempt also served the unconscious purpose of arousing her husband's concern by bringing her plight to his attention in the most forceful possible way.

Let us end with a comment on some of the authors mentioned at the beginning. One psychologist, Lawrence Kohlberg, has made a special study of literary doubles, particularly as portrayed by Golyadkin in Dostoevski's novel *The Double*. He shows that Golyadkin was a timid, ineffectual person, while his double represented his desire to be decisive, witty, and self-possessed. But even more relevant to Mrs. F's case, Kohlberg suggests that "There is reason to believe that an unusual number of writers have experienced autoscopic hallucinations" associated with a wide variety of conditions, such as epilepsy, brain damage, severe migraine, and in some instances schizoid and depressive tendencies without organic involvement. He cites the fact that Maupassant experienced hallucinations of a "duplicate self" in the middle stages of his syphilitic psychosis, and others such as Alfred de Musset experienced similar hallucinations when under emotional stress.

As for Dostoevski, Kohlberg makes this comment: "Surprisingly, the likelihood of Dostoevski having experienced the autoscopic syndrome has not been mentioned in the extensive psychological literature on Dostoevski. Nevertheless there is good reason to believe he actually had these experiences. While the autoscopic syndrome is rare, it is often linked with severe epilepsy of the sort known to have affected Dostoevski." Here is one more proof that in the modern psychological novel, the author frequently draws not only on his observation of other people, but on his own personal, private life, including any mental aberrations he may have experienced.

MADNESS IN TRIPLICATE

For several years Mrs. Nannie Van Hook had rented a run-down, one-room apartment in one of the black ghettos of New York City. Her daughter, Ethel Lee, and her daughter's husband, Robert Jarvis, shared the apartment with her, and all three lived a hand-to-mouth existence. Unable to pay her rent for months at a time, Mrs. Van Hook's landlord had repeatedly threatened her with eviction. Finally the inevitable day arrived, and two policemen appeared at the door, informing her that the landlord insisted that she pack up and be out as soon as possible. Mrs. Van Hook responded that she would leave only if the "Lord God" told her to do so. The policemen said that He had better tell her to go, because they would be back in half an hour and she would have to be out by that time—or else.

As soon as the policemen left, Mrs. Van Hook called Ethel Lee and Robert, who were lying unclothed under her bed. They were not hiding from the landlord or the police but, strange as it may seem, had been *living* in a wooden compartment underneath the bed for three whole years.

When her mother explained that they were being put out of the house, Ethel Lee immediately took charge of the situation. She crawled out of the compartment and, standing up with an effort, reached high above her head in a gesture of supplication, exclaiming, "I am the Mes-

senger. Tell me, Lord God, what is Thy will?" A moment
later her eyes glowed and she shouted, "I am being swept
by a gust of wind. It is God's voice. He is answering me."
The others waited in silence while she listened to the
deity. Finally she said, "He has just told me, 'Take
your possessions and make haste; victory and peace will
be with you.'"

Ethel Lee then turned to the others saying, "Robert
Jarvis, you are the Power and the Strength. You will
lead the way. And you, Mother, must follow along behind us because you are the Keeper." They then prepared to leave. The Messenger wrapped a bed sheet
around her body, and put a white turban on her head.
The Power and the Strength put on his pajamas. The
Keeper put on a dress. Thus attired, the three marched
out of the house and down the street.

The strange procession had not gone more than a few
blocks when they encountered the same two policemen
who had visited Mrs. Van Hook half an hour before. They
were immediately taken to the police station, and from
there transferred to hospitals. The mother and daughter
were taken to Bellevue for observation, and a few days
later committed to Brooklyn State Hospital. Robert Jarvis
was taken to Kings County Hospital and then committed
to Kings Park State Hospital. All three were diagnosed as
schizophrenia, paranoid type, and became permanent residents of these institutions.

The unusual character of this case based on a report
by the psychiatrist S. R. Kesselman is not the fact that
these three people were suffering from religious delusions.
Patients with false beliefs of this type are found in every
large mental institution, and many others live at home, or
wander about from place to place, or attempt to establish
a cult of their own. In fact, religious "manias" are one of
the most common forms of paranoid reaction. When the

patient declares that he is the universal savior or a messenger from God, he is suffering from a delusion of grandeur; if he pictures himself as a martyr bearing the sins of mankind on his shoulders, he is suffering from a delusion of persecution. Many patients are afflicted with both types of delusion.

What *is* unusual about the case is the fact that the illness originated with one of the three victims and spread to the other two. It is a striking example of one of the rarest of all psychiatric disorders: psychosis of association. The French were the first to study this type of mental illness, and in 1877, Ernest Charles Lasègue and Jean Pierre Falret named it *folie à deux,* or double insanity. A small number of such cases are now on record, probably a few more than a hundred, but *triple* insanity, or *folie à trois,* is practically never encountered.

The key to folie à deux or trois is that the aberration is actually transferred from one person to another as if by contagion. We are accustomed to this concept in physical medicine but not in mental medicine. Though some people are afraid they will "catch" mental illness from a disturbed member of the family, they are almost invariably assured that this will not happen. Ordinarily this is sound advice, for severe mental illness is not usually a communicable disease. Certain emotional disturbances, as contrasted with mental illness, however, may be transmitted or induced by the power of suggestion. Among these are cases of hysterical reaction such as tarantism and panic, described elsewhere in this book. (See "The Dancing Plague," "The Phantom of Mattoon," and "Stampede".)

The question is how the illness was transmitted in the Van Hook case—and by whom. Studies of folie à deux have shown that in most instances the delusions are imposed by a dominant person who is already psychotic.

The two individuals (or in this report, three) must be in close association with each other—husband and wife, parent and child, brothers or sisters. A study of over a hundred cases by A. Gralnick revealed the following combinations: two sisters, forty cases; husband and wife, twenty-six; mother and child, twenty-four; two brothers, eleven; brother and sister, six; father and child, two.

The weaker, more dependent person may appear fairly normal at the start, but over a period of time gradually absorbs and accepts the distorted ideas of the stronger individual. The transfer of the delusions from one to the other is due largely to the fact that they are both poorly adjusted individuals who live together in comparative seclusion, have a narrow range of interests, and face the same stresses.

Some psychiatrists believe that the recipients suffer from latent psychotic tendencies which are brought to the surface by the delusions of the stronger personality, just as some people are more prone than others to catch certain physical diseases. Studies have shown that in some cases the individual who adopts the delusions (the receptor) may abandon them if he is separated from the stronger personality (the inductor); in other cases the psychosis persists even after separation.

In the Van Hook family it was not the mother but the daughter who initiated the psychosis. This in itself is unusual since practically all other reports indicate that the mother would be more likely to induce the psychosis since she is a prime source of authority, and the child identifies with her rather than the other way around. At any rate, it appears that all three had long been mildly interested in religion, and had attended various churches without being converted to any particular cult. Though the Father Divine movement was active at the time, they had not even heard of it. However, about three years before their hospitalization, Ethel Lee had experienced what she termed a "revelation." During this episode she claimed that God appointed her to be his "Messenger," and her husband was to be "The Power and the Strength." She also insisted that God had selected her mother as "The Keeper." The latter two were so impressed by this revelation that they accepted these symbolic names and immediately began to govern their lives accordingly.

At the time of the original revelation, Ethel Lee continued to experience auditory hallucinations. She heard the voice of God many times, and reported that He commanded her and her "mate" to live in secret and "not to seek out the sun." They were also ordered to give away all their worldly possessions and were not to "have each other," since sexual relations were considered unclean in the eyes of God. In addition, all three were ordered to abstain from eating meat on Fridays, and to fast completely on Saturdays. On the other days, the diet was to consist almost entirely of yellow corn bread, fried fish, and grease.

Since the mother had been appointed their "Keeper," Ethel Lee and her husband moved into her one-room apartment. And in order to live in secret, and away from the sun, they built a special compartment under the only bed and spent most of their time in it. They carried out the Lord God's "command" by giving away practically everything they owned, including their clothes; and in spite of their close quarters under the mother's bed, refrained from all sexual contact. The mother accepted her role as Keeper to the fullest degree. She alone went out to buy food, prepared it for her two charges, bathed them, and took care of their essential needs. Moreover, she helped them fulfill the command to live in secret by keeping the neighbors away from the house. No one knew that her daughter and son-in-law were living in the room.

Dr. Kesselman examined the three patients in the hospitals, and in compiling their case histories uncovered a number of factors that undoubtedly contributed to their condition. The mother, Nannie Van Hook, forty-seven years of age, had come north about ten years before and had been living on relief ever since. She had separated from her first husband, the father of Ethel Lee, and had later remarried and again separated. She also had a second daughter, Dolores Conquette (called Katie), who had given birth to an illegitimate child, a boy, fathered by Ethel Lee's husband, Robert Jarvis. Mrs. Van Hook's health was fairly good except for a positive Wassermann; she had received treatment for syphilis for some years, but had stopped visiting the clinic three years before because, in her words, she had seen the light and only God could cure her. A few months later a social worker had visited her home and found several people dressed in "fantastic costumes," and apparently participating in a religious ceremony. All of them appeared to be in a trance, including the child, Robert, Jr., who was living with her at the time. Mrs. Van Hook declared that she was no longer interested in the outside world since "When I saw the light, I left the filthy world behind and had nothing to do with the bad people in it."

The follow-up on Mrs. Van Hook confirmed the diagnosis of a communicated psychosis. When questioned, she answered invariably in terms of her delusion. She constantly spoke of the "will of God." For example, when asked if she was happy, her answer was "No; not in this land. I shall be happy wherever my Lord God shall leave me." However, she insisted that the Lord did not speak to her directly, but only through the lips of her daughter, who was freeing her from "false doctrines": "I called upon my Lord God by praying; my prayers and my heart's desire were answered through his Messenger."

Mrs. Van Hook was separated from her daughter in order to break the hold of these delusions, and psychotherapy was administered in the form of explanation of her daughter's illness. Although some improvement occurred, she continued to refer to herself as "The Keeper," and remained obsessed by the peculiar religion which her daughter had developed.

Robert Jarvis also failed to give up his delusions. When interviewed at Kings Park State Hospital, he revealed that he had accepted Ethel Lee's hallucinatory messages as being heaven sent. Speaking in a biblical manner, he continually referred to himself as "The Power and the Strength," to his mother-in-law as "The Keeper," and to his wife as "The Messenger of God." He spoke freely and coherently on impersonal matters, but refused to discuss his relationship with Katie. His facial appearance was stolid and expressionless, and he was emotionally "flat." The diagnosis was the same as for the other two: dementia praecox (schizophrenia), paranoid type.

When Ethel Lee was interviewed in the hospital, she appeared even more actively deluded than her mother and husband, stating that she spoke only when the Lord God Almighty talked through her. Though her speech was retarded and indistinct, she was able to give a fairly clear account of the instructions she had received from the deity, as well as the three years in which she and her husband lived on a special diet and occupied the compartment beneath her mother's bed. Shock therapy was recommended but could not be administered since the only available relative from whom consent could be obtained was Dolores Conquette, and she refused to sign the necessary papers.

On one occasion, a Saturday, the case was presented to a group of students, and Ethel Lee and her mother were brought in for questioning. However, Ethel Lee immediately rose to her feet, faced the group and declared, "I am the Lord God's Messenger; this is the Sabbath, and I can do no work," whereupon she turned and walked out. Her mother immediately declared, "I am the Lord God's Keeper; this is the Sabbath, and I can do no work," and also turned and left. Thereafter the two were never presented on a Saturday.

Dr. Kesselman attempted to trace the factors that led to this triple breakdown. His comments throw considerable light on the case: "It is interesting to suggest the psychodynamics underlying this fantastic situation. In the writer's discussion with the daughter, he learned that she was sexually assaulted by her own father at the age of twelve. She had always been of a schizothymic [withdrawn] temperament, describing herself as 'shy and bashful.' She had a persisting feeling of shame about her relationship with her father, so much so that she resisted the amorous advances of her husband for a long period before her marriage which occurred when she was fourteen. Her husband, as has been noted, was also the father of her sister's illegitimate son who lived with his grandmother, The Keeper, when the mother, Katie (Dolores Conquette), left the household.

"The Keeper also displayed sensitivity and shame about her illegitimate grandson, for the social service agency familiar with the family informed the hospital that for a long period The Keeper refused to permit her grandson to attend school for fear that he would learn the 'false doctrines' of man. Thus, it is somewhat apparent that all three psychotic persons, either consciously or unconsciously, entertained the element of shame. Consequently, when The Messenger presented a plan which would permit all three to withdraw from what was to them a difficult reality, it was readily accepted."

To this tentative explanation we may add another factor that probably accentuated their feelings of shame associated with sex: All three were found to be suffering from syphilis. In addition, it is quite possible that the disease may have had a debilitating effect, thereby lowering their threshold for mental disorder, even though it may not have reached a sufficiently advanced stage to produce psychotic symptoms by itself.

Around the World

The science of anthropology and the global jet have combined to put us in closer touch with cultures which were once beyond our ken. In consequence, interest in the art, folklore, and customs of societies around the world has reached a new peak. One of the important by-products of this trend is a greater appreciation of cultures once dismissed as "primitive" or "backward," and treated with scorn and derision. Today we realize more than ever before that we have much to learn from these societies.

A second by-product, and one that is in keeping with the theme of this book, is a broader concept of human behavior. Not long ago psychology was humorously defined as the study of the college sophomore, since second-year students were so often used as subjects in experiments. Now, however, we are beginning to recognize that it is just as important to compare the behavior of people in widely different cultures as it is to study people in our own society.

One of the many branches of psychology which has benefited from these "cross-cultural" investigations is the study of mental disorders. In fact, a whole new discipline, folk psychiatry, has been developing in recent years.

While it focuses on all aspects of abnormality in other societies, including possible causal factors and treatment by priests and medicine men, it is constantly asking one important question: Are the same types of disorder found throughout the world, or do some societies develop special disorders found nowhere else? The object of the chapters that follow is to throw some light on this question by describing actual cases gathered from widely separated areas such as Africa, Australia, Borneo, Java, Alaska, and China.

THE WILL TO DIE

Marumba was on his way home to his tribe, spear in hand, four pelts swinging from his waist. He had been on a hunting trip beyond the dark mountain that rose where the sun goes down. As he strode along, his head held high, his black skin glowing, the powerful young man looked the picture of health and vigor.

Scarcely forty-eight hours later, Marumba was not the same young man—in fact, he had been transformed almost beyond recognition. He sat in a dark corner of his hut, head bowed and muscles sagging. His face had taken on a deathly pallor, and he stared into empty space with a haunted look in his eyes. Moaning softly, as if in agony, he refused food, drink, and companionship. Outside the hut, his kinsmen were gathering in ominous silence, for they were certain that the spirit of the young hunter would soon depart from his body.

What had wrought this startling change? Was Marumba bitten by a deadly spider? Had he suffered a fatal injury or contracted a tropical disease? The answer to these questions is a flat no. His desperate condition was apparently brought about by black magic, for Marumba had transgressed one of the taboos of his tribe and was paying the penalty for his sin. On his return from his hunting trip, the counselors of the tribe had learned that one of the pelts he brought back was that of a sacred animal, and though Marumba pleaded that he did not realize it was taboo, they nevertheless decreed that he must die.

The tribe's medicine man was sent to Marumba's hut. There he uttered an incantation, drew a piece of bone from his clothing, and pointed it at the young man. From that moment on Marumba, convinced that he was doomed to die, had begun to wither away.

The tragedy of Marumba is based upon actual cases. Though it may seem incredible and wholly foreign to civilized experience, trained observers have attested to the fact that similar incidents occur in many parts of the world. In some instances, as with Marumba, the victim is condemned by a chief or medicine man; in others, he feels he has been cursed by malevolent spirits, or has fallen under the spell of a sorcerer who wishes to eliminate him—but in practically every case, he actually dies within a few hours or a few days at most. As early as 1587, Soares de Souza watched Tupinambas Indians wilt and die after they had been sentenced by the shaman. Similarly, Brazilian Indians, believing in the supernatural power of their chief, have succumbed in a matter of hours after he had made a terrifying augury or prediction. Anthropologists have reported substantially the same phenomenon in Africa, New Zealand, Australia, the islands of the Pacific, as well as in the Caribbean, and particularly Haiti where this form of "black magic" is known as voodoo death.

There is a remarkable resemblance in the accounts of voodoo death in all these widely scattered areas. In 1956, the anthropologist Van der Hoeven, who had made a study of this phenomenon in New Guinea, reported that a sorcerer had been offended by a young Papuan, and in revenge, told the young man that he had placed a *bofiet*, an object poisoned by witchcraft, in his path a few days before. Though the young man was completely healthy, he immediately became extremely ill, refused to speak a word, and seemed entirely detached from his environment. Two days later he was dead. Interestingly, the sorcerer was indicted by a Dutch court and freely admitted that he was guilty. The court recognized that the young man had been "bewitched," and condemned the sorcerer to several years in prison.

Another anthropologist, Leonard, has reported cases from Africa, particularly in the region of the Lower Niger. He writes, "I have seen more than one hardened old Hausa soldier dying steadily and by inches because he believed himself to be bewitched; no nourishment or medicine that was given to him had the slightest effect either to check the mischief or to improve his condition in any way, and nothing was able to divert him from a fate which he considered inevitable. In the same way, and under very similar conditions, I have seen Kru-men and others die in spite of every effort that was made to save them, simply because they had made up their minds, not (as we thought at the time) to die, but that being in the clutch of a malignant demon they were bound to die." Similarly, many cases of death due to violation of taboos have been reported in New Zealand. One Maori woman ate some fruit and was told that it had been taken from a taboo place. She became convinced that the spirit of the chief would kill her—and she was dead before noon the next day. Apparently death can occur even more quickly. According to one student of the Maoris, Tregear: "I have seen a strong young man die the same day he was tapued (tabooed); the victims die under it as though their strength ran out as water."

One of the most vivid accounts of the effect of "bone pointing" is found in *The Australian Aboriginal,* a book by a medically trained investigator, Dr. Herbert Basedow: "The man who discovers that he has been boned by an enemy is, indeed, a pitiable sight. He stands aghast, with his eyes staring at the treacherous pointer, and with his hands lifted as though to ward off the lethal medium, which he imagines is pouring into his body. His cheeks blanch, his eyes become glassy and the expression of his face becomes horribly distorted . . . He attempts to shriek but usually the sound chokes in his throat, and all that one might see is froth at his mouth. His body begins to tremble and the muscles twist involuntarily. He sways backwards and falls to the ground, and after a short time appears to be in a swoon; but soon after he writhes as if in mortal agony, and, covering his face with his hands, begins to moan. After a while he becomes very composed and crawls to his wurley (hut). From this time onwards he sickens and frets, refusing to eat and keeping aloof from the daily affairs of the tribe. Unless help is forthcoming in the shape of a counter-charm administered by the hands of a Nangarri or medicine man, his death is only a matter of a comparatively short time. If the coming of the medicine man is opportune, he might be saved."

The medicine man does not often attempt to save his victim, but when he does, the effect may be as startling as the original spell. The Nangarri goes through an elaborate ceremony before the sick man and his relatives. He then produces a small object such as a pebble or stick or bone which he claims to have taken from the "boned" man. This object, he announces, was the cause of his affliction, and now that it has been removed, there is nothing to fear. The victim, who a moment ago was at the very door of death, raises his head with a supreme effort and gazes at the object with wonderment in his eyes. A few moments later he lifts himself to a sitting position and calls for a drink of water. From then on his recovery is rapid and complete.

What is the rationale behind this remarkable phenomenon? Does the medicine man possess a peculiar power known only to primitive cultures? Or can this power, and the victim's strange reactions, be explained by principles known to modern science?

Though many investigators have reported cases of voodoo death, only one, to our knowledge, has offered a detailed scientific explanation. He is Dr. Walter B. Cannon, America's most celebrated physiologist. In a major article in the *American Anthropologist*, he has discussed several of the cases cited above, and has considered a number of alternative theories before advancing his own. The first hypothesis is poison, and he asks, "May not the fatal result be due to action of poisonous substances not commonly known except to priests and wizards?" To find the answer to this question Dr. Cannon wrote to several physicians who had directly observed the effects of the medicine man's powers. One of them, Dr. P. S. Clarke, had been stationed at a hospital in North Queensland. He related that one day a native who had been working on a sugar plantation came to him stating that he was going to die in a few days since a spell had been cast on him. The doctor gave him a thorough examination and found him completely healthy; nevertheless, during the examination the man became noticeably weaker. His foreman was called to the hospital to give him reassurance, but when he looked at the patient, he said there was nothing he could do since he was nearly dead. The worker expired the next morning, and a post-mortem examination revealed nothing whatever that could account for his death.

Another medical observer, Dr. J. B. Cleland, professor of pathology at the University of Adelaide, wrote Dr. Cannon that "Poisoning is, I think, entirely ruled out in such cases among our Australian natives. There are very few poisonous plants available and I doubt whether it has ever entered the mind of the Central Australian natives that such might be used on human beings." Another investigator, W. L. Warner, pointed out that the Aborigines in the Northern Territory of Australia, where he had observed the effects of bone pointing, were too ignorant to know anything about poisons.

The theory of poisoning, then, is probably groundless. Moreover, it is completely ruled out in those cases where the medicine man counteracts his own "magic" and restores a dying man to health merely by uttering an incantation and pointing an object at him. A rapid recovery of this kind also contradicts the theory of infection or disease. Furthermore, we know of no way a medicine man could transmit an actual disease to his victim by merely pointing a bone at him. Finally, no trace of disease has been found in any of the autopsies that have been performed on the victims.

A number of observers have advanced a theory based on social psychology. They point out that man is essentially a "social animal," and that he needs the support of other human beings. This, they add, is especially true in primitive societies where men must band together to meet a world haunted by spirits which they can neither perceive, control, nor understand. But what happens

when the bone is pointed at the victim? As Cannon puts
it, "All people who stand in kinship relation with him
withdraw their sustaining support. This means that everyone he knows—all his fellows—completely change their
attitudes toward him and place him in a new category.
He is now viewed as one who is more nearly in the realm
of the sacred and taboo than in the world of the ordinary
where the community finds itself." In a word, everyone
regards him as a doomed man, and since there is nothing they can do to help, they leave him alone and
isolated. Moreover, since he is in a highly suggestible
state, he accepts this verdict and co-operates with it by
withdrawing into his hut, waiting for death to overtake
him: "Thus he assists in committing a kind of suicide."

This is not all. The community applies social suggestion
in yet another way. The family helps to convince the
victim that he is bound to die by performing rites of
mourning *before* he is dead! As one observer, Warner,
has expressed it, "An analogous situation in our society
is hard to imagine. If all a man's near kin, his father,
mother, brothers and sisters, wife, children, business associates, friends, and all the other members of the society should suddenly withdraw themselves because of
some dramatic circumstance, refusing to take any attitude but one of taboo and looking at the man as one
already dead, and then after some little time perform
over him a sacred ceremony which is believed with cer-
tainty to guide him out of the land of the living into that
of the dead, the enormous suggestive power of this twofold movement of the community, after it has had its
attitudes crystallized, can be somewhat understood by
ourselves."

Such a situation would doubtless have a drastic effect
even on educated people living in a highly civilized
society, as evidenced by the bitter feelings of rejection

and depression experienced by people who have been discriminated against, blackballed, or otherwise socially ostracized. But think what effect it would have upon fear-ridden Aborigines who are "so primitive, so superstitious, so ignorant that they are bewildered strangers in a hostile world. Instead of knowledge, they have a fertile and unrestricted imagination which fills their environment with all manner of evil spirits capable of affecting their lives disastrously." And add to that, the fixed belief that certain individuals—priests, medicine men, chiefs—possess the magical power to call forth these malicious spirits and avenge any infraction of the tribal law—and the stage is set for the terror that brings on death.

Fear, suggestion, and expectation, then, play important roles in the fate of the victim. But how do they operate? What is the mechanism through which they cause a healthy person to pine away and succumb in a few short hours? Cannon offers a convincing answer. He points out that fear is one of the most deeply rooted and powerful of all emotions, and one of the most pervasive in its effects on the organism. When faced with a threat, the body is thrown into a state of emergency and mobilized for action. In physiological terms, this means that the sympathetic (or sympathicoadrenal) division of the nervous system is working at fever pitch, for in order to supply the energy to meet the threat, it accelerates the heart, discharges adrenalin into the bloodstream, releases sugar from the liver, and dilates the lungs to provide more oxygen. In a word, the sympathetic division speeds up the entire system—and "if this state of extreme perturbation continues in uncontrolled possession of the organism for a considerable period, without the occurrence of action, dire results may ensue."

Cannon points out, further, that while the sympathetic system raises blood pressure at first, it invariably falls to a dangerous level after a few hours of excessive emotional reaction—and this decrease may actually prove fatal. He supports this view with a number of observations. Experiments with cats have shown that when the cerebral cortex is destroyed, the activity of the lower nervous system is uninhibited, and as a result, the animal goes through a "supreme exhibition of intense emotional activity" at the slightest provocation: "The hairs stand on end, sweat exudes from the toe pads, the heart rate may rise from about 150 beats per minute to twice that number, the blood pressure is greatly elevated, and the concentration of sugar in the blood soars to five times the normal." This excessive activity rarely lasts more than three or four hours, for by that time the blood pressure and blood volume have fallen to such a low level that the animal expires.

Cannon compares this reaction to that of combat soldiers suffering from "wound shock." In many cases the blood volume drops to a point where the heart and other essential organs do not receive a sufficient supply of oxygen to maintain their functions; and if this condition continues, it may lead to death in a very short time. Moreover, it has been found that this destructive process is hastened if two other conditions are present. First, the wounded man is more likely to die if he has been deprived of food and water; and second, the outcome is more likely to be fatal if he has been subjected to a particularly terrifying experience such as being buried in a cellar by the explosion of a shell. In cases of this kind shock may set in and death may occur even if the wounds are trivial and no bleeding occurs. Mira, a psychiatrist who examined such cases in the Spanish Civil War of 1936–39, has applied the apt term "malignant anxiety" to the wounded man's state of mind in these fatal cases. In a word, he may be quite literally "frightened to death."

Cannon applies these observations to the study of voodoo death: ". . . a persistent emotional state may induce a disastrous fall of blood pressure, ending in death. Lack of food and drink would collaborate with the damaging emotional effects to induce the fatal outcome. These are the conditions which are prevalent in persons who have been reported as dying as a consequence of sorcery. They go without food or water as they, in their isolation, wait in fear for their impending death. In these circumstances they might well die from a true state of shock, in the surgical sense—a shock induced by prolonged and tense emotion."

Cannon refers to his explanation as a "hypothesis," since at the time of the investigation (1942) he knew of no one who had checked for signs of shock such as rapid, thready pulse, cool, moist skin, low blood pressure, etc. He therefore expressed the hope that medical observers of voodoo death would "conduct at least the simpler tests before the victim's last gasp." Though it appears that such tests have not yet been performed *before* death, significant observations have been made shortly afterward—for, as Arieti and Meth point out in the *American Handbook of Psychiatry*, "The full autopsy reports in these cases have shown signs of vasomotor paralysis." They also comment that even though it is hard to understand how the fear and expectancy of death can actually lead to death, "It could be that a process of autohypnosis succeeds in altering some vital physiologic mechanisms, presumably through some functional alteration of the autonomic nervous system."

Certainly the haunted look in the eyes of the victim and his withdrawal into apathetic isolation suggest that a hypnotic state of mind may be induced by the medicine man as he utters his dire incantations while the victim's gaze is fixed on the ceremonial bone. This theory does not contradict Cannon's view, for it has been demonstrated that blood pressure may be lowered and heartbeat increased or decreased through autosuggestion. This is an area that needs further investigation if we are to arrive at a full solution to the mystery of voodoo death.

PIBLOKTOQ

The description that follows comes from the journals of Admiral Robert E. Peary, whose expedition of 1909 was the first to reach the North Pole: "A married woman was taken with one of these fits in the middle of the night. In a state of perfect nudity she walked the deck of the ship; then seeking still greater freedom, jumped the rail, onto the frozen snow and ice. It was some time before we missed her, and when she was finally discovered, it was at a distance of half a mile where she was still pawing, and shouting to the best of her abilities . . . Then there commenced a wonderful performance of mimicry in which every conceivable cry of local bird and mammal was reproduced in the throat of Inahloo."

Peary found that attacks of this disorder, known as arctic hysteria, or pibloktoq, were not uncommon, and were confined almost wholly to women. In fact, he reported only one case in which a man was afflicted in all the years he lived with Eskimos in the Greenland and polar areas. The episode usually lasts from one to one and a half hours, and ends in a fit of convulsive sobbing. In most cases, the woman then falls into a deep sleep, from which she awakens a few hours later in a perfectly normal state. In rare instances, the victims recover without falling asleep and go about their business as usual. Practically all of them were found to experience a complete amnesia for the episode, and had no recollection of anything that might have precipitated the attack.

A. A. Brill, one of America's first psychoanalysts, became interested in pibloktoq and obtained additional data from one of Peary's most trusted lieutenants, Donald D. MacMillan, a professor of anthropology. MacMillan pointed out that the attacks occurred every day or two, and that eight out of the twenty women on Peary's ship, the *Roosevelt*, were affected. Investigation also revealed that the sudden outbursts were equally violent among women living in the general area, and were particularly apt to occur toward the end of the long winter's night.

MacMillan provided Dr. Brill with a number of details which both corroborate and amplify Peary's description. In a typical case, "A woman will be heard softly singing and accompanying herself by striking the fist of one hand with the palm of the second, making three sounds, one long followed by two short ones. The rhythm and motion continue for some time, during which she usually tears off her clothing, and ends in a fit of crying or screaming in which she may imitate the cry of some familiar animal or bird. No two women act alike; there is a certain individuality in every attack. Some drop down on their hands and knees and crawl around barking like a dog. One woman used to lie on her back in the snow and place some ice on her breasts. Some jump into the water and wade among the ice cakes, all the time singing and yelling. Others wander away from the houses into the hills, beating their hands as if demented." Inahloo herself, whose case was cited above, was more violent than many of the other victims, biting anyone who attempted to restrain her. She also developed her own specialty of attempting to walk on the ceiling like a bird, while uttering bird cries. During the attacks she seemed confused, disoriented, and totally oblivious of her surroundings. Her face became congested and her eyes bloodshot; she also foamed at the mouth and in general appeared "crazy."

Since Peary's North Pole expedition, there have been many reports of pibloktoq and other forms of arctic hysteria. Though the Eskimo inhabitants of Northwest Greenland are most often cited in the literature, similar disorders are quite prevalent in a number of northern societies, particularly in Iceland, the Faroe Islands, the Yukon-MacKenzie region of Alaska, the Kamchatka Peninsula in Northeast Asia, and among the inhabitants of the Kirghiz Steppes in Russia and such Siberian tribes as the Samoyeds and Yakuts. It is interesting that the disorder rarely if ever occurs among Europeans living in the arctic, which suggests that there might be a cultural and perhaps even a physiological element in the etiology (causation) of this condition. We will come back to these questions in a moment.

One of the unique aspects of the disorder is the attitude of the Eskimos toward the attacks. Viewed in terms of our own Western psychiatry, the symptoms appear to be extreme and even psychotic—but to the natives, they constitute only a mild disruption of behavior that can happen to anyone. The outbursts are accepted almost as a matter of course, and the families and friends of the victims do not get overly excited when they occur. Although they help the afflicted person by walking or running by her side to see that she comes to no harm, they seem to feel that the episode is a safety valve for pent-up emotions, a means of getting something out of the system. Perhaps this attitude of unconcern is one of the reasons the attack subsides so quickly and is not transformed into a chronic illness.

But what brings on the attack, and why does it occur among women and not men? Dr. E. F. Foulks, who has made a special study of the syndrome, reports that though the outburst appears suddenly and full-blown, it is usually preceded by a gradual increase in tension and anxiety. During this "prodromal period," the woman withdraws into herself and becomes irritable and uncommunicative. She may brood over the mistakes she made during the past year and the misfortunes she experienced, such as the loss of near relatives, or she may become increasingly fearful about the future. On board ship, an important factor appears to be a gradual intensification of fright during a long period when land is out of sight. These anxieties build up insidiously and the woman is able to keep them under control for a time. Then something occurs that triggers all these tensions at once—a sudden fright, a shocking thought or impulse, a sexual overture—and as a result, her defenses abruptly crumble and she "blows her top."

But why are women, and women alone, afflicted with this disorder, and why do the particular symptoms appear such as tearing off their clothing and running away? A closer look at the psychodynamics of arctic hysteria answers both questions in a fairly satisfactory way. The basic reason why Eskimo women are subject to periods of brooding and anxiety appears to be their inferior status in society. As MacMillan and Peary point out, the Eskimo wife is regarded as the property of her husband, and if he grows tired of her, all he has to do is to say, "There isn't room for you in my igloo," and she has to leave at once. This possibility hangs over her head all the time. But even during her normal, day-to-day life with her husband, she is starved for love and affection and is likely to be subjected to constant abuse. She does not lack sexual satisfaction, or at least sexual activity, but her need for tenderness is rarely fulfilled and she lives in constant fear of being beaten. Brill points out that "the Eskimos may be called an unmoral people in our sense. The woman is as much a part of the man's property as his dog or sledge. They indulge in trial marriage and when things do not run smoothly, they try again and again. By mutual consent wives are often exchanged between friends . . . Under such conditions it is readily comprehensible that whereas the men fully gratify their sexual impulses the women may never experience those elements of love so essential to the feminine nature," for they are "just as capable of loving as a civilized woman."

The social position of woman, then, sets the stage for her acute reactions. It also helps to explain the particular pattern of symptoms that occurs. The sudden urge to run away is the culmination of a smoldering desire for release from servitude. It may also be a bid for sympathy and attention, for she undoubtedly wants to be caught and showered with sympathy and understanding. As Mac-Millan comments, the attack "reminded me of a little child discouraged and unhappy because it imagines that no one loves it or cares for it and therefore runs away." Tearing off clothing to the point of nudity—even in weather forty degrees below zero—may be an unconscious symbolic attempt to be protected by the garment of love. It may also indicate sexual ambivalence: The desire to run away from sex because it means little to her without affection, and the desire to use sex as a means of eliciting attention since her husband was at least interested in her for this reason. The latter theory is partly corroborated by the fact that the only woman in the vicinity who was unmarried, a twenty-five-year-old, had more attacks than anyone else; and another woman had a severe attack of pibloktoq immediately following a rebuff by a white man who had been kind to her. Along this line, Foulks points out that the attacks usually culminate in writhing on the ground and orgasmlike convulsions.

The imitation of animal sounds is somewhat harder to rationalize, but Brill's comments are suggestive. He points out that "Eskimos are children in their grief as in their pleasure," and that, like children, they are subject to crying spells, laughing spells, and screaming spells: "There is hardly anything more childish than the imitation of a dog or bird, or running away into the hills singing or crying." In other words, when Eskimo women are assailed with feelings of anxiety, they have a tendency to revert to infantile behavior. One expression of this regressive tendency is the imitation of animals. This ties up with other regressive disorders such as schizophrenia, in which chronic patients sometimes produce animalistic sounds, a symptom that is termed "aboiement" (literally, "barking").

One more causative factor has been suggested. Investigators have noted that the Alaskan and Siberian diet is deficient in minerals and vitamins, and it has been suggested that periodic fits of madness not only in Eskimos themselves but in their dogs as well may be due in part to their limited nutrition. The greatest deficiency appears to be the lack of sufficient calcium, since the daily intake is only about one third that of the average European. It is a well-known fact that hypocalcemia (chronic lack of calcium) can produce acute mental disorders of various kinds. Foulks therefore suggests that this deficiency may be "a prime triggering factor in producing the symptoms of hysteria." This does not deny the effect of personal and cultural factors such as those outlined above, but rather suggests that these factors determine the particular form which the disorder takes in arctic regions. It also suggests that the solution to the problem of causation may lie in a collaboration between medical, psychoanalytic, social, and environmental factors. This "multidisciplinary approach" is one of the most important trends in present-day psychiatry and psychology.

Finally, our first question: Is pibloktoq a unique disorder? The individual symptoms are not unique—in fact, they are found in mental and emotional disorders around the world. Tearing off clothes is common among manic patients and patients suffering from schizophrenic excitement; and exhibitionism is a well-recognized sexual deviation with neurotic overtones. The compulsion to run away is found in a hysterical condition known as fugue, or "flight," and has been given the name poriomania— and the patient generally has complete amnesia for the episode, as in pibloktoq. Imitative behavior is a common symptom in some forms of schizophrenia, and also in a number of "exotic" disorders such as latah, which is found not only in Malay, but in Siberia as well, and may be related to arctic hysteria. Acute attacks of fear and rage, together with fugue, are one of the symptoms that occasionally occur in psychomotor epilepsy.

But though the individual symptoms are not unique, the *pattern* of symptoms appears to be quite individual. Brill and most other investigators reject the idea that pibloktoq is a form of epilepsy, which would put it in the class of brain disorders. He favors the view that it is hysterical in nature, and compares it to the *grande hystérie* found in the Western world, particularly in the beginning of the present century. This disorder is almost exclusively confined to the female and is characterized by unrestrained emotional outbursts of a highly dramatic character. The typical hysterical personality tends to be immature, and uses infantile methods of coping with anxiety and gaining attention and sympathy such as temper tantrums or weeping spells. Some hysterical women become subject to full-fledged attacks of hysteria in which they almost deliberately lose control over themselves, scream and shout, and act as if they were beside themselves. As in arctic hysteria, they may also finish the episode with a fit of convulsive sobbing or, in some cases, an actual convulsion.

These reactions leave little doubt that pibloktoq is a form of hysteria. But it is *arctic* hysteria, a syndrome that stems from internal and external stresses that are characteristic of the northern environment and the insecure, fear-ridden position of woman in Eskimo society.

A DISORDER CALLED KORO

About a dozen years ago a young Chinese peasant (we'll call him Wu-Ling) was admitted to the Central Civil Hospital in Batavia (now Jakarta), Java, with an advanced case of tuberculosis. Before initiating a treatment program, the physician gave Wu-Ling a complete examination from head to foot, during which he was surprised to find a crude splint attached to the young man's genital organ. The splint consisted of a piece of wood held in place by two loops of cord tied around the penis, plus a piece of heavy wire wrapped around the base of the organ to keep the wood securely in place.

Within a day or so, the peculiar apparatus was brought to the attention of Dr. P. Van Wilfften Palthe, a physician engaged in anthropological research in the area. He at once suspected that Wu-Ling might be suffering from koro, a strange disorder which he had heard about but had never actually seen.

Dr. Palthe immediately came to the hospital, examined the splint, and asked Wu-Ling why he wore it. The young man insisted that if he did not wear it, his penis would shrivel up and disappear into his stomach—and if that happened, he would immediately collapse and die. He had tried holding on to the organ, but this kept him home and prevented him from earning his livelihood in the rice fields. He then told the doctor that he had heard that other men had the same fear of losing the penis, and that some of them bought a special clamp to keep it in place. However, he did not know where to obtain the clamp and was too poor to afford it anyway. He had therefore devised one of his own making.

This account confirmed the fact that Wu-Ling's disorder was a genuine case of koro, the term for "shrink" in the Buginese language of the neighboring island of Borneo. Further inquiry, however, revealed that among the Chinese the condition was known as *shook yong*, which literally signified "shrinking penis." Palthe found that the morbid fear, or phobia, of losing the penis and dying generally comes on suddenly and lasts for several days or even weeks. The first reaction, as with Wu-Ling, is to prevent the organ from "shooting into the belly" by holding it in a vicelike grip. The patient soon becomes fatigued, however, and calls upon others to help him. His wife, if he has one, is the first to come to his assistance, and she holds the organ with her hand (and in some cases in her mouth) as long as she can. When she tires, the patient's relatives and friends gather in a circle around him and solemnly take turns holding the organ. As Palthe points out in an article on the subject, "They must all see to it that the penis is not released for a single instant; otherwise *in it shoots* and death follows inevitably! After long, weary hours of vigil, an attack gradually wears off, but is repeated again and again."

The instrument to which Wu-Ling referred is called a *lie teng hok*, and is a wooden device used by goldsmiths and apothecaries in weighing powdered metal. It is shaped somewhat like scissors, and the penis is placed between the two prongs, with a ring to tighten its hold. The disorder is so common among the Chinese that the device is in considerable demand, since it can be worn as long as the phobia lasts.

Chinese doctors, however, disapprove of its use except in cases of emergency. They claim that it does nothing to cure the disease itself, and that this can only be accomplished by applying principles of medicine which have been handed down from generation to generation for many centuries. This tradition is based on the belief that the world is governed by two forces, yang and yin. Yang is the male principle, and the word stands not only for masculinity but for the spirit of heaven, the sun, day, warmth, the living, the positive, and the strong. Yin, the female principle, stands in opposition to yang, and is expressed by birth, the moon, night, cold, death, the negative, and the weak. It follows that when the penis, the masculine organ, shrinks and disappears, the yin principle takes over completely and death is bound to follow. According to Chinese medicine men, the disease in which this occurs, shook yong, can be cured in one way only—by taking yang medicines. They therefore prescribe such concoctions as ground rhinoceros horn, a mixture of gunpowder and arak, powdered tin blended with sulphur, and selected medicinal herbs which are believed to restore masculinity.

If these medications work, they work only by suggestion—and this is quite possible, since the disorder is psychological and not physical in nature. And if they do not work, there is no evidence whatever that the dread consequences of the "disease" will take place. As Dr. Palthe puts it, "No one ever saw anybody die of a penis retracted into the belly, but that does not in any way lessen the strength of the belief in such a possibility. The disease *exists* because it *must* exist! This is, in fact, always the course of logic in the primitive folklore: the penis is the center, the essence of life; a corpse, then, has no penis, it is retracted into the belly. This argument is then inverted and they say, 'Whenever the penis exhibits the tendency to retraction, whenever it is seen to start shrinking, danger threatens. If it should actually succeed in disappearing into the belly, that means death.' This collective fantasy is a typical product of primitive reasoning; the mystic 'pars pro toto' (a part taken for the whole) idea perpetuates in the face of all factual evidence the belief that a corpse has no penis, for surely it *could* not have one! The conclusion drawn therefrom is of the same nature, irrefutably, although no one has ever seen a patient die of shook yong with his own eyes, and although there are all over China, even at the present, eunuchs enough, who have been deprived of their penis as well as their testes, to be a clear and definite living disproof of the truth of the reasoning."

What, then, produces this phobia and this fantasy? As Dr. Palthe points out, koro, or shook yong, is actually an anxiety neurosis, and the anxiety arises from sexual conflicts. These conflicts may be due in some cases to infidelity, or in others to urges or actual practices which the patient regards as perverted or sinful. Feelings of guilt are probably involved in every instance, and it is these feelings that generate the fear that the patient will be punished not only by losing his penis but by losing his life as well, since his heritage says that masculinity means life and the deprivation of masculinity means death.

There is evidence that though this phobia is based on feelings of guilt, it may in some cases be precipitated by a real or fancied physical condition. Some patients have reported that they began fearing the loss of the organ when they indulged in sexual acts at too early an age, or at times when they were too fatigued or weak to carry through. In Wu-Ling's case, excessive masturbation appears to have brought the fear to the surface. When questioned about his sex life, he admitted that he had always had difficulties in his relationship with women, and that he had been too timid to associate with them. As a consequence, he had led a celibate life and had released his sexual tension through frequent masturbation. His parents, however, had become aware of this habit, and warned him that if he continued to masturbate excessively, his penis would shrivel up and shoot inside—in other words, they threatened him with shook yong. Although their admonition made a deep impression on Wu-Ling, he found that he was unable to cease the practice, and as a result became so filled with anxiety over the dire consequences that he finally resorted to anchoring down his organ with a makeshift splint.

Anyone familiar with psychoanalytic theory will be bound to note the similarity between the koro phobia and the concept of castration anxiety. Palthe himself calls the disorder "a living example of Freud's castration complex." The fear of being deprived of one's genital organs is central in the Freudian theory of psychosexual development, and is intimately associated with another key concept, the Oedipus complex. Briefly, Freud held that between the ages of three and seven, every boy symbolically re-enacts the ancient myth of Oedipus in which the Greek king was doomed to slay his father and marry his mother. In the Freudian theory this means that the boy falls in love with his mother and regards his father as a deadly rival. Since this incestuous love is sexual in nature, he then acquires an unconscious fear that his powerful rival will punish him by depriving him of his guilty organ.

As pointed out in *The Encyclopedia of Human Behavior,* three other factors tend to intensify this fear: First, "the boy may have dreams or fantasies that his rival, the father, has lost his own penis, and guilt feelings aroused by these thoughts make him afraid that he will be deprived of his own penis in retaliation"; second, "this fear is fed by threats, reproaches, or physical punishment, which is ordinarily practiced during this period. This may have a particularly strong effect on boys who have incest fantasies involving the mother during masturbatory activity. It must be recognized that outright castration threats are seldom made. However, because of his latent anxieties, the child transforms warnings against masturbation such as 'It will make you sick' into the fear that he will lose his penis"; and third, "This fantasy is intensified when he discovers, through games like 'Doctor,' that girls do not possess a penis. This suggests that the organ can actually be taken away."

As they develop, most boys resolve the Oedipus situation and rid themselves of castration fear by gradually identifying with their father and by forming sexual attachments to girls of their own age. Some, however, remain "fixated" at the Oedipal stage and as a consequence, they remain bachelors, live with their parents, spend their lives looking fruitlessly for, as the song says, "A girl just like the girl who married dear old dad," marry a woman much older than themselves, or adopt the characteristics of the mother and become either a latent or an overt homosexual. Moreover, these men may be haunted by an unconscious castration anxiety for the rest of their lives —an anxiety that evidences itself in dreams, fantasies, and neurotic behavior symbolically related to sex.

Freud did not confine castration fear to the male, although he offered few details on the feminine form of the complex. He did point out, however, that girls become attached to their father and develop feelings of hostility toward their mother. He also held that they unconsciously feel that they have been deprived of a penis as a punishment for sexual interest in the father, and they often blame the loss of the organ on their rival, the mother. In light of this theory, it is interesting that women in Borneo and other parts of Southeast Asia have been found to suffer from a feminine equivalent of koro in which the principal symptoms are the feeling that their breasts are shriveling up and that their labia are being sucked inward.

On the face of it, the male form of the Freudian theory would seem to apply to Wu-Ling—except for the important point that we do not know anything about his relationship to his father and mother. Nevertheless, a strict Freudian would probably suspect or assume that the Oedipus complex was operating in his case, and that the phobia was therefore produced by an incestuous desire for his mother and a fear that he would be deprived of his penis as punishment for this guilty urge. The warning that the penis would shoot into the belly would, then, be the Indonesian cultural equivalent of the castration complex. On that assumption, the orthodox Freudian might conclude that the existence of koro is concrete evidence that the psychoanalytic interpretation applies in Eastern as well as Western societies.

But it is important to recognize that many non-Freudians have denied the applicability of the Oedipus situation and the castration complex in *both* cultural areas, the occidental and the oriental. Alfred Adler, one of the first to break away from Freud, felt that if rivalry between the boy and his father does arise, it stems from the boy's desire to prove that he is at least the equal of his father in strength and attractiveness—and if the girl becomes attached to the father and hostile to the mother she does so out of a desire to reject feminine inferiority and identify with the superior status of the male in our society. Karen Horney, and other non-Freudians, deny that the Oedipus complex and castration fear are either normal or universal. If they do develop, she maintains, they are expressions of a neurotic relationship fostered by parents who caress their children erotically, allow them to witness their own sexual relations, or adopt provocative and seductive attitudes toward their children of the opposite sex.

Whether or not one accepts the psychoanalytic interpretation, the koro phobia accentuates several significant facts about human behavior. First, it demonstrates that primitive as well as "advanced" peoples place special emphasis on sexual potency. In all cultural areas, the individual's "self-concept" is intimately dependent on sexual ability. Second, the sex organs are an area of special sensitivity, and any threat to these organs—in actuality or in fantasy—is particularly disturbing. Third, neurotic conflicts may be expressed in sexual terms in the East as well as the West. And fourth, sexual taboos of one kind or another—against incest, excessive masturbation, etc.—are probably found in every society.

Koro, or shook yong, is not simply a cultural curiosity, but an expression of these four fundamental aspects of human behavior.

Animals and Men

The comment has frequently been made that psychologists have learned almost as much about human nature from animals as from men. We would not know nearly as much about the learning process if the lowly rat had not run thousands of miles of mazes. Our knowledge of conditioning was derived largely from Pavlov's dogs and Skinner's pigeons. An untold number of apes and monkeys have contributed to our understanding of the structure of the human brain and the way it is used in thinking and solving problems. Animals are the psychologist's best friends.

Experiments with animals, then, have helped us gain much of our knowledge of human behavior. But beyond experimentation lies the case approach, the one we are using in this book. And we could find no better way to close these chapters than to report on three dramatic cases that show some of the more unusual ways that man relates to animals.

The stories have been chosen not because they illustrate the obvious fact that most of us have a deep interest in animals of one kind or another, but because they shed light on some of the extremes of human behavior—which has been the theme of this book. One of the stories will show how close a tie there can be between man and animal; another will deal with a strange disorder that is likely to disappear because the animal involved is in danger of extinction; and the third will revolve around an elderly educator who devoted the last years of his life to teaching a four-footed pupil, apparently with remarkable success.

RELUCTANT HUSBAND

The wedding had taken place that morning, and as she prepared for "the first night," Lucy looked back on the gala affair. At the time she had been so excited that now it was hard to re-create all the details. But she did recall detecting a touch of envy beneath the smiles of some of her bridesmaids, for John had long been the most eligible bachelor in the office, and several of the girls had been interested in him. About a year before, however, he had begun to date her and after an on-and-off courtship had finally proposed. She could not help allowing herself a moment of triumph, for John was not only good looking and an excellent horseman, but was highly intelligent and clearly "on the way up."

As these thoughts passed through Lucy's mind she began to notice that John was taking an interminable time getting ready for bed. At first she said nothing about it, for fear of appearing overeager. But when he continued to dally, she ventured the question, "Aren't you ever coming to bed?" He then began to complain that he must have drunk too much champagne and was suffering from an excruciating headache; "Maybe if I sit up for a few minutes, it will go away." The minutes, however, stretched into an hour, and by that time Lucy, fatigued from her strenuous day, had fallen into a deep sleep.

The next night there was another excuse, and the next still another. During the day John appeared relaxed and content, and the two enjoyed the many activities of a happy honeymoon. But as night approached, Lucy invariably found that a change came over her husband. He became distant, detached, and obviously upset. Finally she gathered the courage to ask him if he had any regrets about the marriage, reminding him that he had taken over a year to propose and perhaps was even now uncertain of his feelings. He assured her that he had no regrets whatever and loved her dearly. That night he seemed particularly nervous and apprehensive—but he finally consummated the marriage.

Lucy was surprised at John's apparent nervousness, for he appeared to be a highly sophisticated and self-confident young man. However, since she was somewhat nervous herself, she tried to understand his behavior, assuming that he was less experienced than he appeared to be.

But the problem did not stop there. As the marriage went on, John reacted more and more violently. After every act of intercourse he would sit on the edge of the bed, wring his hands, and exclaim that it was wrong of him to do so, and that he must not do it again! At first Lucy took this strange behavior as a personal affront, but after thinking it over she decided that he must have some kind of emotional problem which he needed time to overcome. Though puzzled and perplexed, she decided to endure the peculiarity rather than make an issue of it.

As time went on, the marriage became better established, but there was no improvement in sexual relations. However, on one of the infrequent occasions when intercourse did occur, Lucy conceived. When the child was born, she devoted herself so wholeheartedly to it that she became less disturbed about the problem with her husband. Meanwhile, he had made rapid progress in his profession and was soon recognized as one of the town's leading citizens. His fortunes continued to rise, and he became prosperous enough to indulge his one great desire, that of owning a fine riding horse. After considerable searching, he found a young mare and had a stable built on his property. The animal was a great source of pride to him, and he would often discuss its good points with his wife and neighbors.

Life became more settled for the couple, but the sexual problem persisted and took a new turn. John had ceased wringing his hands after each act of intercourse, but instead would jump up from the bed, dress, and leave the room, returning an hour or so later in a quiet and composed state of mind. For an explanation of this unusual behavior, here is an excerpt from the original report of this case as it was given by the psychiatrist Karl A. Menninger:

"One night for reasons which she was unable clearly to explain, his wife resolved to follow him upon one of his mysterious disappearances from their bedroom. She trailed him to the stable where to her utter amazement she observed him in the act of cohabiting with his mare. She was most of all impressed by the fact that not only did the man show the utmost evidence of affection for the mare, kissing and fondling her as if she were a woman, but the mare showed definite and unmistakable signs of responding to his maneuvers with sexual pleasure.

"The wife was thunderstruck by her discovery, so much so that she confronted her husband with it immediately. He fell on his knees before her, broke into loud sobbing, confessed that his behavior had gone on since several years before their marriage, and that his great distress in marrying her was not his shame about it, but his feeling that he was being unfaithful to the various mares with whom he had love affairs and sexual relations."

Incredible as this revelation appeared to her, Lucy was forced to accept it, for she had actually witnessed evidence of her husband's perverse attachment. Disgusted and repelled by the episode, she was tempted to call an end to the marriage on the spot. But her husband was so genuinely penitent and guilt-ridden that she decided to continue, provided he got rid of the mare as soon as possible. He readily agreed, vowing that he would lead a normal life from that moment on.

True to his word, John sold the mare and did everything possible to convince his wife that he had conquered his perversion. To demonstrate his interest in her, he stayed home every night and was more attentive than he had ever been. "For a time," Menninger relates, "all was well. Then, contrary to his promise, he became interested in another mare and purchased her over his wife's protests. He assured his wife that he would not become involved in a sexual interest in this mare, that it was a good investment, and that it looked silly for a man who had been a horse fancier as long as he had to refrain from as good a purchase as this was, etc. Ultimately, the same situation developed again. He became more and more passionately attached to the mare, petted and caressed her in a manner which his wife, in the light of her knowledge, found unbearable. He then began disappearing at night for short periods in as surreptitious a way as possible to continue his affair with the mare."

This time Lucy gave her husband an ultimatum: If he did not give up the mares completely and permanently, she would file a suit for divorce. The threat and the fear that he might be publicly exposed threw him into a panic, and he resolved to break away from his sexual deviation once and for all.

Dr. Menninger concludes his case report with these words: "He again sold his beloved mare, and once more assumed the role of a good husband, meanwhile maintaining an outward demeanor such that no one in the community ever suspected any of these discoveries, so far as his wife knew. She continued to live with him until she discovered that he was clandestinely continuing to practice bestiality with various horses. Upon this discovery she left him flatly, arranging for separate maintenance, promising to refrain from suing him for divorce and exposing him on condition that he pay her properly and remain away from her and the child."

The case of John and Lucy (the names and narration are the author's) raises some compelling questions about the prevalence of different types of sexual relations between man and animal. Studies of bestiality (also termed zooerasty, zoophilia, and sodomy) indicate that it is more common than many people recognize. Kinsey and his collaborators reported that 8 per cent of all males and 17 per cent in rural areas admitted to at least one full sexual experience with animals. The percentage in rural areas rises to 50 per cent when the definition is not confined to actual intercourse, but includes such practices as stimulation through friction against the animal and masturbation of the animal. Bestiality is far more common among males than females, with whom it usually takes the form of self-masturbation through bodily friction with the animal, which has been given the technical name of *frottage* (French for "rubbing").

The Encyclopedia of Human Behavior gives some further data on this deviation: "Sexual contact with animals appears to be a universal phenomenon, since laws and taboos concerning bestiality are found in practically all societies. Most religious codes, including the Old Testament, condemn the practice, but it is permitted in a few societies, particularly during initiation ceremonies. In our culture the practice usually results from observing coitus between animals. Boys and young men find this form of voyeurism sexually stimulating, and some decide to experiment with animals themselves. If they do not have an adequate opportunity for heterosexual relations, or if others around them engage in this behavior, they may make a regular practice of bestiality."

An extremely wide variety of animals has been used as sexual objects in different cultures. In our society mares and dogs are probably the most common, but other farm animals such as ducks and geese may serve the purpose. In a Canadian Indian tribe, the Salteaux, sexual relations with the following animals have been reported: woman with dog, and man with bear, caribou, porcupine, and even the female moose just after it has been shot. The Mohaves extend this list to include heifers, sows, hens, and female asses. In Peru the practice is so prevalent among llama herders that there is a law forbidding men to herd these animals unless they are accompanied by women. North African natives have been found to engage in the sadistic practice of having coitus with hens while twisting the animals' neck in order to reach orgasm as it flutters to death. In addition, the origin of syphilis has been attributed to bestial relations, and some Arab tribes seek to cure this disease by having relations with mares (a variant of the myth that gonorrhea can be cured by coitus with a virgin). And in Indochina, an animal may not be sacrificed if it has had relations with a human being, since this would make it the "wife" of a human, and therefore human itself.

One last question is whether bestiality is a psychiatric disorder. The answer is, not in and of itself. It depends on the circumstances and motivation. The young country boy who engages in this practice on a dare or simply as an experiment is probably within the limits of normality, hazy as they are. But if he continues the practice compulsively, and as he grows up prefers relations with animals to relations with women; or if he is virtually incapable of normal relations—as was the case with John —he is undoubtedly suffering from an emotional disturbance.

Two types of explanation are generally given for this disorder. The first is that the individual (male or female) feels sexually or socially inadequate and as a result develops a fear that he will not be able to perform successfully, and/or a fear of rejection if he tries to establish an intimate relation with the opposite sex. These fears are often repressed and therefore operate on an unconscious level. Most individuals do not realize they exist unless they undergo psychotherapy (which John refused). Many authorities believe this pattern also applies to other sexual deviations such as voyeurism, exhibitionism, and pedophilia (sexual activity with children).

The second type of explanation is based on the theory of psychoanalysis. According to Freud, every child develops an Oedipus complex early in his psychosexual growth. As mentioned in "A Disorder Called Koro," the term refers to an erotic attraction to the parent of the opposite sex, accompanied by feelings of rivalry and hostility toward the parent of the same sex. ("Electra complex" is sometimes used for the girl's attachment to her father.)

The child, however, feels guilty about the attachment, and may seek to resolve this conflict on an unconscious level by transferring his sexual feelings to an animal. This would mean, quite simply, that some people not only develop a special interest in animals such as horses, but eventually become sexually involved with them. Menninger himself accepts this theory, stating that "some private totems represent the secret retention of a forbidden loved object in a substituted form, and the enacting of these feelings toward them characteristic of the childhood epoch. It is as if a boy, sexually aroused by his mother or sister, but forbidden by circumstances and prohibitions from gratifying his instincts, displaced his fantasies to animal intimates of his childhood life. They can make no protest, they can be approached surreptitiously and, moreover, they have the right to expect affection which is commonly encouraged toward domestic animals."

The relationship with animals is usually abandoned before the child reaches maturity, for "later, more desirable objects present themselves and the child either loses interest or is forced by public opinion of his comrades to relinquish sexual utilization of the beloved animal. Probably in the majority of cases, certainly in the majority of cases of city-bred people, these affections never extend beyond mild, one might almost say, platonic friendliness, or occasional sporting enthusiasm." However, in a small minority the attachment is expressed in full-fledged sexual relations with animals not only in childhood but in adulthood as well—perhaps because the "Oedipal conflict" has never been adequately resolved.

We are left, then, with two types of explanation for bestiality among adults: fear of inadequacy or impotence, and unconscious substitution of animal relationships for human relationships. Which of these applies to John?

Menninger emphasizes the second alternative, but does not support this conclusion with evidence from the young man's life history (presumably because he was not psycho-analyzed). It may well be that he felt guilty about sexual relations with his wife because of his long and intimate association with horses, and the guilt might have given rise to a fear that he would be rendered impotent with her as a punishment for violating the moral code. This may have set the stage for continuing his sexual involvement with mares, an involvement that probably stemmed from long-standing fears and conflicts. In this way the two theories might be combined into one.

MAN INTO BEAST

"The soul of these tiger-men, who in outward appearance are in no way different from ordinary men, is said at times to dwell in a tiger . . . Although I had come across a good many things that were far beyond the bounds of probability, I was still extremely skeptical about these stories until two years ago when a curious thing happened to me. I found myself in a little place near Tomati [Hindustan] where I had gone to settle some disputes. The natives there showed me a tiger-man whose soul, they said, had 'gone into his tiger' for the time being. He seemed like a drunken man, lay in his hut, took no food, and only gave confused replies when questioned. In fact, he appeared to be, as they said, 'without a soul.' On the third day his condition changed quite suddenly, and he appeared in my tent perfectly active and full of life but in great mental distress. My interpreter translated his explanations. He, or rather the tiger in which he had lived for the last three days, had attacked a man a few miles north of where we were, and he besought us to go there quickly in case it might still be possible to bring aid to his victim. Weeping, he protested over and over again, 'I did not want to do it, but the tiger was so strong.' Something made me follow the man. After a short march we came upon the terribly mauled body of a Burmese. And nearby was the trail of a tiger . . ."

This fantastic tale, quoted in a book by Herbert Tichy entitled *Tibetan Adventure*, does not end here. Its denouement stretches credulity even further. The narrator, a "cool, level-headed Englishman," continued his story after a thoughtful silence, "I know for certain that two months ago English friends shot a very fine tiger, and at precisely the same moment when they killed the tiger, without any external cause whatever, the tiger-man died in Tomati. I know the exact minute, my agent swears it and is a most accurate person."

This account might easily be dismissed as pure hearsay, primitive superstition, or a typical traveler's tale. But even if we maintain that finding the mauled man was mere coincidence, and even if we insist that no one could really know that the tiger and the man died at precisely the same moment, we are still left with some intriguing questions: How prevalent is the tiger-man belief? How does this supposed affinity between man and beast develop? Is it a symptom of mental disorder? Are there other myths of a similar nature?

Tiger-men, and leopard-men as well, have been found in two general localities: The Naga district situated between Assam and Burma—the locus of the story just quoted—and in large parts of West Africa. There is a marked contrast between the beliefs and associated practices in the two areas, and they will therefore be described separately.

In the Assam-Burma region of Hindustan, the tradition takes a thoroughly benign form in spite of the fact that the Nagas are wild and picturesque savages. The tiger-man (and rarely tiger-woman) is a deeply disturbed individual who suddenly comes to believe that his soul has been projected into the body of a particular tiger, and that consequently he is responsible for everything the tiger does. C. P. Mills, who has lived and worked in the Assam hills, notes that "It is sometimes said that the affliction is catching, and that a man can become a leopard-man by habitually consorting with a leopard-man. It usually happens, however, that the symptoms occur in a man willy-nilly for no apparent reason. It should be clearly understood that no one wants to become a leopard-man. It is a most infernal nuisance. For one thing it is exceedingly fatiguing, for the man is exhausted by the activities of his leopard. For another thing, leopard-men are always getting into trouble. Suppose I am a leopard-man. My leopard goes and kills someone's pig. The owner of the pig rather naturally comes and abuses me. Not only that, but if he can he will shoot or spear my leopard, in which case I shall die."

Being a tiger-man, then, is more than a nuisance, it is downright dangerous. Mills goes on to point out that tiger-men lead highly nervous lives, not only because they are held responsible for the actions of their soul mate, but because "an injury to the leopard or tiger involves an injury to the man to whom it belongs. Wounds are believed to appear on the human body corresponding to wounds on the animal body . . . It should be understood that the wound on the human body does not appear simultaneously with that inflicted on the animal, but some days later, when the man has learnt of the condition of his leopard or tiger." He illustrates this point by citing the case of a man named Saiyi who heard that a tiger had been found wounded, and announced that it was his animal. He immediately took to bed and within three days had to be carried to the government hospital on a stretcher. The doctors found that he was suffering agonizing pain from two swellings, one on either side of the stomach, which he claimed corresponded to the entrance and exit holes of the bullet which had hit the tiger. The man eventually died in the hospital.

But why do men project their soul into a tiger or leopard? There are two answers to this question, one in terms of the folk beliefs of the region, the other in terms of modern psychology. Among the Nagas, the belief stems from two sources: their theory of the soul, and the tiger legends of the district. The Nagas view the soul as an entity that may become detached from the body—what J. G. Frazer calls the "external soul." If it leaves the body and takes up an abode in the Land of the Dead, it will never return, for the owner dies. On the other hand it may depart from the person's body temporarily, as it does in dreams. Or it may be captured by an evil spirit, in which case the owner becomes ill, and can get his soul and his health back only by performing appropriate ceremonies. In still other cases, however, the soul may temporarily abide in the body of a tiger or a leopard (or "little tiger"), since the Nagas maintain that there is an intimate connection between these animals and human beings.

The explanation of this connection has been handed down from generation to generation. According to their folklore, a man, a spirit, and a tiger were born of the same mother. However, the offspring differed in three basic ways: The man preferred his meat cooked, the spirit just dried his in the smoke, and the tiger ate his raw. These differences caused so much friction that eventually the family split up and the three offspring went their separate ways. However, the bond between man and tiger remained strong, and different tribes developed their own versions of the relationship. Among the Angami Nagas, for example, tigers are held in such great respect that if a tiger dies, a period of mourning is proclaimed and the entire village performs the rites reserved for an older brother. Among the Chang Nagas, one entire clan is made up of tiger-men and tiger-women. According to their tribal legend, this clan was spared by the tigers during the Universal Deluge when all men and animals were crowded on the tops of the highest mountains, and ever since they have regarded themselves as tiger-folk. Among the Lhota Nagas, only the medicine man is a leopard- or tiger-man. Most common, however, is the belief of the Sema Nagas studied by Tichy and Mills. It is their belief that the soul may leave the body during sleep, or more rarely in waking life, and reside for a time in the body of a particular tiger—and that while it is in the tiger, the man is not only aware of all its actions, but responsible for them.

What is the psychological explanation of the tiger-man belief among the Hindustani? There is little doubt that the entire phenomenon can be attributed to a combination of fear and suggestibility. First, the entire region has long been infested with man-killing tigers, and natives who could not cope with their anxiety in any other way sought to allay their fear of the ferocious animal by identifying with it. By sharing their soul with the tiger or leopard, they gained a feeling of power and security —but at the same time they had to pay the price of taking responsibility for the animal's destructive behavior.

Second, stories of this marauding beast were passed from person to person and inflamed the imagination of the natives to a point where the animals' activities occupied a major part of their dreams and fantasies—and since they made little if any distinction between fact and fantasy, reality and dream, they could readily believe that there was a special bond between the tiger and themselves.

Third, some of the natives undoubtedly suffered from hallucinations and attempted to explain their state of mind by claiming that they were possessed by a tiger, just as mentally ill people in the Middle Ages attributed their symptoms to possession by demons. Fourth, it is very likely that many tiger-men were afflicted with hysteria, a neurotic disorder involving a high degree of suggestibility. Hysterical reactions are known to be particularly common in the region between Assam and Burma, and it is also significant that hypnosis, which is based on the power of suggestion, is widely practiced in some of the villages, including Tomati. The pains and swellings suffered by tiger-men like Saiyi can readily be explained as hysterical symptoms, since they have many parallels in the West as well as in the East. A suggestible husband may identify so completely with his pregnant wife that he suffers morning sickness or even labor pains. Swellings and even blisters have been produced by hypnotic suggestion. And stigmata, or the wounds of Christ, are generally attributed to a combination of emotional identification and extreme suggestibility. (See "The Unhealing Wounds.")

Fifth, another disturbance involving a high degree of suggestibility is frequently seen in this area: catalepsy. During a cataleptic episode, the patient's skeletal muscles become semirigid, and he remains in one position for many minutes or even hours. If his arms or legs are moved by others, they stay in the same position, however awkward it may be, like the limbs of a jointed doll. The disorder may be accompanied by a trance state, and though the victim appears stuporous to the outsider, he may actually be experiencing vivid fantasies and hallucinations. When he awakens from the cataleptic trance, the native in this region may say that his soul has been transported into his tiger, and he will give a graphic description of the animal's behavior while it was in his body. He will tell, for example, how he was trapped and managed to escape, or how he rescued his mate, or how he hunted and killed his prey. These accounts may be so convincing to his fellow tribesmen that if the tiger-man claims that his animal is in a certain locality, they may tie him up before embarking on the hunt, believing that in this way they will impede the animal's movements.

Sixth, the death of the tiger-man can also be explained by the power of suggestion. As D. H. Rawcliffe points out in *The Psychology of the Occult*, "His belief that the death of a tiger must be followed by his own is part and parcel of his mental background, fixed ineradicably in his mind by centuries of tribal superstition." Moreover, it is important to note that he does not begin to suffer until *after* he has learned that the tiger has been shot. But when he has been told about the fate of his "animal familiar," he immediately feels that he himself has been wounded, and therefore expects to suffer and even die. There is good reason to believe, as the physiologist Walter B. Cannon has shown in his study of voodoo death, that suggestion and expectation can have such a powerful effect on the vasomotor system, which controls the heart, that the victim may wither away and die within a few days or even a few hours. (See "The Will to Die.")

Although the tiger- and leopard-men of the Burma-Assam region are frequently blamed for the depredations of their animal familiars, they are actually harmless and rather pathetic creatures. If they inflict any injury it is only on themselves, for they probably produce the wounds which they claim to correspond to the wounds suffered by their animal. The self-mutilation occurs during their trance state in response to fantasies and hallucinations.

In sharp contrast to the timid and troubled tiger-men of Hindustan, the leopard-men, hyena-men and crocodile-men of West Africa organize themselves into secret societies that prey upon their fellow tribesmen. There is apparently no limit to their sadistic attacks. As Rawcliffe points out, "They deliberately foster belief in their lycanthropical powers by dressing in the skin of the wild animal, leaving tracks in the ground pertaining to the animal-fetish of the secret society in question, and leaving their victims torn and lacerated in imitation of a wild beast. Such practices for the most part serve merely to gratify a ghastly cruelty, inspired and directed by the local ju-ju-man or witch doctor. The unfortunate victims frequently have their entrails torn out while they still live. Such secret societies were often cannibalistic—they practiced devouring parts of the human anatomy such as the heart, eyes and liver, and the more tender parts of the flesh. The trails leading away from the scene of the crime would be those of a hyena or leopard or crocodile, but after some distance the tracks of the human foot would supplant them to leave no doubt that it was the leopard-man or hyena-man who had been at work. The terror created by such methods in the minds of the primitive blacks can well be imagined. Furthermore, if one of the lycanthropists was shot or wounded, it is easy to see how stories of lycanthropical metamorphosis might spread. A state of extreme emotional tension and high suggestibility and expectation would be aroused among the local population, in which delusions and even visual hallucinations might occur, giving further impetus to the myth of actual lycanthropical transformations." It might be added that suggestion plays a large role in inducing these hallucinations and delusions, for the incantations of the witch doctor, accompanied by the monotonous beating of the drums, undoubtedly produce a hypnotic effect on the frightened natives.

Finally, we have clear evidence that lycanthropy is more prevalent than many people realize, particularly in societies where superstition prevails. It has been traced to biblical days—for example, Nebuchadnezzar, king of ancient Babylon, suffered from the delusion that he was a wolf. From the fifteenth to the seventeenth centuries the werewolf delusion reached epidemic proportions in isolated areas of Italy and other Western countries. In fact, it was so common that the term lycanthropy itself means "wolf-man," although it is now applied more generally to any delusion involving the transformation of man into beast. A representative example is the lycanthrope who was reputed to commit acts of violence in a mountainous region of Italy. When he was captured and brought to trial, he insisted that he was really a wolf in man's clothing. During the examination the judge asked why his skin was smooth instead of hairy, and he explained in a confidential tone of voice that in his case the hairy coat grew inward instead of outward.

During the epidemic of lycanthropy that occurred in continental Europe, the victims of this disorder were subjected to unspeakable cruelty and brutality. We now realize that many, if not all of them, were suffering from mental disorders; but at that time the authorities held that they were possessed by Satan, and sought to extract confessions of wrongdoing by inflicting excruciating torture upon them. As an example, the wolf-man who claimed he wore his hairy coat inside was sentenced to amputation of his arms and legs to convince him of the error of his ways—but he died unconvinced. Boquet, the chief magistrate of a district of the Jura Mountains of France, boasted that he had more than six hundred lycanthropes and demonolaters burned at the stake in the year 1541. Among them were many reputed witches accused of sexual misconduct. According to his own statement, "Ugliness and depravity are shown by Satan in his carnal knowledge of these sorceresses. To some he appeared in the form of a black man; to others, as some beast or other—dog, cat, he-goat, or ram." In his article on "Psychiatry Through the Ages," Stone makes this comment, "The lycanthrope and some of the witches were probably cases of dementia praecox [schizophrenia], while the orgies they confessed to possibly represented the illusions or hallucinations or actual reports of pagan rites still practiced in isolated hamlets which Christianity did not penetrate deeply."

To show that lycanthropic illusions were practically universal, we end with a note on animal delusion in the Far East. In her book entitled *Hysteria: The History of a Disease*, Ilza Veith states, "No single figure has had as important a role in Chinese and Japanese fantasy as that played by the fox." At first this animal was a benign creature, but later the Japanese adopted the traditional Chinese belief that foxes were demons who could "either enter human beings and take possession of their souls, or themselves assume human appearance in order to exert their influence on others." That influence was a baneful one and was believed to account for all types of psychic ills including not only insanity, but such sexual disorders as frigidity, impotence, nymphomania, and satyriasis.

As an example, Veith cites the case of a young girl who suddenly became insane and showed unmistakable signs of "fox possession." When subjected to searching questions, the answers were given by a voice recognized as that of a fox, who revealed that "her mother, a widow, had illicit intercourse with a silk merchant who often passed the night in her house. After having made these revelations, the fox 'went out of' the patient, the silk merchant fled, the widow was sent back to her native village, and the girl, now completely restored, went to the house of relatives. This case suggests that the weight of the guilt and knowledge of her mother's improper conduct so preyed upon her as to cause emotional disturbance. Unable because of considerations of filial piety or fear of loss of face to reveal this secret, she unconsciously took refuge in the fox disguise and so achieved her purpose."

Apparently, possession by a fox was a convenient way of explaining mental aberrations. And undoubtedly our picture of the vixen, or female fox, as a mischief-maker stems from this ancient superstition, just as the men and women of Hindustan blamed their ills on their soul mate, the tiger.

THE MYSTERY OF
THE THINKING HORSE

The scene was a paved courtyard surrounded by high apartment houses in the northern part of Berlin, and the year was 1904. A group of people were standing around with their eyes riveted on a stately Russian trotting horse. Beside him, on the right, stood a seventy-year-old man with a white beard, wearing a long gray coat and a slouch hat. For the second time that day, Wilhelm Von Osten, who looked more like a schoolteacher than a horse trainer, was putting his charge through his paces. And well he might look like a teacher, for instead of issuing the usual commands to turn, stop, etc., he was asking such questions as "How much is two and three?" and "I have a number in mind. I subtract nine and have three as a remainder. What is the number I had in mind?" And to each question Clever Hans, the horse, would tap out the correct answer with his right foreleg.

Practically everyone has witnessed remarkable performances by animals in circuses or vaudeville houses. Lions obey the whip of their trainer, monkeys ride unicycles, dogs jump through flaming hoops, and some even bark the answers to simple mathematical problems. But Von Osten's horse was apparently in a class by himself, as a few excerpts from an account of his feats will indicate: "He had, apparently, completely mastered the cardinal numbers from 1 to 100 and the ordinals to ten, at least. Upon request he would count objects of all sorts, the persons present, even to distinctions of sex. Then hats, umbrellas, and eyeglasses. Even the mechanical activity of tapping seemed to reveal a measure of intelligence. Small numbers were given with a slow tapping of the right foot. With larger numbers he would increase his speed . . . The four fundamental processes were entirely familiar to him. Common fractions he changed to decimals, and vice versa; he could solve problems in mensuration—and all with such ease that it was difficult to follow him if one had become somewhat rusty in these branches.

"The following problems are illustrations of the kind he solved: 'How much is 2/5 plus 1/2?' Answer: 9/10. (In the case of all fractions Hans would first tap the numerator then the denominator; in this case, therefore, first 9, then 10.) 'What are the factors of 28?' Whereupon Hans tapped consecutively 2, 4, 7, 14, 28."

But mathematics was not Hans's only field of accomplishment, nor was tapping his only mode of expression. He would answer a question that required a yes by nodding his head, and one that required a no by shaking it from side to side. Right, left, up and down were indicated by turning his head in these directions. If a gentleman in the audience raised his right arm, and Von Osten asked which arm was raised, he would promptly make a movement to the right—even though, viewed from his own standpoint, it appeared to be on the left. He also seemed to be able to distinguish colors. His master would hang colored cloths on a line, and ask him to bring red or blue or green. He would walk over to the line, and almost invariably bring the right cloth in his mouth.

The range of Hans's apparent accomplishments was so great that a few more excerpts from the above-mentioned report might be in order. "Taking into account his limited means of expression, his master had translated a large number of concepts into numbers, e.g., letters of the alphabet, the tones of the scale, and the names of playing cards were indicated by taps. In the case of the playing cards one tap meant 'ace,' two taps 'king,' three 'queen,' etc."

Number translation opened up new areas which Von Osten developed during the four years he devoted to teaching his four-footed protégé: "If a series of placards with written words [in German] were placed before the horse, he could step up and point with his nose to any of the words required of him. He could even spell some of the words. This was done by the aid of a table devised by Von Osten in which every letter of the alphabet, as well as a number of diphthongs, had an appropriate place which the horse could designate by means of a pair of numbers. Thus in the fifth horizontal row, 's' had first place, 'sch' second, 'ss' third, etc., so that the horse could indicate the letter 's' by tapping first 5, then 1, 'sch' by 5 and 2, 'ss' by 5 and 3. Upon being asked 'What is the woman holding in her hand?' Hans spelled without hesitation: 5,2; 3,2; 4,6; 3,7; i.e., 'Schirm' (parasol)."

Several of Hans's other feats were equally startling. He seemed to know the value of all the German coins. And he was apparently completely familiar with the entire calendar, for he could not only tap out the date of any day mentioned, but answer such questions as "If the ninth day of a month comes on a Tuesday, what is the date for the following Thursday?" He could also tap out the time to the minute, and answer the question "Between what figures is the small hand of a watch at five minutes after half-past eight?" Though horses are not noted for their visual acuity, he would tap out the number of windows on a distant house or the number of children climbing over a neighboring roof. But perhaps most astonishing of all, he seemed to possess the rare quality of absolute pitch, for he would not only tap out "c" or "d" when Von Osten sang or played these notes on a mouth organ, but "without difficulty he analyzed compound clangs into their components; he indicated their agreeableness or disagreeableness and could inform us which tone must be eliminated to make consonants out of dissonants . . . Finally he was familiar with no less than thirteen melodies and their time."

These illustrations appear to indicate that Hans always gave the correct answer—but that was not the case. He occasionally slipped, though in most cases he corrected his mistake when the question was repeated. He seemed to have particular difficulty when the answer was "1" or when a very large number of taps was required. Mood and temper also appeared to play a part. Von Osten pointed out that Hans was quite high-strung and would become stubborn or tease his questioner by deliberately giving the wrong answer to the simplest questions. Also, "Whenever anyone asked a question without himself knowing the answer, Hans would indulge in all sorts of sport at the questioner's expense." His owner attributed these vagaries to sensitivity and high spirits.

Von Osten's attitude toward his remarkable animal was vastly different from that of a circus trainer or vaudeville performer. He never used the whip, but only gentle encouragement plus frequent rewards of bread or carrots. As a former mathematics teacher, he looked upon Hans as an apt pupil who was worth thousands of hours of patient teaching. As time went on, he became convinced that he was writing a new chapter in the history of education by developing the latent capacities of a "dumb animal" whom no one had ever attempted to educate in any systematic way. Moreover, he refused to exploit Hans by exhibiting him on a stage, or by accepting money for the demonstrations he gave in his courtyard and he was always ready to have him examined by scientists and even ringmasters, for his only interest lay in exploring the animal mind to the fullest possible degree.

In spite of the fact that Von Osten never sought publicity of any kind, word of the horse's accomplishments soon got around, and article after article appeared in the press and even in scientific journals. His name was sung on the vaudeville stage, his picture appeared on postcards and liquor labels, and replicas of Clever Hans soon became available in toy stores. Many noted zoologists, naturalists, and horse fanciers who had observed Hans became convinced of his ability to count and solve mathematical problems. Others maintained that Von Osten had developed a set of tricks which somehow controlled the animal and deceived a gullible public.

The controversy assumed huge proportions and practically every conceivable theory was advanced to explain the phenomenon. Two monographs attributed his apparent mathematical ability to rote memory, and called him simply a "four-legged computing machine." Some writers insisted that he was totally unable to analyze musical chords, but had sufficiently acute vision to notice which stops on the mouth organ were closed, and had learned to give a certain number of taps for each of them. They also maintained that he could not actually tell time but had merely learned the necessary number of taps by heart since he was always asked the time at the same hour of the day—although this was actually contrary to fact. Others, on the other hand, denied him the "glory" of a tenacious memory and held that he was merely reacting to signals given by his master. But they were totally unable to describe the nature of these signals and fell back on the suggestion that they had "something to do" with his slouch hat, his long coat, eye movements, the tone of his voice, or the way he thrust his hand into his pocket filled with the carrots he used as a reward. Still others were sure the explanation lay in "thought waves" radiating from the master's brain, or "hypnotic influence," or simply "the power of suggestion."

This welter of conflicting explanations only served to make Hans's performance more of an enigma than ever. And to top it all, two further facts deepened the mystery. First, Von Osten permitted other people to question Hans in his presence, and many of them were able to elicit the correct answers. And second, certain individuals, particularly the naturalist K. G. Schillings, who spent a great deal of time with the horse, were able to elicit the answers even when Von Osten was not present! Together, these two facts seemed to suggest that the animal was not merely responding to signals, but had truly been taught to think for himself.

The case of Clever Hans aroused so much interest that two commissions composed not only of outstanding naturalists, psychologists, and other scientists, but also circus trainers familiar with all the tricks of the trade, were set up to investigate the mystery of the thinking horse. Here is an excerpt from the report submitted by one of these commissions: "In spite of the most attentive observation nothing in the way of movements or other forms of expression which might have served as a sign could be discovered . . . As a result of these observations the undersigned are of the opinion that unintentional signs of the kind which are at present familiar are likewise excluded. They are unanimously agreed that this much is certain: This is a case which appears in principle to differ from many hitherto discovered, and has nothing in common with training, in the usual sense of that word, and therefore it is worthy of a serious and incisive investigation."

Shortly after this report appeared, an experienced psychologist, Oskar Pfungst, accepted the commission's challenge and asked Von Osten to permit him to make a thorough study of Hans's reputed abilities. The permission was readily granted, and Pfungst embarked on a varied series of tests and observations which proved to be a model of psychological investigation at its best. His procedures and results have been thoroughly recorded in the book *Clever Hans,* from which we have been quoting.

Pfungst at once decided that the only way to solve the mystery was to introduce carefully controlled conditions and to conduct tests that would rule out the possibility that the horse's errors were due to chance. His first step was to befriend the horse—and fortunately he discovered that in a short time the animal responded to his own questions as readily as to those of Von Osten and Schillings. His second step was to determine whether Hans was capable of thinking independently. He did this by confronting the animal with two general types of problems: those in which the experimenter did not know the answer ("procedure without knowledge") and those in which he did ("procedure with knowledge"). Each of the problems had to be answered in one of three ways: by tapping, by movements of the head, or by walking over to the object designated—which covered all the ways Hans had apparently been taught to respond.

The details of all these experiments need not be given, but a few examples will suffice. In one test, the horse was asked to tap numbers printed on cards and exposed to his view. The results showed that his answers were practically always correct when the experimenter could see the numbers, and practically never correct when they were hidden from his view. The same occurred when words or single letters were used instead of numbers. When Hans was asked to add or subtract, he almost always succeeded if the experimenter knew both the question and the answer, but when Pfungst and Von Osten each whispered a number in his ear separately (and without telling the other what it was), he invariably failed. Similarly, Pfungst proved that he was unable to solve color problems or answer questions on music when the experimenter did not know the answer. He therefore concluded from these and other experiments that "Hans can neither read, count, nor make calculations. He knows nothing of coins or cards, calendars or clocks, nor can he respond, by tapping or otherwise, to a number spoken to him even a moment before. Finally, he has not a trace of musical ability."

The results of the tapping tests indicated that the horse

was unable to work alone, and must have perceived certain stimuli which served as cues to the answer. But what *were* these cues? Since experts contend that horses have extremely acute hearing the suggestion was made that the experimenter might unintentionally whisper the answer under his breath—a form of involuntary "inner speech." This possibility was ruled out by having the questioner keep his mouth and nose closed, and by putting lined ear muffs on the animal's ears. In both cases Hans continued to give the right answer if the questioner knew what it was. Next, the possibility of visual cues was examined—and here the results were entirely different. If the questioner stood behind the horse he would either give a totally incorrect answer or would "make the most strenuous efforts to get a view of the questioner." And if the animal wore large blinders he would almost invariably fail. The same occurred if the experimenter and the horse were separated by a canvas tent.

In the course of these experiments Pfungst made two revealing observations. First, the horse never looked at the persons or objects he was called upon to count or at the words he was to read, but would always keep his eyes fixed on the questioner. And second, when Pfungst himself peered closely at Von Osten as he was posing questions, he suddenly discovered that the old man was giving the animal signals which no one had noticed. In his own words, "These signs were minimal movements of the head on the part of the experimenter. As soon as the experimenter had given a problem to the horse, he involuntarily bent his head and trunk slightly forward and the horse would then put the right foot forward and begin to tap, without, however, returning it each time to its original position. As soon as the desired number of taps was given, the questioner would make a slight upward jerk of the head. Whereupon the horse would immediately swing his foot in a wide circle, bringing it back to its original position."

Pfungst, however, did not merely accept this explanation and call it a day, but verified it in a further series of tests. By careful observation he confirmed the fact that every time Von Osten obtained a successful response, he made the same minute movements. Then he showed that Schillings, who enjoyed equal success with Hans, made exactly the same movements—and other experimenters who were *less* successful frequently made "belated or precipitate jerks." Then Pfungst had the others observe *himself* as he posed the questions, and found to his utter amazement that he, too, made the same involuntary movements!

Ever the careful experimenter, Pfungst then embarked on a further series of tests as final proof of his observations. He showed that if the questioner stood rigidly erect he elicited no response from Hans, and if he stooped over slightly, as in writing notes, the horse would immediately begin to tap, whether or not he had been asked a question.

But why did the questioner bend forward when he posed his question, and straighten up when the horse had made the correct number of taps? The answer now seemed "ridiculously simple." As the questioner finished posing his problem, he would look down, ever so slightly, to observe the horse's foot more closely, and automatically and almost imperceptibly straighten up when he had given the proper number of taps. He then proved that he could obtain either correct or totally incorrect responses by *voluntarily* controlling his own tendency to bend over and straighten up.

These observations were further confirmed in a variety of ways. He showed that the horse's reactions became confused if the questioner stood more than a few feet away, where the animal would have trouble perceiving these minimal movements. He disproved the theory that thrusting the hand in the pocket for carrots served as a signal by showing that Hans would make no response at all if he did this without making the appropriate head and body movements. And he found that the animal's tendency to tap faster when given a large number was not due to an understanding of the number itself, but to the inclination of the questioner's head: Von Osten always bent farther forward when the number was large. As further proof of this point, Pfungst found that when he himself acted as questioner, he could control the rate of tapping by varying the inclination of his body. And finally, he ruled out the theory of "thought waves" by having twenty persons concentrate on the answers to a series of twenty-one problems, while he himself served as questioner *without* knowing the answers. Hans failed every one of the problems except two—and these he presumably tapped correctly by chance alone.

It will not be necessary to dwell on all the problems which Hans solved by movements of the head or by approaching objects, since the principles are the same as in the case of tapping with his foot. Pfungst found that when the horse was asked questions concerning up, down, right, and left, he answered correctly only when the questioner involuntarily moved his head in the appropriate direction. The same for picking out colored cloths or words on printed placards. He would always keep his eyes on Von Osten as he walked toward these objects, but was completely at sea when they were placed very close together, or when his master was asked to turn his back or face in the wrong direction.

These observations, and others on the same order, conclusively demonstrated that Hans was not reacting to the content of the questions but only to the involuntary bodily movements of the questioner. But why were these movements made—and how did the horse learn to respond to them?

Pfungst sought the answer to the first question through introspective analysis of his own movements as well as laboratory experiments performed on a large number of subjects. His first discovery was that these "expressive movements," as he termed them, were not only involuntary but practically uncontrollable, for "even after I had discovered the nature of these movements and had thus become enabled to call forth at will all the various responses on the part of the horse, I still gave the signs in the earlier involuntary manner." He then demonstrated that Hans responded as promptly to questions which he articulated *inwardly* as to those he spoke aloud—and more than that, he was able to obtain any answer he wished, no matter how incorrect, simply by "focusing consciousness with a great degree of intensity upon the answer desired." For example, if he asked Hans, "How many angles has a hexagon?" he was able to obtain three different answers—6, 2, and 27—by focusing on each of them in turn.

The word "intensity" is the key to the whole problem, for he discovered that the expressive movements which prompted the horse to start tapping occurred only when he experienced a "high degree of tension of expectancy," and that when the correct number of taps had been made, this state of tension was suddenly and automatically relaxed, producing the slight head jerk that served as a signal to the horse to cease his tapping. These observations explain the horse's high percentage of success, but also his failures with the number 1 and with large numbers. The difficulty with number 1 was due to the fact that "it is not easy to relax attention immediately after having just begun to concentrate"; and his inability to cope with large numbers was due to difficulty in maintaining the necessary tension for long periods of time.

In the laboratory experiments that followed his introspective approach, Pfungst devised a unique and imaginative technique. He decided to *take the part of the horse himself*, and invited twenty-five persons of varying sex, age, nationality, and occupation to serve as questioners—without informing them of the purpose of the procedure. In a counting experiment, for example, he had the questioners stand within view at his right and think of a number or arithmetic problem with a high degree of concentration. When he observed what he thought was the starting signal, he would begin tapping his right hand, and when he perceived what he thought to be the final signal, he would stop the tapping. The results of these experiments were dramatic. With the exception of only two individuals, each subject was found to make the same involuntary movements and, significantly, they were both scientists "whose mode of thought was always the most abstract." What is more, he found that his answers, like Hans's, were practically always correct. Needless to say, his subjects were dumbfounded by his ability to "read their minds." And even when they were initiated into the secret, they found it difficult and in some cases impossible to inhibit their involuntary expressive movements.

The fact that so many subjects made the same movements explained why the horse was able to give correct answers to questions posed not only by his trainer but by many strangers as well. This did not prove that Hans was capable of abstract thought, as many people believed, but merely showed that the same stimulus frequently elicited the same automatic response.

As a final step in these thoroughgoing experiments,

Pfungst sought to confirm his results quantitatively. He adapted an apparatus originally intended for recording involuntary tremors to the measurement of his subjects' head movements, and also employed a pneumograph to register the respiratory changes that usually accompany tension and release of tension. He continued to act the part of the horse, and the two types of reaction were automatically recorded by a moving pen. Although there was some variation among his subjects, the results were generally impressive. They revealed that the head movements were amazingly minute—scarcely a hairbreadth—since they varied between 2.3 mm and .1 mm, and averaged only 1 mm! This explained why they had not been detected by the other investigators.

Moreover, the respiratory records proved to be a good indication of the subject's degree of concentration and tension, for they revealed that breathing tended to be shallow, irregular, or altogether inhibited until the correct number was reached, and at that point the subject usually inhaled deeply, and in doing so, raised his head. On the other hand, if the subject's concentration lapsed, the curve invariably indicated this fact, and in these cases Pfungst (acting as the horse) was unable to give the correct answer. Mistakes also occurred if the experimenter became fatigued, reacted prematurely or belatedly, or miscalculated the answer to the problem. Like Hans, Pfungst proved to be a faithful and automatic mirror of the questioner's involuntary reactions. Here, then, was conclusive proof of his theory.

One question remains: How did Hans learn to respond to these extremely minute movements? In the first place, the horse possesses a far greater capacity for perceptual discrimination than is generally recognized. In spite of the fact that his vision is not notably keen, and his eyes are on the side of his head instead of the front, he seems to have learned to make the most of his visual capacities in the interest of self-preservation. As Pfungst points out, "We can also readily appreciate how indispensable in the struggle for existence a well-developed power of perceiving moving objects must be to horses (and most other animals) in their natural condition and habitat." Moreover, the horse is particularly aware of movement, especially after he has been carefully trained. G. M. Beard, the first scientist to prove that many so-called mind readers are really muscle readers, states that "Every horse that is good for anything is a muscle reader; he reads the mind of his driver through the pressure on the bit, though not a word of command is uttered." This is explained by the fact that when the rider merely *thinks* of turning his horse in a certain direction, his thought is automatically and involuntarily translated into minute movements which guide the horse in the appropriate direction even before he gives the command.

In addition, the horse possesses other qualities which make him amenable to training: keen hearing, a capacity for concentrated attention, an ability to form and retain simple associations, and the capacity to respond to kindness, patience, and encouragement, especially when the training process is reinforced by frequent rewards of food, a procedure which is now termed operant conditioning. Undoubtedly, Clever Hans possessed all these qualities in an exceptional degree.

Now for a word about the teaching process which Von Osten used. He first taught Hans to bring cloths of different colors or touch them with his nose by leading him to each color separately and by calling it by name. Later, he would remain in his place (but well within the horse's side view) and gaze intently at the desired cloth in order to see whether the horse would select the color he demanded. Hans might fail a hundred times, but as soon as he succeeded he received a reward. These successes convinced Von Osten that he was learning to discriminate colors by name, although actually the rewards only had the effect of encouraging the animal to watch his master and follow his line of vision and the position of his head more closely.

A similar type of procedure was used in other phases of the learning process—for example, whenever his master pronounced the word "left," he pulled the horse's head to the left by means of a bridle or offered him a reward on the left side. This simply established a tendency to respond in a specific way; but later on, when he asked a question involving "left," the horse did not respond to the word itself, but to the fact that his master automatically moved in that direction. It is an interesting fact that Charles Darwin was one of the first to point out that whenever you wish an object to move in a certain direction it is almost impossible to inhibit an unconscious, involuntary movement in that direction.

Von Osten was apparently totally ignorant of this principle, or was so convinced that his horse was learning to think that he overlooked it completely. But it is a principle that has been increasingly recognized by psychologists, and termed either motor automatism or ideomotor behavior. As pointed out elsewhere in this book, such automatic behavior explains a variety of common phenomena such as the operation of a Ouija board and the divining rod, as well as our tendency to move with the players as we observe a ping-pong game. (See "Nom de Plume," "The Forked Stick," "Personality Parade.")

In attempting to teach his horse to count, Von Osten employed a method long used by trainers of show horses: tapping with the foot. He first rewarded Hans for tapping in response to his command, then planted wooden pins in the ground (first one, then two, then three) and raised the horse's foot as many times as the count demanded. Next, he stood at the horse's side and commanded him to tap three. We can only reconstruct what happened the first time—which was crucial—but very probably his master bent forward to watch the tapping more closely and unconsciously straightened up when Hans reached the third tap. The horse was probably startled at the latter movement, and therefore ceased tapping. At this point he received a carrot as reward, and this was instrumental in establishing an association between the sight of the upward jerk and the act of ceasing to tap. This process was repeated many times, and the horse gradually learned to attend more and more closely to the upward jerk and to more minute movements made by Von Osten as his tension and excitement decreased.

Once this procedure was established, Von Osten began to "instruct" his horse in "solving" more and more difficult problems—but since the technique was fundamentally the same in the entire process, it is unnecessary to elaborate on it further. Suffice it to say that Hans proved to be an extraordinarily patient animal and rarely rebelled against the tedious procedure. As he continued to "progress," "the old man believed himself to be a witness of a continuous organic development of the animal's soul—a development which in reality had no other existence than in his own imagination." In his eyes, "he saw the animal's intelligence steadily increase, without having the slightest notion that between his words and the response in movements of the horse, there were interpolated his own unconscious movements—and that thus instead of the much desired intellectual feats on the part of the horse there was merely a motor reaction to a purely sensory stimulus."

When the details of Oskar Pfungst's experiments were

published, his explanations were universally acclaimed by the scientific world. But there was one man who could not bring himself to accept his conclusions. That man was Wilhelm Von Osten.

Bibliography

WALTER MITTY IN THE FLESH

American Psychiatric Association: *Diagnostic and Statistical Manual, Mental Disorders.* Washington, D.C., 1952.

Brill, A. A., New York *Journal*, October 30, 1926.

Cleckley, H. M., "Psychopathic States," *American Handbook of Psychiatry*, S. Arieti (ed.). New York: Basic Books, 1959, vol. I, Chap. 28.

Greenacre, Phyllis, "The Relation of the Impostor to the Artist," *The Psychoanalytic Study of the Child*, Ruth F. Eiffler (ed.). New York: International Universities Press, 1958, vol. 13, 521–40.

Goldenson, R. M., "Antisocial Reaction," *The Encyclopedia of Human Behavior: Psychology, Psychiatry, and Mental Health* New York: Doubleday & Company, Inc., 1970, Vol. I, 86–90.

Heaton-Ward, W. A., "Psychopathic Disorder," *Lancet*, 1 (1963) 121–23.

Hynd, A., "The Fabulous Fraud from Brooklyn," *Grand Deception: The World's Most Spectacular and Successful Hoaxes, Impostures, Ruses and Frauds*, Klein, A. (ed.). Philadelphia: J. B. Lippincott Company, 1955, 62–71.

McKelway, St. C., *The Big Little Man from Brooklyn.* Boston: Houghton Mifflin, 1969.

Weyman, Stanley, as quoted in New York *Journal*, October 30, 1926.

Wirt, R. D., P. F. Briggs, and J. Golden, "Delinquency-Prone Personalities, III, The Sociopathic Personality: Treatment," *Minnesota Medicine*, 45 (1962), 289–95.

PERSONALITY PARADE

Mühl, A. M., "Automatic Writing as an Indicator of the Fundamental Factors Underlying the Personality," *Journal of Abnormal Psychology*, 17 (1922), 166–83.

FORGOTTEN LIFE

Henderson, D., R. D. Gillespie, and I. R. C. Batchelor, *Textbook of Psychiatry*. London: Oxford University Press, 1962.

Jastrow, J., *The Subconscious*. New York: Houghton Mifflin Company, 1906.

McDougall, W., "Four Cases of 'Regression' in Soldiers," *Journal of Abnormal and Social Psychology*, 15 (1920), 136–56.

Sidis, Boris, *The Psychology of Suggestion*. New York: D. Appleton & Company, 1909.

NOM DE PLUME

Brown, R., *Unfinished Symphonies*. New York: William Morrow & Co., 1971.

Cory, C. E., "Patience Worth," *Psychological Review*, 26 (1919), 397–406.

Curran, P. L., "A Nut for Psychologists," *The Unpartizan Review*, 13 (1920), 357–72.

Flournoy, Théodore, *From India to the Planet Mars: A Study of Somnambulism with Glossolalia*. New York: Harper & Brothers, 1900.

Jastrow, Joseph, *Wish and Wisdom: Episodes in the Vagaries of Belief*. New York: D. Appleton-Century-Crofts, 1935.

Litvag, Irving, *Singer in the Shadows: The Strange Story of Patience Worth*. New York: Macmillan, 1972.

Prince, W. F., *The Case of Patience Worth*. New Hyde Park, N.Y.: University Books, 1964.

Worth, Patience, *The Sorry Tale: A Story of the Time of Christ*. New York: Henry Holt & Company, 1917.

——, *Light from Beyond; Poems by Patience Worth*, Herman Behr (ed.). Brooklyn, N.Y.: Patience Worth Publishing Company, 1923.

THE LETTER

Barber, T. X., "Antisocial and Criminal Acts Induced by Hypnosis," *Archives of General Psychiatry,* 5 (1961), 109–20.
Brenman, M., "Experiments in the Hypnotic Production of Anti-Social and Self-Injurious Behavior," *Psychiatry,* 5 (1942), 45.
Erickson, M. H., "An Experimental Investigation of the Possible Anti-Social Use of Hypnosis," *Psychiatry,* 2 (1939), 391–414.
Kline, M. V., "The Dynamics of Hypnotically Induced Anti-Social Behavior," *Journal of Psychology,* 45 (1958), 239.
Lyon, W., "Justification and Command as Techniques for Hypnotically Induced Antisocial Behavior," *Journal of Clinical Psychology,* 10 (1954), 288.
Rowland, L. W., "Will Hypnotized Persons Try to Harm Themselves or Others?" *Journal of Abnormal and Social Psychology,* 34 (1939), 114.
Watkins, J. G., "Anti-Social Compulsions Induced Under Hypnotic Trance," *Journal of Abnormal and Social Psychology,* 42 (1947), 256.
Wells, W. R., "Experiments in the Hypnotic Production of Crimes," *Journal of Psychology,* 11 (1941), 63.
Weitzenhoffer, A. M., *Hypnotism: an Objective Study in Suggestibility.* New York: John Wiley & Sons, Inc., 1953.

THE UNHEALING WOUNDS

Beyer, E., "The Enigma of Therese Neumann," *Catholic World,* Feb. 1952, 359–66.
Graef, Hilde, *The Case of Therese Neumann.* Westminster, Md.: Newman Press, 1951.
Hamilton, F., "Is There a Miracle at Uptergrove?" *Maclean's Magazine,* Sept. 15, 1950.
Imbert-Gourbeyre, A., *La Stigmatisation.* Paris, 1894.
Pattie, F. A., Jr., "The Production of Blisters by Hypnotic Suggestion: A Review," *Journal of Abnormal and Social Psychology,* 36 (1941), 62–72.
Rawcliffe, D. H., *The Psychology of the Occult.* London: Derricke Ridgway, 1952.
Siwek, P., *The Riddle of Konnersreuth.* Milwaukee: Bruce Publishing Company, 1953.
——, "Therese Neumann," in Catholic Encyclopedia. New York: McGraw-Hill Inc., 1967.

Sureck, D., "Therese Neumann of Konnersreuth," *Coronet,* 43 (Dec. 1957), 160–64.

THE FORKED STICK

Barrett, W. F. and T. Besterman, *The Divining Rod: An Experimental and Psychological Investigation.* London: Methuen, 1926.
Carpenter, W. B., "On the Influence of Suggestion in Modifying and Directing Muscular Movement, Independently of Volition," *Proceedings of the Royal Institution of Great Britain,* 1 (1852), 147–53.
Dale, L. A. et al., "Dowsing: A Field Experiment in Water Divining," *Journal of the American Society for Psychical Research,* 45 (1951), 3–16.
Gardner, M., *In the Name of Science.* New York: G. P. Putnam's, 1952.
Indian Journal of Engineering, editorial, May 1, 1926.
Jacobson, E., "The Electrophysiology of Mental Activity," *American Journal of Psychology,* 44 (1932), 677–94.
James, W., *The Principles of Psychology.* New York: Henry Holt & Company, 1890.
Jastrow, J., *Wish and Wisdom.* New York: D. Appleton Century-Crofts, 1935.
Maby, J. C. and T. B. Franklin, *The Physics of the Divining Rod.* London: G. Bell and Sons, 1939.
——, "The Physics of the Divining Rod," a review, *Nature,* August 3, 1940, Vol. 146, 150.
Ongley, P. A., "New Zealand Diviners," *New Zealand Journal of Science and Technology,* 30 (1948), 38–54.
Rawcliffe, D. H., *The Psychology of the Occult.* London: Derricke Ridgway, 1952.
Report on the Work of the Water Diviner to the Government of Bombay, October 1925–January 1927.
Taylor, F. N., *Small Water Supplies.* London: B. T. Batsford, 1911.
Thomson, J. J., *Recollections and Reflections.* New York: The Macmillan Company, 1937.
Vogt, E. Z., "Water Witching: An Interpretation of a Ritual Pattern in a Rural American Community," *The Scientific Monthly,* (Sept. 1952), 175–86.
Vogt, E. Z. and R. Hyman, *Water Witching, U.S.A.* Chicago: University of Chicago Press, 1959.
Watson, J. B., *Psychology from the Standpoint of a Behaviorist.* Philadelphia: J. B. Lippincott Company, 1924.

DECISION

Erickson, M. H. and L. B. Hill, "Unconscious Mental Activity in Hypnosis: Psychoanalytic Implications," *Psychoanalytic Quarterly,* 13 (1944), 60–78.

A QUARTET OF PRODIGIES

Galton, F., *Hereditary Genius.* London: Macmillan, 1869.
James, William, *On Vital Reserves.* New York: Henry Holt & Company, 1911.

BREAKING POINT

Maazel, M., "What to Do About the Child Prodigy," *Etude,* 68 (Aug. 1950), 12.
Manley, J. L., "Where Are They Now? April Fool!" *The New Yorker,* Aug. 14, 1937, 22.
Scheinfeld, A., *Your Heredity and Environment.* Philadelphia: J. P. Lippincott Company, 1965.
Sidis, Boris, *Philistine and Genius.* New York: Moffat, Yard, 1911.
Wiener, N., *Ex-Prodigy: My Childhood and Youth.* New York: Simon & Schuster Inc., 1953.
Wilson, S., "The Freedom to Explore," *Saturday Review,* March 28, 1953, 10.

MAN VS. MACHINE

Bousfield, W. A. and H. Barry, "The Visual Imagery of a Lightning Calculator," *American Journal of Psychology,* 45 (1933), 353–58.
Goldenson, R. M., "Prodigy," *The Encyclopedia of Human Behavior: Psychology, Psychiatry, and Mental Health.* New York: Doubleday & Company, Inc., 1970, Vol. II, 1009–13.

VIRTUOSO

Abbott, E. B., "The Miraculous Case of Blind Tom," *Etude,* 58 (Aug. 1940), 517.
Brawley, B. G., *The Negro Genius.* New York: Dodd, Mead & Company, Inc., 1937.

Garrison, W. B., "Blind Tom: Mystery of Music," *Coronet*, July 1952, 55–56.
Podolsky, E. (ed.), *Encyclopedia of Aberrations*. New York: Citadel Press, 1953.

A FLAIR FOR DATES

Horwitz, W. A., C. Kestenbaum, E. Person, and L. Jarvik, "Identical Twin–'Idiots Savants'–Calendar Calculators," *American Journal of Psychiatry*, 121 (1965), 1075–79.
Scheerer, M., E. Rothmann, and K. Goldstein, "A Case of 'Idiot Savant'; An Experimental Study of Personality Organization," *Psychological Monographs*, 58 (1945), Number 4.

THE DANCING PLAGUE

Baglivi, G., *The Practice of Physick*. London: A. Bell, 1723.
Gloyne, H. F., "Tarantism: Mass Hysterical Reaction to Spider Bite in the Middle Ages," *American Imago*, 17 (1950), 29–41.
Mackay, C., *Extraordinary Popular Delusions and the Madness of Crowds*. London: Office of the National Illustrated Library, 1852.
Sigerist, H. E., *Civilization and Disease*. Ithaca, N.Y.: Cornell University Press, 1943.
Stern, E. M., "She Breaks Through Invisible Walls," *Mental Hygiene*, 41 (1957), 361–71.

THE PHANTOM OF MATTOON

Goldenson, R. M., "Hysterical Personality," *The Encyclopedia of Human Behavior: Psychology, Psychiatry, and Mental Health*. New York: Doubleday & Company, Inc., 1970, Vol. I, 588.
Johnson, D. M., "The 'Phantom Anesthetist' of Mattoon: A Field Study of Mass Hysteria," *Journal of Abnormal and Social Psychology*, 40 (1945), 175–86.

A BOOM IN TULIPS

Brown, Roger, *Social Psychology*. New York: The Free Press, 1965.
Mackay, C., *Extraordinary Popular Delusions and the Madness of Crowds*. London: Office of the National Illustrated Library, 1852.
Posthumus, C. W., "The Tulip Mania in Holland in the Years 1636 and 1637," *Journal of Economic and Business History*, 1 (1928), 434–66.

STAMPEDE

Adler, Alexandra, "Neuropsychiatric Complications in Victims of Boston's Cocoanut Grove Disaster," *Journal of the American Medical Association*, 123 (1943), 1098–1101.

Brown, R., *Social Psychology*. New York: The Free Press, 1965.

Cantril, H., "Causes and Control of Riot and Panic," *Public Opinion Quarterly*, 7 (1943), 609–79.

Coleman, J. C., *Personality Dynamics and Effective Behavior*. Fairlawn, N.J.: Scott, Foresman and Company, 1960.

Foy, E. and A. F. Harlow, *Clowning Through Life*. New York: E. P. Dutton & Company, Inc., 1928.

Fritz, C. E., "Disasters Compared in Six American Communities," *Human Organization*, 16, No. 2 (1957), 6–9.

Schultz, D. P., "An Experimental Approach to Panic Behavior: Final Report to the Group Psychology Branch," Office of Naval Research, Aug. 15, 1966.

Veltfort, H. R. and G. E. Lee, "The Cocoanut Grove Fire: A Study in Scapegoating," *Journal of Abnormal and Social Psychology*, 38 (1943), 138–54.

DOUBLES NUMBER ONE AND TWO

Newman, H. H., *Multiple Human Births*. New York: Doubleday, Doran & Company, Inc., 1940.

Newman, H. H., F. N. Freeman, and K. H. Holzinger, *Twins: A Study of Heredity and Environment*. Chicago: University of Chicago Press, 1937.

STRANGE ENCOUNTER

Bakker, C. B. and S. E. Murphy, "An Unusual Case of Autoscopic Hallucination," *Journal of Abnormal and Social Psychology*, 69, No. 6 (1964), 646–49.

Goldenson, R. M., "Autoscopic Syndrome," *The Encyclopedia of Human Behavior: Psychology, Psychiatry, and Mental Health*, Vol. I, 142–43.

Kohlberg, Lawrence, "Psychological Analysis and Literary Forms: A Study of the Doubles in Dostoevsky," *Daedalus* (Spring 1963), 345–62.

Lippman, C. W., "Hallucinations of Physical Duality in Migraine," *Journal of Nervous and Mental Disease*, 117 (1953), 345–50.

Lukianowicz, N., "Autoscopic Phenomena," *Archives of Neurology and Psychiatry,* 80 (1958), 199.

Prince, M., *The Dissociation of a Personality.* New York: Longmans, Green & Company, 1905.

Rosenfield, Claire, "The Shadow Within: The Conscious and Unconscious Use of the 'Double,'" *Daedalus,* (Spring 1963), 326–44.

Thigpen, C. H. and H. M. Cleckley, "A Case of Multiple Personality," *Journal of Abnormal and Social Psychology,* 49 (1954), 135–51.

——, *The Three Faces of Eve.* New York: McGraw-Hill Book Co., Inc., 1957.

Todd, J. and K. Dewhurst, "The Double: Its Psychopathology and Psychophysiology," *Journal of Nervous and Mental Disease,* 122 (1955), 47–56.

MADNESS IN TRIPLICATE

Goldenson, R. M., "Folie à Deux," in *The Encyclopedia of Human Behavior: Psychology, Psychiatry, and Mental Health.* Vol. I, 468–69.

Gralnick, A., "Folie à Deux—The Psychosis of Association: A Review of 103 Cases and the Entire English Literature with Case Presentations," *Psychiatric Quarterly,* 14 (1942), 230–63.

Kesselman, S. R., "Folie à Trois—Psychosis of Association," *Psychiatric Quarterly,* 18 (1944), 138–52.

THE WILL TO DIE

Arieti, S. and J. M. Meth, "Rare, Unclassifiable, Collective and Exotic Psychotic Syndromes," *American Handbook of Psychiatry,* S. Arieti (ed.). New York: Basic Books, 1959. Vol. I, Chap. 27.

Basedow, H., *The Australian Aboriginal.* Adelaide: F. W. Preece, 1925.

Cannon, W. B., "'Voodoo' Death," *American Anthropologist,* 44 (1942), 169–81.

Cleland, J. B., "Disease Amongst the Australian Aborigines," *Journal of Tropical Medicine and Hygiene,* 31 (1928), 233.

Hoeven, J. A. van der, "Psychiatrisch-Neurologische Beobachtungen bei Papuas in Neu Guinea," *Archives of Psychiatry,* 194 (1956), 415.

Leonard, A. G., *The Lower Niger and Its Tribes.* London: The Macmillan Company, 1906.

Warner, W. L., *A Black Civilization, A Social Study of an Australian Tribe.* New York: Harper & Brothers, 1958.

PIBLOKTOQ

Aberle, D. F., "Arctic Hysteria and Latah in Mongolia," *Annals of the New York Academy of Science*, 2 (1952), 291.

Brill, A. A., "Piblokto or Hysteria Among Peary's Eskimos," *Journal of Nervous and Mental Disease*, 40 (1913), 514–20.

Foulks, E. F., "Arctic Hysteria—A Research Problem," *Pennsylvania Psychiatric Quarterly*, 8 (1968), 50–55.

Peary, R. E., *The North Pole*. New York: Frederick Stokes Company, 1910.

A DISORDER CALLED KORO

Goldenson, R. M., "Castration Complex," *The Encyclopedia of Human Behavior: Psychology, Psychiatry and Mental Health*. New York: Doubleday & Company, Inc., 1970, Vol. I, 187–88.

Palthe, P., "Psychiatry and Neurology in the Tropics," in C. D. De Langen and A. Lichtenstein, *A Clinical Textbook of Tropical Medicine*. Batavia: G. Kolff, 1936.

RELUCTANT HUSBAND

Goldenson, R. M., "Bestiality," *The Encyclopedia of Human Behavior: Psychology, Psychiatry, and Mental Health*. New York: Doubleday & Company, Inc., 1970. Vol. I, 157–58.

Menninger, K. A., "Totemic Aspects of Contemporary Attitudes Toward Animals," *Psychoanalysis and Culture: Essays in Honor of Géza Róheim*, G. B. Wilbur and W. Muensterberger (eds.). New York: International Universities Press, 1951.

MAN INTO BEAST

Cannon, W. B., " 'Voodoo Death,' " *American Anthropologist*, 44 (1942), 169–81.

Mills, C. P., "The Were-Tigers of the Assam Hills," *Journal of the Society for Psychical Research*, 22 (1922), 387.

Rawcliffe, D. H., *The Psychology of the Occult*. London: Derricke Ridgway, 1952.

Roth, W. E., Review in North Queensland Ethnology Bulletin, No. 5 (1903), 27–31.

Stone, S., "Psychiatry Through the Ages," *Journal of Abnormal Psychology*, 32 (1937), 131–60.

Tichy, H., *Tibetan Adventure*. London: Faber and Faber, 1938.
Veith, I., *Hysteria: The History of a Disease*. Chicago: University of Chicago Press, 1965.

THE MYSTERY OF THE THINKING HORSE

Beard, G. M., "Physiology of Mind Reading," *Popular Science Monthly*, 10 (1877), 459–73.
Pfungst, O., *Clever Hans: The Horse of Mr. Von Osten*. New York: Henry Holt & Company, 1911.

INDEX